RUNNING
SCARED

*Why America's Politicians Campaign Too Much
and Govern Too Little*

by ANTHONY KING

MARTIN KESSLER BOOKS

THE FREE PRESS
New York   London   Toronto   Sydney   Singapore

THE FREE PRESS
A Division of Simon & Schuster Inc.
1230 Avenue of the Americas
New York, NY 10020

Manufactured in the United States of America

10 9 8 7 6 5 4 3 2 1

Library of Congress Cataloging-in-Publication Data
King, Anthony Stephen.
    Running scared: why America's politicians campaign too much
and govern too little / Anthony King.
        p.   cm.
    Includes bibliographical references and index.
    ISBN 0–684–82730–1
    1. Electioneering—United States. 2. Politicians—United States.
    3. Democracy—United States. 4. United States—Politics and
    government.   I. Title.
JK2281.K53   1997   96–8623
324.7'0973—dc20   CIP

ISBN 0–684–82730–1

For Seth H. Dubin
and all of his family:
Dorothy, Tom, Ellen and Andy

CONTENTS

ACKNOWLEDGMENTS

My principal debt of gratitude is to Giles Alston, without whose assistance this book could not—and would not— have been written. He prepared briefing materials and bibliographies, supplied documents and checked references with tremendous skill and energy. He also suggested lines of thought that had not previously occurred to me and also prevented me from making a considerable number of mistakes. I owe more than I can say to Dr. Alston's devotion to duty, good humor and profound knowledge of American politics.

Patrick O'Hagan, then an undergraduate at Harvard, also provided assistance at an early stage of the research, as did Jack Kneeshaw of my own university, the University of Essex. I am grateful to Sarah Bayes for putting the whole book on disk (and for insisting that she was enjoying reading it while she did it). Thomas Christiansen organized my interview with Brigitte Schulte and was excellent company on our trip to Bonn.

For granting me interviews, and for contributing an enormous amount of both information and understanding, I am grateful to Sir Alan Haselhurst of the British House of Commons, to Brigitte Schulte of the German Bundestag and to three members of the United States Congress: Dick Armey, Barney Frank (who expressed some doubts about my central thesis) and David E. Price (who endorsed it enthusiastically). Steny Hoyer, another member of the U.S. Congress, and one of his staff, Betsy Bossart, kindly agreed to meet Giles Alston. I also benefited from pleasant lunchtime conversations with David S. Broder and E. J. Dionne, Jr., both of the *Washington Post*.

I am also extremely grateful to three academic institutions in the United States which provided me with generous hospitality during the course of my thinking and writing: the Brookings Institution in Washington, D.C., where, thanks to Thomas E. Mann, I spent several agreeable weeks; the John F. Kennedy School of Government at Harvard where, thanks to Robert D. Putnam and Albert Carnesale, I was able to spend a profitable month in 1993; and the Department of Government at Harvard which, thanks to Paul E. Peterson and Susan J. Pharr, provided me with a home away from home for another month in 1995. Harvard appears to have the reputation in the United States of being a rather stuffy and standoffish place. I did not find it so; I found it very friendly and congenial.

Seven friends, two British and five American, were kind enough to read the manuscript of the book in its entirety. The two British were my wife Jan King (who knows an infelicitous phrase when she sees one) and my Essex colleague David McKay (who has a good claim to being Europe's leading expert on American politics). The five Americans were Seth H. Dubin, Morris P. Fiorina, Gary C. Jacobson, Richard E. Neustadt (though he, being married to a peer of the realm, probably counts as half British by now) and, not least, Bruce K. Nichols of The Free Press. All saved me from many errors of grammar, fact and interpretation. I wish to express my warmest gratitude to all of them—while, of course, granting them the usual absolution.

This book is intended for the general reader, but any professional political scientist who happens to come across it will immediately recognize my principal intellectual debts. They are to R. Douglas Arnold, Morris P. Fiorina, Alan Ehrenhalt, Gary C. Jacobson, David R. Mayhew, Paul E. Peterson and Nelson W.

Polsby. Anything good about this book is mainly their doing; whatever is wrong with it is mine. I am very grateful to Doug, Mo, Gary, Dave, Paul and Nelson. My only regret is that I have not met Mr. Ehrenhalt.

Finally, I must express my sadness that Martin Kessler, formerly of Basic Books and latterly of Martin Kessler Books at The Free Press, did not live to see the book through to completion. He warmed to my original idea and gave me much encouragement. I think he would have approved of the final product. I certainly hope so.

University of Essex
Wivenhoe Park
Colchester, Essex
England

INTRODUCTION

Most people take for granted the main features of the country in which they live. In the United States, Old Glory is flown everywhere and is treated with an almost religious reverence; there are speed limits on almost every street and highway, enforced by men carrying guns; total strangers at the hotel checkout say, "Have a nice day." In Great Britain, by contrast, the Union Jack is seldom flown, and almost no one regards it as a national icon; there are speed limits, but they are rarely enforced; the police do not carry guns; and the man or woman at the checkout desk, while usually perfectly polite, is most unlikely to express an interest in whether or not one has a nice day. It is only knowledge of foreign countries that makes our own country seem mysterious, that reveals it as having distinctive characteristics that require to be explained. As Rudyard Kipling said of his native land, "What should they know of England who only England know?"

There is one feature of politics in the United States with which every American citizen is completely familiar. It manifests itself on lapel badges, in television commercials, on car bumper stickers and on billboards in city centers and along state highways throughout the length and breadth of the land. It can be heard

1

on the radio and, at higher decibel levels, coming from loud-speakers on the back of pickup trucks. It is the phenomenon of the never-ending election campaign.

Americans do not merely have elections on the first Tuesday after the first Monday of November in every year divisible by four. They have elections on the first Tuesday after the first Monday of November in every year divisible by two. In addition, four states have elections even in odd-numbered years. Indeed there is no year in the United States—ever—when a major statewide election is not being held somewhere. To this catalog of general elections has of course to be added an equally long catalog of primary elections (forty-three presidential primaries in the year 1996 alone). Moreover, not only do elections in the United States occur very frequently: the number of posts legally required to be filled by them is enormous—not just the presidency of the United States but the post of local consumer advocate in New York. It has been estimated that in the United States at the present time there are no fewer than half a million elective offices filled or waiting to be filled.

Indeed the holding of elections in America has given birth to a major industry, akin to the auto industry or the fast-food industry. Those employed in it include registration officials, the printers of ballot papers, the manufacturers of voting machines, campaign buttons, T-shirts and bumper stickers, campaign consultants, pollsters, advertising copywriters, party officials, workers in individual candidates' campaigns, the producers of television commercials, press reporters, television commentators, election analysts, computer programmers and manufacturers and, of course, the elected officials themselves. No one has ever attempted to estimate the total annual "output" of the American elections industry, but, especially in presidential election years, it must make a substantial contribution to the nation's gross domestic product.

Americans take the existence of their elections industry for granted. Some like it; some dislike it; most are simply bored by it. But they are all conscious of it, in the same way that they are conscious of Mobil, McDonalds, *Larry King Live,* Oprah Winfrey, the Dallas Cowboys, the Ford Motor Company and all the other symbols and institutions that go to make up the rich tapestry of American life. In a meaningful sense, America is *about* the holding of elections.

To a visitor to America's shores, however, America's elections industry and its seemingly never-ending election campaign present a largely unfamiliar spectacle. In other countries, election campaigns have both beginnings and ends. Amazingly, there are even periods, often prolonged periods, when there are no election campaigns taking place at all. There are other features of American elections that are also unfamiliar. In few countries are elections and election campaigns as financially costly as they are in the United States. In none is the role of organized political parties so limited.

America's never-ending election campaign, together with other aspects of the functioning of American electoral politics, has one crucial consequence that is little noticed but vitally important for the functioning of American democracy. Quite simply, the American electoral system places America's elective politicians in a highly vulnerable position. Individually and collectively, they are more vulnerable, more of the time, to the vicissitudes of electoral politics than are the politicians of any other democratic country.

The full argument of this book will unfold gradually as we go along; but its essence can be stated at once and very briefly. We will argue that America's elective politicians are more continuously worried about their electoral futures than are the politicians of any other country; that they therefore devote more of their time to electioneering; and that their conduct in office is more continuously governed by electoral considerations. We will argue further that American politicians' constant and unremitting electoral preoccupations have deleterious consequences for the functioning of the American system. They consume time and scarce resources. Worse, they make it harder than it would otherwise be for the American system as a whole to deal with some of America's most pressing problems. American citizens often complain that their system is not sufficiently democratic. We will argue that, on the contrary, there is a sense in which the system is too democratic and ought to be made less so.

In the pages that follow, we will set out the argument in detail. Before we do, however, four important preliminary points need to be made.

The first is that, for reasons of time and space, this book deals solely with American national-level politics. Were the analysis to be extended to state and local politics, it would probably turn out to have even greater validity. But that is for others to decide.

The second is that this book does not call for, and would not presume to call for, sweeping changes in the American Constitution or in the broader American political order. The American political system is one of the most successful and enduring in the world. It would be a rash person who would tinker lightly with its basic elements. Europe, Asia, Africa and Latin America have few political lessons to teach the United States; and there is no reason to suppose that the problems addressed in these pages require changes in the American system more profound than many others that have taken place in recent years.

The third point is that, although this book is written by a foreigner, a Canadian citizen who happens to live in Great Britain, it is not written in any spirit of moral or intellectual superiority. On the contrary, Canada teeters permanently on the brink of national disintegration, while Britain is in a state of seemingly irreversible secular decline. Americans over the years have had quite enough of Brits and others telling them how to run their affairs. This author has no wish to prolong either their agony or their irritation. What follows is—and should be read as—the work of a candid friend.

The fourth and final point is probably the most important. Archilochos long ago pointed out that, whereas the fox knows many things, the hedgehog knows only one big thing. The fox is undoubtedly the superior creature since there are so many things in the world to be known. Nevertheless, this book is the kind of book that a hedgehog with tunnel vision might write. In order to clarify and simplify the argument, it focuses on "one big thing": American politicians' electoral vulnerability. In so doing, it undoubtedly slights many other equally important factors and considerations and offers an account that, while accurate so far as it goes, is extremely partial.

So be it. The fox knows many things but does not know everything. The hedgehog is not completely blind. There may be some virtue in a book that, precisely because it is written by a foreigner, focuses on one big and very important thing that most Americans, because they are so accustomed to it, tend not to notice.

Having thus introduced the argument briefly and at a somewhat abstract level, we begin by looking in more detail at the careers of three politicians who, because they have all been elected to public office in a democracy, are all at some degree of electoral risk. But it turns out that one of them, the American, is at a much greater degree of risk than either of the other two.

1

THREE POLITICIANS AT RISK

No single individual can be typical of every one of a country's politicians; but some are more typical than others, and the three politicians whose stories we tell in this chapter can stand for the great majority of their colleagues. They have served in their country's national legislature for a considerable number of years; their careers have quietly prospered, but none is a national celebrity; and their legislative districts are reasonably safe (or have been in the past) for the party to which they belong. Most of their legislative colleagues, reading the accounts that follow, would undoubtedly detect many points of difference between their own careers and those of the three described here; but they would probably also say, "Yes, that's broadly right. I recognize the general outline."

Sir Alan Haselhurst is a British M.P., a Conservative member of the House of Commons, arguably the world's oldest legislative assembly. He has sat there since 1970, with a brief interval between 1974, when he lost his original seat, the highly marginal constituency of Middleton and Prestwich in Lancashire, and

6

1977, when he was returned to the House at a special election (or, as the British say, "by-election") for Saffron Walden in Essex, some forty miles northeast of London. Before his first election to Parliament, Haselhurst, after attending Oxford, earned his living as a manager in the textile and chemical industries; and during his three years out of the House in 1974–77 he set up his own business as an industrial consultant, as well as working as an assistant to a former cabinet minister.

Despite his continuing connections with business, Haselhurst is, and always has been, a career politician. Politics is his first love; he is committed to it as a profession. He finds it possible, but he also finds it exceedingly unattractive, to contemplate a life outside politics. During the 1960s he was prominent as national chairman of the Young Conservatives, then a thriving and much publicized youth organization. When he lost his original seat in 1974, rather than accepting full-time employment he set up as a business consultant chiefly in order to be able to pursue his political career. He missed Parliament when he was not there.

But, although a career politician, Haselhurst is by no stretch of the imagination a political careerist. He has always stood proudly on the liberal wing of his party. In the 1960s he attacked those Conservatives who sided with the white-supremacist regime in Rhodesia when it unilaterally declared its independence from Britain. In the 1970s he made public his unhappiness about the direction in which Margaret Thatcher was taking the party. In the 1980s he helped form a group within the party, called Centre Forward, which aimed to counterbalance the influence of Thatcher and the Tory right. He rebelled in the House of Commons on a number of occasions against the Thatcher government. For his pains, he was denied ministerial office under both Thatcher and her successor, John Major. He remains an influential and respected backbencher, but only a backbencher. He received his knighthood, becoming Sir Alan, only in 1995, long after many of his contemporaries had been similarly rewarded.

Haselhurst's Saffron Walden constituency is tiny by American standards but quite large by British ones. Comprising three small market towns—Halstead, Great Dunmow and Saffron Walden itself—and upwards of a hundred villages, it has an electorate of roughly 70,000. The constituency's rural peace is disturbed only by the presence on its southern fringe of Stansted, London's third international airport. Saffron Walden is, in addition, politically peaceful. It has been Conservative for generations, and Haselhurst is only its third M.P. in more than half a century. His illustrious predecessor, R. A. ("Rab") Butler, represented Saffron Walden uninterruptedly from 1929 until 1965 and served in the governments of Winston Churchill, Sir Anthony Eden, Harold Macmillan and Sir Alec Douglas-Home as, among other things, education minister, chancellor of the exchequer, home secretary and foreign secretary. Haselhurst might once have hoped to follow in Butler's ministerial footsteps. Alas, it was not to be.

Haselhurst did not have to fight a primary in order to become the Conservative candidate for Saffron Walden; nor did he have to conduct a campaign of any kind. Instead, following the unexpected death of Peter Kirk, Rab Butler's successor as the local M.P., in 1977, he was one of more than two hundred Conservative hopefuls who "put their names forward" for consideration by the Saffron Walden Conservative Association. On the basis of the various would-be candidates' written applications (plus, presumably, a few informal phone calls), the executive of the association whittled down the original number of applicants to about twenty, of whom Haselhurst was one. All twenty were then invited to attend an evening drinks party in a Great Dunmow hotel—in, as it happens, sweltering heat—and each of them was interviewed individually the following day. Only four of the twenty survived this second stage of the process; and, once again, Haselhurst was among them.

The grand climax of the nomination proceedings took place a few days later when the four short-listed candidates appeared before the 150-strong local executive council. Each made a short speech, and a question-and-answer session followed. Haselhurst performed third of the four and was chosen on the second ballot after one of the other would-be candidates had been eliminated.

He thinks he may have won partly because one of the questions from the audience slightly irked him and he suddenly found himself speaking with more passion and conviction than before. The final selection meeting took place on June 12, 1977. The special election took place only four weeks later, on July 7. Haselhurst, like his Conservative predecessors, won easily.

Three points about Haselhurst's nomination are worth noting. The first is that Haselhurst was not a local man; he did not live locally, was not closely connected with the constituency and, before throwing his hat in the ring, did little more than "mug up" on local issues. Haselhurst saw himself principally as a national politician, and that was what the Saffron Walden Conservatives were looking for. The second is that only about 150 people—a very small number—took part in his selection as a candidate, and all were political activists and members of the local Conservative party. The third, already referred to, is that Haselhurst felt no need to conduct any kind of preselection campaign. Prior to the final meeting of the executive council on June 12, he wrote no letters, made no phone calls, issued no press releases, delivered no speeches and appeared not at all on radio or television. The whole nomination process was essentially a private affair—not secret, but private. Indeed Haselhurst got the impression that any efforts on his part to lobby the 150-odd selectors would be ill received. *He* would make his appearance before them. *They* would make the decision.

The relationship between Alan Haselhurst and the Saffron Walden constituency over the decades since 1977 has been close. Haselhurst is what is known in Britain as a "good constituency member." Although he was new to the district in 1977, he bought a house in a village near the town of Saffron Walden shortly after his election and still commutes most days between his constituency home and the House of Commons. Although his home number is not listed in the phone book, a lot of local people know it by now, and Haselhurst goes out of his way to make himself accessible at home, in London and at regular constituency "surgeries," where individual constituents can come to

him with their problems. He attends numerous local Conservative party functions and has frequent meetings with farmers,
charitable groups, local business people and so on. He regards
Saffron Walden as "a smashing place to be," inhabited by "thoroughly nice people." The feeling is largely reciprocated.

The great bulk of Haselhurst's constituency service he provides personally. He has only a small office at the House of Commons and no office at all in his district. His staff—if that is not
too strong a word—consists of his wife Angela, who acts as his
secretary, and a student, who is working for him for a year between leaving school and going on to university. Even in his capacity as a member of the House of Commons Select Committee
on Transport, he has no one to help him. He himself thinks
M.P.s should have three full-time staff: one to act as personal secretary and organizer of the member's schedule, one to help on the
constituency side and one to help on the policy side. The only
other backup Haselhurst has consists of the modest offices of the
Conservative association in Saffron Walden, which help with
some constituency matters and through which constituents can
contact their M.P. if they so choose. Haselhurst's constituency
operation is, to say the least of it, "hands on."

Fund-raising plays a part, but only a small part, in the political
life of any British M.P. The strict limits placed on campaign expenditures at the local level, and the total ban in Great Britain on
political advertising on radio and television, mean that only relatively small sums need to be raised and not a great deal of time or
energy needs to be devoted to raising them. The total amount
spent on promoting Alan Haselhurst's candidature in the Saffron
Walden constituency during the 1992 election campaign was a
mere £7,875.13 (approximately $12,000). Haselhurst attends
Conservative fund-raising fetes, suppers and bazaars, and at election times he writes a few letters to local friends and business
people soliciting donations. But that is all his fund-raising activities amount to. He certainly does not employ a professional
fund-raiser or fund-raising firm.

Campaigning in Saffron Walden is likewise conducted in a

low-key and sporadic way. In one sense, Haselhurst is out campaigning all the time: his constituency service is intended, of
course, to serve the people of his constituency, but it is also intended to impress on them continually the fact that he is doing a
good job as their M.P. But, in another sense, he, like most other
members of Parliament, campaigns only very seldom. General
elections in Great Britain take place only every four or five years,
primary elections are unknown and, except in some highly marginal constituencies, election campaigns tend to be very short,
lasting a matter of weeks rather than months. In the whole of a
typical decade, an M.P. like Alan Haselhurst would expect to
spend no more than twelve weeks, at most, on the hustings. Not
surprisingly, Haselhurst feels no need to employ a press secretary
(even if he could afford one). When he does campaign, it is very
much as the standard-bearer of his party. All of his election materials stress that he is "your Conservative candidate," and at election times the north Essex countryside suddenly blossoms with
small placards adorned with Alan Haselhurst's portrait framed in
Conservative blue.

How might Haselhurst lose his seat? One possibility is that he
might be rejected by the electorate. The voters of Saffron Walden
might turn to the candidate of another party, say Labour or the
Liberal Democrats. In a seat as safe for the Conservatives as Saffron Walden, that possibility seems, and is, very remote; and, in
the improbable event that it did happen, it would almost certainly be because the voters of Saffron Walden had turned against
the Tory party nationally, not because they had turned against
Alan Haselhurst locally. After two decades in the constituency,
Haselhurst is quite clear that all his hours and days devoted to
constituency service, if they have any electoral impact at all, have
one only at the margins, affecting a few hundred voters, at most.
There probably is an "incumbent effect" in Saffron Walden,
which does work in Haselhurst's favor; but it amounts to very little. As elsewhere in Great Britain, most voting in the Saffron
Walden constituency is party voting.

The other way in which Haselhurst might lose his seat is if he lost the confidence of the present-day equivalent of the group that originally selected him as their candidate: the 150-odd leading figures in the local Conservative association. If the association were to deny him renomination and he would therefore cease to be the official Tory candidate for the constituency, he would almost certainly go down to defeat. Indeed he would probably not even bother to run again. The relationship between the M.P. and his local party activists is thus crucial. The member's career turns on it.

Fortunately for Haselhurst and most other British M.P.s, the relationship is usually, in practice, a fairly easy one to sustain. The member needs his party supporters, but they also need him; rows in the local party are unpleasant and potentially electorally damaging; and, not least, a conscientious member usually builds up over time a fund of personal good will and substantial networks of friends and well-disposed acquaintances. Cases of non-readoption are by no means unknown; but they are rare.

In Haselhurst's case, the chances of his not being readopted as the Saffron Walden Conservative candidate approach zero. He likes the local Tories. They like him. They, like him, tend to be on the Tory party's liberal wing. The only time the relationship came under any strain was in 1985, when Haselhurst helped found Centre Forward, the avowedly anti-Thatcherite organization in the party. Roughly a hundred people—somewhat more than usual—turned up at a routine meeting of the association, and one member asked whether the association should not perhaps contemplate finding another candidate; but the one member found no support at all among the rest of those present, and the matter soon blew over. Nowadays Haselhurst is almost automatically readopted as the candidate before each general election—"as the need arises."

As must be evident, the relationship between a British M.P. like Haselhurst and his local party is rather like a marriage. Both sides have to work at it and take it seriously. Of course they do. But, provided the M.P., in particular, works at it and provided nothing goes desperately wrong, the marriage is likely to last.

The possibility of the M.P. not being renominated always exists in the background as a theoretical possibility; but it very seldom becomes a real threat. Haselhurst and others like him do not live in perpetual fear that their "spouse"—their local party activists— will suddenly divorce them and go off with someone else. So far as their local party is concerned, they have, for all practical purposes, security of tenure.

Needless to say, the effects of this security are enhanced by the four- or five-year life of most British Parliaments. Haselhurst was asked what he thought the effect would be—both on him personally and on British government—if, instead of lasting four or five years, Parliaments typically lasted only two years. The thought had obviously never occurred to him before, and he looked aghast:

> It would be hopeless. We suffer from too much short-termism already. It would make it very hard to take the tough decisions. You would live in a frenetic atmosphere, and you would probably start to magnify the importance of the single-issue voter, the person who says "If you don't do what I say, I won't vote for you." It would be an impossible situation.

If Alan Haselhurst is "married" to the Conservative party and the majority of voters in Saffron Walden, so Brigitte Schulte is "married" to the Social Democratic party and the majority of voters in the Forty-first electoral district of the German Federal Republic. Located southwest of Hannover, District Forty-one is based on the medium-sized industrial town of Hameln—and, since most Germans cannot begin to remember the numbers of all their legislative districts, District Forty-one is usually referred to as, simply, "Hameln."

Hameln is considerably larger than Saffron Walden. It covers an area of nearly two thousand square miles, comprises two counties, Hameln-Pyrmont and Holzminden, and has an electorate of roughly 190,000, compared with Saffron Walden's 70,000. Hameln is also considerably more urban than Saffron Walden. In the nineteenth century it was a predominantly agricultural region, but now it is dotted with cities and towns producing such goods as furniture, chemicals and electronics. It is also something of a banking and commercial center. However, despite its industrialization, the economy of the district is by no means dominated by industrial giants. Most local firms are small or middle-sized, or else are branches of national firms. Family enterprises are common. Like other parts of Germany, Hameln was hit by the mid-1990s recession; but it remains a prosperous area, one that people are not anxious to leave.

Its political traditions are staunchly Social Democratic. Until the Social Democratic Party (SPD), along with all of the other democratic parties, were suppressed by the Nazis in 1933, Hameln was an SPD bastion; and, when the federal republic was founded in 1949, it reverted to its Social Democratic allegiance almost as though nothing had happened. The district has been securely in the Social Democrats' hands ever since. None of the other parties, the Christian Democrats, the Free Democrats or the Greens, stands a chance.

But Hameln's main claim to fame is neither economic nor political but legendary. It was in Hameln that the mysterious stranger known to the English-speaking world as the Pied Piper of Hamelin made his dramatic appearance toward the end of the thirteenth century. The town was infested with rats. The Pied Piper promised, for a fee, to get rid of them. He did. He lured them by the thousands to their deaths in the river that still flows through the town:

> From street to street he piped advancing,
> And step for step they followed dancing,
> Until they came to the river Weser
> Wherein all plunged and perished!

But the townspeople refused to pay the promised fee, whereupon the Pied Piper again played on his pipe, and all of Hameln's children followed him eastwards out of the town and into oblivion. It is said that only two of them were ever seen again. One was blind, the other deaf. To this day, the people of Hameln reenact the story of the Pied Piper every summer and Hameln's shops display fierce little toy rats and rats made out of chocolate.

Unlike Alan Haselhurst, who was a virtual stranger to Saffron Walden when, along with the two hundred others, he applied for that seat, Brigitte Schulte has lived in the district for all of her adult life. A school teacher and later a school principal by profession, she was still in her twenties when she became an active local SPD member. Over the following decade, she became a prominent figure in local government in the Hameln area, eventually becoming leader of the SPD group on one of the local councils. She knew everyone in the Hameln SPD; everyone in the Hameln SPD knew her. When the time came, as it soon did, she did not begin by seeking the Bundestag nomination of her party; it sought her.

In 1974, when Schulte was still only thirty-one, Hameln's sitting member of the Bundestag, Heinz Frehsee, announced his intention to retire at the next election. He had been a member of Germany's national legislature for twenty-seven years. Immediately the leading members of the local party began a search for his successor; and one of the first people they thought of was their bright young teacher colleague, who had the additional advantage of being a woman. ("We don't have enough women in the parliament," she recalls one of her supporters saying. "Why not you?") Brigitte Schulte herself was less enthusiastic; she had just become principal of a local school, and her then husband was not at all keen on her becoming a full-time politician. But the pressure on her to run intensified over the following weeks, and gradually she came round to the view that she not only wanted to run, she desperately wanted to win.

Although from the beginning there were five candidates in the field, three from inside the district, two from outside, it soon became clear that Schulte had only one serious rival for the nomination: a senior civil servant from Bonn. For six weeks, during the fall of 1975, all five contenders toured the constituency, meeting party members, making five-minute speeches, answering questions and participating in political discussions. The numbers present varied. Sometimes the group was small; on one occasion it numbered more than three hundred.

On the basis of what they saw and heard about the five contenders, the roughly six thousand members of the SPD in Hameln then chose delegates to attend the final selection meeting, which was held on a cold winter's night in December 1975. The procedure adopted was similar to that in Saffron Walden, with contenders who got the fewest votes being eliminated until one of the five had an absolute majority. In the event, Schulte and the man from Bonn were well ahead on the first ballot and Schulte won outright on the second. Schulte remembers precisely how many members were present on the night of her triumph: 189.

The process that led to Brigitte Schulte's nomination for Hameln was thus, as in Saffron Walden, an entirely intraparty process. No one who was not a party member was involved. The main difference between Schulte's experience and Haselhurst's was that she, unlike him, had to campaign actively to secure the nomination. But, even so, the campaign was not remotely like an American primary. There were no posters, no billboards, no radio spots, no TV commercials. For Schulte, in particular, the campaign was largely a face-to-face affair, conducted among people whom, because of her local connections, she mostly knew already. The outcome of the ensuing general election, held in October 1976, was a foregone conclusion, at least in District Forty-one. Brigitte Schulte won with a majority of 15,000 over her Christian Democratic opponent. She has been a member of the Bundestag ever since.

She takes her work as Hameln's representative extremely seriously. On the one hand, she gets great pleasure out of serving the people of her district; on the other, Hameln provides her with a secure political base. Although her main home is now in Bonn and she spends most nights during the week there, she tries to spend most weekends—and often whole weeks during parliamentary recesses—working in the district. She has a house in Hameln as well as her home in Bonn, and she goes out of her way to make herself available on an individual basis, as well as making the usual rounds of visits to local businesses, hospitals, schools, trade union branches and so on. She keeps in close touch with the local SPD. Compared with Haselhurst, she is fortunate in having adequate staff support. In addition to a personal secretary and two people who work for her on the policy side (Schulte is a member of the Bundestag's budget and defense committees), she maintains two district offices, one with two staff in Hameln town itself and one with a single staff member in Holzminden, roughly thirty miles away. In effect, she is her own press secretary, having good relations with the half-dozen local newspapers in the district and writing for them regularly. Perhaps surprisingly, she does not receive a great deal of old-fashioned constituency correspondence. People know they can come and see her in her district office.

As in Saffron Walden, election campaigns in Hameln are low-key affairs. German national elections take place roughly every four years, and the quadrennial election campaigns are largely fought nationally. The fact that Hameln is such a safe district for the SPD also lowers the temperature. In 1990, for example, Brigitte Schulte's campaign for the October Bundestag elections did not begin until mid August, after the summer holidays. Money is no problem, partly because not much of it is needed. The candidate herself contributes modest sums out of her own pocket, but otherwise she finds it easy to raise money from local SPD members, many of whom are generous donors, and also from local businesses, some of which donate money to the candidates of all the major parties. The parties themselves, as in most European countries, are subvented directly from state funds. Schulte's total campaign expenditure during the 1994 Bundestag election amounted to roughly 55,000 DM (approximately $37,000). She could not usefully have spent more.

Schulte's assiduous constituency service makes little difference to the overall outcome of elections in District Forty-one; any candidate of the SPD would be bound to win. But it does provide her with a welcome—and measurable—bonus. Half of Germany's

Bundestag members are chosen, like Schulte, to represent American-style geographical districts; but, under Germany's system of proportional representation, the other half are chosen from lists of party candidates. The individual voter in Germany thus has two votes: one for his or her local Bundestag candidate and one for his or her preferred party. It follows that, in every district, the difference between the two tallies of votes—for candidates and for parties—provides every local candidate with a quite precise measure of his or her local popularity (or lack of it). Schulte is understandably proud of the fact that by the 1990s the difference between the SPD list vote in Hameln and her own personal vote had grown to a gratifying 3.3 percent.

Given that Hameln is so safe for the SPD, the crucial political relationship for Schulte, as for Haselhurst, is that between her and her local party. If that relationship is a good one, she is completely safe. If not, not. Schulte is on the moderate wing of her party: pro-private enterprise, pro-nuclear power and pro-NATO. She was a strong supporter of the former SPD chancellor Helmut Schmidt but has been less enthusiastic about some of the more recent SPD chancellor-candidates, notably Oskar Lafontaine. Fortunately for her, as for Haselhurst, the great bulk of her local party is of the same persuasion. Some SPD members of the Bundestag—and some Greens—are under considerable pressure to vote in parliament the way their local party supporters want them to, contrary to their own convictions. But Schulte is under no such pressure. In addition, because of the close correspondence between her views and those of her local party, and also because of the cordial personal relations between them, her renomination by the local SPD before every election is assured. She has never been challenged for her party's nomination; she has never even imagined that she might be. The mandatory nomination meeting, which takes place roughly twelve months in advance of every national election, is largely a formality. All the indicators are that Brigitte Schulte can remain Hameln's Bundestag member for as long as she wants to. In the politics of Hameln, she is a sort of benign Pied Piper.

One of her special interests, relevant to her membership of the Bundestag defense committee, is her membership of the North Atlantic Assembly. As a NATO parliamentarian, she frequently meets colleagues from the U.S. Congress and is well aware that the terms of members of the House of Representatives last only two years. The thought that Germany might likewise adopt two-year terms appalls her. That, she says, "would be terrible." Both German governments and individual Bundestag members would be under constant electoral pressure. "I," she says, shaking her head, "would certainly not stand for the Bundestag any more." Fortunately, there is no suggestion in Germany that the members of the Bundestag should be reelected every two years. The suggestion currently being canvassed is, on the contrary, that the maximum legal life of each Bundestag should be extended, as in some German states, from four years to five.

Such are the political worlds of Alan Haselhurst and Brigitte Schulte. To enter the political world of Steny H. Hoyer, the U.S. congressman from the Fifth District of Maryland, is to enter a completely different world. Election campaigns are no more than episodes in the political lives of Haselhurst and Schulte. In Hoyer's they play a continuous and wholly inescapable part. Indeed almost the only thing that he and Schulte have in common is that, although Hoyer is of Danish origin, both of them have German names. Hoyer happens to be the name of a big German trucking firm.

Steny Hoyer, as much as Haselhurst but even more than Schulte, is a career politician, someone who not merely lives off politics but lives for politics. His adult life and his political life are almost coextensive. A lawyer by profession, Hoyer was first elected to the Maryland state senate in the same year, 1966, that he graduated from Georgetown Law School. In 1978, after a dozen years in the legislature (during which he rose to become the state's youngest-ever senate president), he decided to run for statewide office, but was defeated in his bid for the lieutenant governorship when the gubernatorial candidate on whose ticket he was running lost in the state Democratic primary. His career in elective politics temporarily stalled, he accepted a nominated appointment to the Maryland Board of Higher Education.

However, bad luck was soon followed by good. In 1981, less than two and a half years after Hoyer's defeat for the lieutenant governorship, the Fifth Congressional District of Maryland was declared vacant when the incumbent member, Gladys Spellman, failed to recover from a heart attack she had suffered during the previous year's election campaign. No fewer than nineteen candidates ran in the Democratic primary that followed, but Hoyer won, defeating his principal rival, the former congressman's husband, by fewer than two thousand votes out of the 46,224 that were cast. The primary was held in April. The special election was held only a few weeks later, in May 1981, and once again Hoyer won. Probably because his Republican opponent was strongly backed by the national GOP and because the election took place in the wake of the March 1981 attempt on President Reagan's life, Hoyer's margin of victory was much smaller than Spellman's had been—he took only 55 percent of the vote compared with her 80 percent—but he was still able to capitalize on the built-in Democratic advantage in the district. That advantage still exists. He continues to be able to capitalize on it.

That said, the Fifth District that Hoyer represents today is not the Fifth District that he was first elected to represent in 1981. Haselhurst and Schulte have been lucky in that the constituency boundaries of both Saffron Walden and Hameln have remained substantially unaltered over the past three decades. It could have been otherwise. In Great Britain, in particular, redistricting takes place approximately every ten years, and the effects on individual constituencies—and their members—can be devastating. Haselhurst has been lucky to escape. Hoyer has not been so fortunate. In 1991, as a result of the 1990 U.S. census, the Maryland state legislature had to redraw the boundaries of the state's congressional districts. It did so by, on the one hand, carving a new, largely African-American district out of Hoyer's old Fifth District and, on the other, adding to the old Fifth a large swathe of territory in the south of the state. The constituents Hoyer lost were mostly black, urban and liberal; those he gained were mostly white, rural and considerably more conservative. Overnight the proportion of African-Americans in the Fifth District fell from more than 50 percent to less than 20 percent. Overnight, too, a totally safe district for the Democrats became considerably more marginal. In the 1980s, following the 1981 special election, Hoyer never got less than 72 percent of the vote in his district. Since 1992 he has never gotten more than 59 percent.

Like his old one, Hoyer's new district totally lacks reality as a community. Whereas Saffron Walden is idyllic and remarkably homogeneous and Hameln is rich in folklore and almost equally homogeneous, the Fifth District of Maryland, like most U.S. congressional districts, exists simply as lines on a map. It meanders from part of Anne Arundel county, containing large chunks of suburban Washington, D.C., in the north, to Calvert, Charles and St. Marys counties in the south, with part of Prince George's county, also containing large chunks of suburban Washington, in between. With a total population of roughly 600,000 and a voting-age population of nearly half a million, it is a large district, much larger than either Saffron Walden (with 70,000 voters) or Hameln (with 190,000). It is also extremely diverse, comprising college professors and students (the University of Maryland's largest campus, at College Park, is in the district), service personnel (the Patuxent Naval Air Warfare Center is a major defense facility), large numbers of federal employees and, in parts of the three southernmost counties, a considerably poorer rural population. Washington's famous Beltway cuts through the district's northwestern tip.

The consequence of the Fifth District's size and diversity, and of its politically greater marginality since 1991, is that Steny Hoyer has to function, whether he likes it or not, as a veritable reelection machine. Unlike Haselhurst and Schulte, he can take nothing for granted. If they are "married" to their constituencies, Hoyer's relationship with his is more like that of a salesman operating in a highly competitive and potentially unpredictable market. He has always to be wary. He has always to be alert.

For someone in Hoyer's position, constituency service is not mainly a matter of duty (though, of course, it is a duty and one that most congressmen enjoy performing); rather, it is mainly a matter of electoral survival. Hoyer has not merely to serve his constituents and to protect their interests; he has to be seen to be doing so. The job of being what the British, in their rather languid way, call a "good constituency member" is an intensely demanding one in the United States, and it demands vigilance and ingenuity as well as goodwill and a willingness to work hard.

Steny Hoyer's performance since 1981 as the member of Congress for the Fifth District has been little short of magnificent— and, understandably, he advertises the fact. At one level, he and his staff provide a comprehensive service to constituents as individuals. Like Haselhurst, but unlike Schulte, Hoyer actually lives in the district—he drives to and from work every day—and as a result he frequently meets constituents in the evening, often bringing their problems back to the office with him the next morning. His Capitol Hill office receives approximately four hundred pieces of district-related mail each week (someone has the job of counting them), and all that require a response receive one. One member of his staff, the legislative correspondent, deals full time with constituency mail. Before the 1991 redistricting Hoyer felt the need of only one district office (the old district was relatively compact as well as being close to Washington), but he now has two, one in Greenbelt to cover the suburban parts of the district and one in Waldorf to cover the southern and more rural parts. Out of a total staff of seventeen—compared with Haselhurst's one and a bit, and Schulte's six—five of them work full time in the district.

At another level, Hoyer has been tireless in championing the cause of federal employment—and federal employees—in the district. The brief biographical sketch distributed by his office notes that "he has been the author of numerous bills and amendments to protect the pay, benefits and rights of federal government employees," and he has consistently (and successfully) backed the extension of the Washington Metro into his two suburban counties. The new National Archives building at College Park is called the Steny H. Hoyer Building, and it was a major coup for Hoyer when the Internal Revenue Service decided in 1991 to consolidate twenty-eight separate District of Columbia offices into one big complex in Prince George's county.

But probably Hoyer's greatest district-related triumph came in the mid 1990s when he succeeded in reversing an initial recommendation by the Defense Department's Base Closures Commission that the Patuxent Naval Air Test Center (as it was then called) should be either drastically reduced in size or else closed altogether. Far from being closed, the Patuxent Naval Air Warfare Center (as it has since been rechristened) has been expanded and turned into a full-service naval facility. It is now the district's largest employer. Hoyer's success in saving the center was not only good for southern Maryland's economy; it was, as he himself says, highly "*visible.*"

In a district as disparate and politically marginal as the Maryland Fifth has become, visibility is a high priority. Neither Haselhurst nor Schulte employs (or could afford to employ) a press secretary; neither of them sends out (or could afford to send out) a regular district newsletter. Hoyer does both. The press secretary organizes ad hoc press conferences and interviews with the local media; Hoyer makes extensive use of the television studios in the House of Representatives press gallery. Once a year, a constituency newsletter is mailed to every address in the district, at a cost to the taxpayer, including printing, of roughly $50,000. Inside the newsletter is a form which constituents can return for further information on such issues as education, defense and women's health. From the forms that are returned, Hoyer's office has built up a database for targeted mailings to groups of about eight thousand constituents at a time.

This need to be visible arises directly out of the fact that Hoyer's congressional seat is almost continuously at risk. Haselhurst fights a general election every four or five years; Schulte fights one every three or four years; Hoyer fights one every twenty-four months (and of course the 1991 redistricting markedly reduced his margin of safety). Moreover, Haselhurst and Schulte can count on their party's renomination; neither really has to think about it. Hoyer can also be pretty confident of retaining his party's nomination; but, unlike the others, he has constantly to fight for it. In the eight election years from 1982 through 1996, Hoyer had to contend with primary opposition on no fewer than seven occasions; only in 1988 was he unopposed. To be sure, his margins of victory have invariably been enormous; usually he has won at least 80 percent, sometimes more than 90 percent, of the primary vote. Nevertheless, the possibility of defeat, or at least of serious political embarrassment, is ever present. An election campaign, however one-sided, has to be fought.

Hoyer's campaigns in the Fifth District thus have no beginnings and no ends. They are like a conveyor belt, an ongoing operation. Asked how soon after each election he began to think about the next one, he replied laconically, "That night." It never leaves his mind—or that of most other congressmen—that after every November election there are only 730 days until the next one. Hoyer also believes that whether or not he carries the Fifth District depends ultimately on him. He reckons that the Democrats' built-in advantage over the Republicans in the district has now been reduced to no more than 45 percent Democratic to 40 percent Republican and that the remaining 15 percent are up for grabs. For the purposes of capturing that 15 percent, constituency service, campaigning and visibility are crucial. In 1994, when there was a strong Republican tide flowing elsewhere in the country, but when Hoyer in the Fifth District actually increased his margin of victory, constituency service and campaigning probably made all the difference. "That was when the personality factor really came into play." In a district like the Fifth, it is not enough for the incumbent to run as the candidate of his party. He must run on his personal record. In his campaign advertising, does Hoyer stress mainly himself or his party? The answer is unequivocal: "Myself."

Campaigning in this ceaseless and highly personal way costs a great deal of money. The taxpayer indirectly contributes something (for example, the cost of Hoyer's newsletters), but not much. Most of the money that someone like him needs to spend on campaign staff and equipment, on printing, on roadside advertising and on TV and radio commercials, he has to raise on his own, whether from his party's congressional campaign committee, from political action committees (PACs) or from favorably disposed individuals. The money is needed not only for campaigning; it is also needed for the purpose of deterring serious potential challengers from entering the race, both in the primary and in the election in November. It is largely for fundraising purposes that a Hoyer for Congress Committee is kept more or less permanently in being. In addition, Hoyer himself spends an average of about eight hours a month—a full working day each month—talking directly to potential donors on the phone or in person. The amount of time devoted to fund-raising naturally tends to increase as the election approaches.

In fact, Hoyer probably needs to spend less time fund-raising than most members of Congress. By the mid 1990s he was a long-serving member of the House and also an established figure in the Democratic congressional leadership. He used to have to ring up potential donors and say, "My name's Hoyer. I'm having a fund-raiser. Is there a chance you might come?" Now the donors themselves say, "Hoyer's having a fund-raiser. We'd better go." In addition, Hoyer's mainly liberal voting record on bread-and-butter domestic issues means that he has the financial backing of a number of important labor unions, via their PACs. In 1996 he ranked eighth among all House Democrats in the volume of PAC contributions he received. It almost goes without saying that the amounts he succeeds in raising, and that he needs, are, by European standards, colossal. In 1992 Alan Haselhurst spent approximately $12,000 on his reelection campaign. In 1994 Brigitte Schulte spent approximately $37,000 on hers. In the same year, 1994, Steny Hoyer spent $1,295,542 on his, a great deal of it on purchasing television time. The transatlantic difference remains large even when allowance is made for the substantially larger number of voters in Hoyer's district.

Hoyer's political life differs from that of Haselhurst and Schulte in yet another respect. It is scarcely an exaggeration to say that Haselhurst and Schulte enjoy total autonomy in their legislative lives, at least so far as their constituents and their local constituency parties are concerned. They can join whatever committees in the legislature they like. They can promote whatever bills and make whatever speeches they like. They can also vote as they like—though of course the presumption in Great Britain and Germany, as in most parliamentary systems, is that they will normally vote with their party. The only issue on which Haselhurst says he would have felt constrained by his constituency was over proposals that were made in the 1970s to expand Stansted airport, on the southern edge of Saffron Walden, into a major international airport. The great majority of his constituents were vehemently opposed. Fortunately, he was too. (In the event, the expansion went ahead anyway, and opposition protests in Saffron Walden have long since died down.)

Hoyer also enjoys some degree of autonomy. His constituents are not interested in, or even aware of, much that goes on in Congress; and many of Hoyer's personal causes are relatively uncontroversial in constituency terms. For example, Hoyer is a senior American member of the Commission on Security and Cooperation in Europe (the so-called Helsinki Commission), and in 1990 he played a major part in piloting through Congress the far-reaching Americans with Disabilities Act. As a member of the House leadership in 1993, he defied a substantial portion of constituency opinion when he helped promote passage of the North American Free Trade Agreement (NAFTA) legislation. Nevertheless, it is probably fair to say that, to a far greater extent than Haselhurst and Schulte, Hoyer has constantly to look over his shoulder. He must continuously adjust his behavior in Congress to the requirements of ensuring his reelection.

His choice of committee assignments provides a good illustration. In 1983, having succeeded in winning a seat on the powerful House Appropriations Committee, Hoyer chose to sit on two of its subcommittees. One dealt with Labor, Health and Human

Services, and Education, the other with the Treasury, the U.S. Postal Service and General Government. Both choices made perfect sense given the old Fifth's liberal leanings and the preponderance of federal employees within it. In 1985, for similar district-related reasons, he added a third subcommittee: that on the District of Columbia. However, in 1991, when it was clear that the new Fifth District would include several large military bases (and would no longer include so many suburban voters), he traded his place on the D.C. subcommittee for one on the subcommittee dealing with military construction projects. It was from that base that he opposed closure of the Patuxent naval facility. Since the U.S. Government Printing Office is a large employer in his district, it is also not surprising to find that Hoyer is a member of the congressional Joint Printing Committee.

It is less clear to what extent Hoyer has adjusted his congressional voting in response to his new district's requirements. He himself claims he has not—that even before 1991 he held hawkish positions on crime, defense and the need for a balanced budget. Against that, the box scores kept by such organizations as the *National Journal* indicate a substantial rightward shift in his voting record between 1990 and 1992. Whatever the truth of that matter, there can be no doubt that after 1991 Hoyer had to reorient a good deal of his legislative activity. The threat of base closures in his new district brought that issue to the fore, and environmental issues in the new district, with its many miles of shoreline along Chesapeake Bay and the Potomac River, are far more salient now than they were in the old district.

Finally, what distinguishes Hoyer, not least, from Haselhurst and Schulte is that Hoyer is not only a full-time election-winning machine; he is also, in a way that they are not, a full-time, powerful legislator. Backbench members of the British House of Commons and the German Bundestag are not really "legislators" in the full American sense of the term; except on rare occasions, they have little independent capacity either to pass laws or to exert substantial influence on their country's executive branch. Rather, their role, as rank-and-file members of their party in parliament, is either to support the incumbent administration of the day if it is "theirs" in party terms or to oppose it if it is not. What is most striking about members of the U.S. Congress is that they are *both* members of the most powerful legislative assembly in the world *and,* simultaneously, subject to intense and continuous electoral pressure of a kind unknown elsewhere. It is with the causes and consequences of this unremitting electoral pressure in the United States that the rest of this book is mainly concerned.

One simple summary statistic begins to make the point. Between his first election for Saffron Walden in 1977 and the end of 1996, Sir Alan Haselhurst fought a total of five elections. Between her first election for Hameln in 1976 and the end of 1996, Brigitte Schulte fought a total of six elections. By contrast, between his first election for Maryland's Fifth District and the end of 1996—a considerably shorter period than in the case of either Haselhurst or Schulte—Steny H. Hoyer fought a total of no fewer than fifteen elections (seven primary and eight general elections). That simple but startling contrast is no mere epiphenomenon, no mere happenstance without wider political significance. On the contrary, it goes, as we shall see, to the heart of many of American government's current frustrations—and to many Americans' current frustrations with government.

Hoyer, like both Haselhurst and Schulte, was asked what he thought of American congressmen's two-year terms. His reply was diplomatic. "The two-year cycle," he said, choosing his words carefully, "*is* a distraction, but it does offer the value of connection with the district." One of his assistants was less diplomatic. Asked what she thought of the two-year cycle, punctuated by primaries, she replied simply: "It's absurd."

2

WHY AMERICAN POLITICIANS
ARE VULNERABLE

The careers of the three politicians described in the last chapter are at one level, of course, unique; but at another level they are typical of the careers of the majority of elected politicians in their countries. It is time therefore to spell out in more detail, and on a broader canvas, the ways in which American elective politicians differ from their brethren and sisters in other major democracies. The fact is that all politicians in all countries run scared some of the time. The unique characteristic of elective politicians in the United States is that practically all of them run scared practically all of the time. Why?

They do so, as will emerge, not for any one reason but for a whole combination of reasons—reasons that in practice powerfully reinforce each other. Politics and government in the United States are marked by the fact that American elected officials have, in many cases, very short terms of office *and* face the prospect of being defeated in primary elections *and* have to run for office primarily as individuals rather than as standard-bearers of their party *and* have continually to raise large sums of money in order to finance their own election campaigns. Some of these factors operate in some other countries. There is, however, no other country in which all of them operate and operate simultaneously. The cumulative consequences, as we shall see, are both pervasive and profound.[1]

We look first at the question of the lengths of terms for the holders of political offices. The Constitution of the United States sets out in one of its very first sentences that "the House of Representatives shall be composed of members chosen every second year by the people of the several states." When they decided on a term of office as short as two years for House members, the framers of the Constitution were setting a precedent that has, in the event, been followed by no other major democratic country. In Great Britain, France, Italy and Canada the constitutional or legal maximum for the duration of the lower house of the national legislature is five years. In Germany and Japan the equivalent term is four years. Only in Australia and New Zealand, whose institutions are in some limited respects modeled on those of the United States, are the legal maxima as short as three years. In having two-year terms, the United States stands alone.

The legal maxima prevailing in other countries are, to be sure, somewhat misleading. In most parliamentary systems, provision is made for the possibility of dissolving the national legislature before its term is up and for the holding of national elections ahead of schedule. The incumbent government may itself possess the power of dissolution, as in Great Britain and the other "Westminster model" countries; or there may be special, and more elaborate, arrangements for bringing about parliament's dissolution, as in France, Italy and Germany. In consequence, the actual duration of the legislatures in almost all democracies apart from the United States tends to be shorter—sometimes considerably shorter—than the prescribed maximum. In France, for example, the average duration of National Assemblies since 1960 has been 3.5 years as opposed to the constitutionally permitted five.

However, too much should not be read into such shorter averages. What tends to happen in most parliamentary democracies is that longish periods of considerable legislative stability are punctuated by periods of narrow or nonexistent parliamentary majorities, in the course of which several elections are held within a short space of time. In Canada, for instance, three national elections were held in the four years between 1962 and 1965, when no party or combination of parties was able to form a stable majority in the House of Commons. Similarly in France, the shortish average life of National Assemblies since 1960 is largely accounted for by two unusual periods when pairs of legislative elections were held within two or three years of each other: in 1967–68, when President de Gaulle was contending with an unprecedented wave of industrial and student unrest, and in 1986–88, when a Socialist president, François Mitterrand, briefly "cohabited" with a right-wing dominated National Assembly. Such examples apart (and excluding Australia and New Zealand), the norm in most parliamentary democracies is for the national parliament to remain in existence for between roughly three and a half and four and a half years.

One implication of this contrast between the U.S. House of Representatives and most other democratic parliaments is immediately obvious—and is a theme of much American political journalism. When a U.S. congressman takes his House seat in the January of the year following his successful election or reelection, he already knows that he faces a further electoral contest before the end of the following year—that is, in less than twenty-two months' time. For example, David S. Broder, in a routine-seeming piece in the *Washington Post,* wrote:

> Democratic lawmakers returned to Capitol Hill yesterday voicing concern that the problems plaguing the Clinton administration may cripple his legislative program and bring them grief in the 1994 election.[2]

But what was remarkable about Broder's report, at least in the eyes of a foreign observer, was that it was published in early June 1993—only six months into the life of the new Congress. In most other countries, such disturbing thoughts enter legislators' minds, if at all, only at a far later stage in the political cycle.

Members of the United States Senate are, of course, in a quite different position. Their constitutionally prescribed term of office, six years, is very long by anyone's standards. But from our point of view senators' six-year terms are not all they seem. In the first place, so pervasive is America's electioneering atmosphere that even newly elected senators begin almost at once to lay plans for their reelection campaigns. Senator Daniel Patrick Moynihan of New York recalls that when he first came to the Senate in 1977 his fellow members, when they met over lunch or a drink, usually talked about politics and policy. Now they talk about almost nothing but the latest opinion polls. In the second place, the fact that under the American Constitution the terms of one third of the senators end every two years means that, even if individual senators do not feel themselves to be under continuing electoral pressure, the Senate as a whole does. *It*, the Senate, may not be up for reelection every two years; but one in three of *them* are. The same *Washington Post* report by David Broder in June 1993 continued:

> The Clinton agenda looks shaky in the Senate, especially after interim Sen. Bob Krueger (D-Tex.) was beaten 2 to 1 by Republican challenger Kay Bailey Hutchison in Saturday's [June 5's] special election. The massive defeat sent shock waves through Democratic ranks and heightened fears among Democrats that they could lose their majority and their chairmanships next year, when 21 Democrats and 13 Republicans face voters.[3]

Despite the Founding Fathers' original intentions, the Senate's collective electoral sensibilities increasingly resemble those of the House.

There is, of course, one elected American policymaker—the most important of them all—who does enjoy a term of office roughly comparable to that of elected officeholders in other countries: the president himself, with his fixed term of four years. Indeed the president of the United States is in practice considerably more secure than the heads of government in most other countries because, unlike him (impeachment apart), they can be ousted not merely at national elections but during the long intervals between them. As strong a leader as Great Britain's Margaret Thatcher fell as the result of a coup inside the Conservative party in 1990. French prime ministers come and go (though presidents stay). Prime ministers in Italy seldom last for more than a year or two.

As in the case of the Senate, however, all is not as it seems. Just as the internal life of the Senate, despite its stability as an institution, is at all times colored by the electoral preoccupations of one third of its members, so the man in the White House, and all those around him, operate in a political environment colored by the electoral preoccupations of congressmen and senators. *Their* electoral concerns are of necessity a central feature of *his* calculations. As David Broder's report indicated, the president's agenda looked "shaky" in Congress in 1993 precisely because Democrats on Capitol Hill were worried about their seats.

Moreover, all the evidence suggests that in recent decades presidents themselves, despite the apparent security of their fixed and relatively long terms, have come to see their own tasks in increasingly election-oriented ways. Ronald Reagan's White House, especially in the first few years, was organized at least as much for campaigning as for actually governing; and Bill Clinton in 1993 brought with him to the White House a group of advisers, and also a mindset, that was sharply focused on electoral considerations. Amid the swirl of meetings that surrounded the preparation of Clinton's first economic plan in February 1993, less than four weeks after his inauguration, an economic adviser was heard to complain, "The campaign people act as if 1996 is tomorrow"—and, bizarrely, the campaign people themselves were, as many witnesses have testified, central to the making of the plan.[4]

To this analysis one partial caveat needs to be entered. Whereas the heads of government in most democracies can stand for reelection (or renomination) more or less in perpetuity, the president of the United States, under the terms of the Twenty-second Amendment to the Constitution, can stand for reelection only once. A president who serves two terms is thus subject to electoral pressure, bearing directly upon him as an individual, during only half of his total period in office. His second term is, for him personally, an "elections-free zone." Once again, however, the implications are not as far-reaching as they might seem. Even if the president himself is in his second term and therefore not running for reelection, most of those with whom he has to do business on Capitol Hill are. He may have quit the electoral arena; but they have not—and his conduct in office continues to depend, not on him alone, but on *their* assessments of *their* electoral prospects. A president in his second term may also be keen, as Reagan undoubtedly was, that he should be succeeded by another president from the same party. Even if the electoral stakes in question are no longer his own, he is very likely to continue to have them. Elections inevitably cast their shadows even over those who are retiring from the political field.[5]

Many of America's most important individual decision makers thus have shorter terms of office than their opposite numbers in almost any other democratic country; and both the presidency and Congress as institutions are continuously affected, in the ways just described, by the presence within the system of these short legislative terms. By virtue of that fact alone, both the individual politicians in the United States and the American governmental system as a whole are continuously subjected to a level of electoral pressure that, by international standards, is extraordinarily high.

But there is more to it even than that. Not merely do American congressmen, senators and would-be presidents have to compete in general elections in order to attain office. They have, in addition, to be prepared to compete in primary elections for the purpose of securing their party's nomination. In other words, they have to be prepared to jump not just one electoral hurdle to attain office: they have to be prepared to jump two (or even three in the eleven states that allow for runoffs in primaries). And the existence of this extra hurdle places American politicians in a completely different position from that of elective politicians in *all* other democratic countries.

Most Americans seem unaware of the fact, but the direct pri-mary—a government-organized popular election to nominate candidates for public office—is, for better or worse, an institution peculiar to the United States. Neither primary elections nor their functional equivalents exist anywhere else in the democratic world. They have the effect, it goes without saying, of adding a further di-mension of uncertainty and unpredictability to American elective politicians' already uncertain and unpredictable world.

Party nominations everywhere except in the United States are in the hands of the political parties themselves; and the political par-ties in almost all other democracies function for most practical purposes as private clubs or associations.[6] Parties in most other countries can be compared with private companies which, so to speak, manufacture "products"—candidates for public office—which the "consumers"—or voters—either "buy" or not as they choose. State regulation of these private "companies" is usually minimal. Only in Germany, among the major western democra-cies, are the parties regulated by the law to any substantial extent.

More important for our purposes, the participation of the mass electorate in the selection of party candidates for office is completely unknown outside the United States. To be sure, some individual parties—the French Socialists and the British Labour party, for example—do permit all of their dues-paying members to take part in the process of selecting candidates; but relatively few parties outside the United States go even this far. The norm is for nominations to be made by local, regional or national party caucuses. Those involved in the process in other countries are all usually party delegates or other kinds of party officehold-ers, and they may well number only a few dozen or, at most, a few hundred. For example, the British Conservative party has dominated British politics for most of the twentieth century; yet, as we saw in the case of Alan Haselhurst, Conservative parlia-mentary candidates are initially selected—and are then usually sustained in their positions—by groups of local activists that sel-dom number more than fifty or sixty. In Italy, the national exec-utive of the historically dominant Christian Democratic party met centrally (and secretly) to arrange the party's entire national candidates list.

The practical consequences are immensely significant. In most countries outside the United States, the individual legislator or other holder of public office, so long as he or she is reasonably conscientious and does not gratuitously offend local or regional party opinion, has no real need to worry about renomination. To be sure, cases of parties in countries like France, Germany and Canada refusing to renominate incumbent legislators are not unknown; but they are relatively rare and tend to occur under unusual sets of circumstances. The victims are usually old, idle or alcoholic. In practice, legislators and other officeholders outside the United States normally find that retaining their party's confidence is not at all difficult.

The contrast between the rest of the world and the United States could hardly be more striking. To the American congressman or senator, or even president, the possibility of not being renominated as the result of a primary election—and therefore of not being reelected—is ever present. The possibility of losing a primary may seem remote; but it can never be entirely dismissed as a possibility, even in the safest districts and states. Most elective politicians in other countries are singly vulnerable: to the whim of the general electorate. Elective politicians in the United States are thus doubly vulnerable: to the primary electorate as well as the general.

There was a time when primaries, even in the United States, were by no means universal. As recently as the early 1950s, the laws of Connecticut did not provide for them. But since then primaries have been mandatory or readily available in all fifty states.[7] They can take place, depending on state law, at any time between March and October in any election year. Moreover, contested primaries involving incumbent officeholders, though not the norm, are far from infrequent. In 1978 no fewer than 104 of the 382 incumbent members of the House of Representatives who sought reelection faced primary opposition. In the following three elections, the figures were: 93 out of 398 in 1980, 98 out of 393 in 1982 and 130 out of 409 in 1984.[8] More recently, in 1994, nearly one third of all House incumbents seeking re-election, 121 out of 386, had to face primary opposition. In the Senate in 1994 the proportion was even higher: 11 out of 26.[9] Even those incumbents who did not face opposition could seldom be absolutely certain in advance that they were not going to. The influence of primaries in the United States—and the possibility of primaries—is pervasive. As we shall see, the fact that incumbents usually win is neither here nor there.

To frequent elections and primary elections must be added another factor, which contributes powerfully to increasing the electoral vulnerability of politicians in the United States: the relative absence of what we might call "party cover."

In most democratic countries, the fate of most politicians depends, not primarily on their own endeavors, but on the fate—locally, regionally or nationally—of their party. If their party does well in an election, so do they. If not, not. The British term "swing," with its air of fatal—and impersonal—inevitability, captures well the manner in which politics in most such democracies is conducted.[10] The individual politician's interests and those of his party are bound up together. The individual has an undoubted stake in not damaging his party; but at the same time, so long as he remains his party's candidate, he has a good deal of room for maneuver. He need not concern himself excessively with his personal political standing, with his votes in the legislature (which will normally be party votes) or with local campaigning. He is likely to want to be attentive to his constituents—out of a sense of duty or because, in a marginal seat, his reelection may depend on voters' memories of services rendered and favors received—but his close ties to his party mean that his sensitivities to his district will usually be only as great as he wants them to be and will tend, by American standards, to be limited.

There are exceptions to this general rule. In elections to the Japanese House of Representatives under Japan's traditional electoral system, each electoral district had between three and five seats; but each voter had only a single vote. The major parties, knowing that each voter had only a single vote but wanting to win as many of each district's seats as they could, typically nominated as many candidates as they reckoned had a decent chance of winning (say, three in a four-member district). The result was that each party's candidates were forced, in form as well as in fact, to compete against each other. Not surprisingly, candidates finding themselves in this situation developed in their districts their own personal support organizations (known as *Koenkai*). Candidates in Italy's multimember districts likewise have to run against one another and likewise, and for the same reasons, conduct highly personalized campaigns.[11]

Despite these exceptions, however, America's elective politicians remain the odd men out. They are, almost literally, out on their own—not only in relation to politicians in most other countries, but also in absolute terms. The factor of party still matters in American electoral politics, but less so than anywhere else in the democratic world. As a result, American legislators seeking reelection are forced to raise their own profiles, to make their own records and to fight their own reelection campaigns. If the term "swing" captures well the relative impersonality of British electoral politics, the term "entrepreneur"—with its connotations of aggressive individualism—captures perfectly the style that actual and would-be elective politicians in the United States are forced to adopt. It is no accident that the term has caught on so completely—and that it has caught on only in America.

Gary C. Jacobson, a leading student of American electoral politics, puts the point eloquently:

The most striking feature of contemporary congressional elections is the ascendant importance of individual candidates and campaigns. . . . Congressional campaigns are overwhelmingly candidate centered. Although national parties have recently expanded their efforts to recruit and finance candidates, most serious congressional aspirants operate, of choice and necessity, as individual political entrepreneurs. The risks, pains, and rewards of mounting a campaign are largely theirs. Most instigate their own candidacies, raise their own resources, and put together their own campaign organizations. Their skills, resources, and strategies have a decisive effect on election outcomes.[12]

The candidate's party is a background factor. It is the candidate himself who is in the foreground.

Visual imagery reinforces the point. In Italy and other countries on the continent of Europe, the political parties' posters—and only the parties' posters—are neatly displayed on official billboards, with a special allocation of space given to each party. In the United States, it can sometimes be virtually impossible for an outside observer to discover the partisan affiliation of an individual candidate, even one running for an important statewide office.

Nonpartisan individualism among candidates is matched—and partly caused—by nonpartisan individualism among voters. In other countries, few voters deviate in the ballot box from their current party preference. In America, millions do (or in fact do not have a party preference). The incidence of "split-ticket voting" in the United States—unknown, and indeed physically impossible, in most other countries—has soared since the 1960s, as has the proportion of voters who claim they identify with one party but who nevertheless vote for another. In the 1950s, the proportion of party identifiers in House and Senate elections who defected from their party at individual elections seldom rose above 10 percent; since the mid 1970s it has seldom fallen below 20 percent.[13] Congressmen and senators know this. They know that their future depends on who *they* are and what *they* do. In America, their party does not provide them with a place to hide.

This absence of party cover, entailing a very high degree of electoral exposure, is occasioned partly by another feature of American politics that most Americans take for granted but that is in fact extremely unusual: the low levels of party cohesion (and certainly of party discipline) in the U.S. Congress. The levels have risen substantially in recent years, especially following the Republican sweep in the midterm elections of 1994; but they are still low by international standards. In the great majority of the world's legislatures, most members of the same party vote in the same way most of the time on all resolutions, bill and amendments. To know how party member A voted is, most of the time, to know how party member B voted. This is true in countries as geographically and ethnically diverse as Canada and Australia and even in Japan, where Dietmen of the same party normally cast their legislative votes as one, even though many of them may be electoral rivals in the same district. One consequence is that, in most countries, legislators' constituents and their political opponents do not spend time poring over the details of roll-call votes in the legislature. There is no point. They yield little or no information of interest. Most of the time, they merely record that legislators A, B and C voted, as usual, with their party.

Yet again, the contrast with America could hardly be greater. In September 1994 *Time* magazine published a report under the headline "Evolution of a Crime Bill." Underneath brief descriptions of the four key congressional votes on the crime bill in question there was a box headed "How you were represented." Subscribers to the magazine were told how their senior senator, their junior senator and the House representative from their district voted on the four occasions. Nonsubscribers were told: "If this were your personal subscription copy of TIME magazine, this space would contain the voting record of your congressional Representative and two Senators on these issues."[14] Only in America would a leading news magazine think it worthwhile to provide such information. The effect on Congress—and therefore on the American system of government as a whole—may be imagined. Congressmen and senators are continually aware that their constituents—or at least potentially significant minorities of their constituents—are looking over their shoulders as they cast their roll-call votes. How they cast those votes may well determine their electoral future.

Frequent general elections, the existence of primary elections and the absence of strong, cohesive national parties are not, however, the only factors that render American elective politicians peculiarly vulnerable—that increase their exposure to the vicissitudes of electoral politics. In addition, candidates for public office in the United States are largely required to find the means of funding their own election campaigns—and American election campaigns are among the most expensive in the world.

In most democratic countries, either or both of two factors strictly limit the role that money plays in elections. First, in many countries, such as Germany, France and Italy, the national government directly subsidizes the national party organizations and also, in many instances, helps defray the election costs of individual candidates. Second, in those countries, but also in many others, including Great Britain, Canada and New Zealand, strict legal limits are placed on the total amount of money that may be spent on campaigns (at least by individual parliamentary candidates), and the government also provides free air time for candidates and parties. In many countries, including Great Britain, it is illegal for candidates and parties to advertise on radio and television, apart from their limited allocations of free time.[15] Whether by means of subsidy or limits on campaign spending, individual candidates are thus substantially relieved of the need to engage in extensive fund-raising on their own account.

The only major democracy in which candidates for office are required to raise money on anything like the American scale is Japan. Members of the Japanese Diet have not only to maintain their own local support organizations (which may be funded partly by the party faction they belong to); they also have to meet the very high additional costs—the large staffs, the extra office space, the wining and dining of constituents and the wreaths for funerals and the opening of new businesses—that are associated with being a successful Diet member. A leading U.S. student of Japanese politics, seeking to account for the prodigiously high cost of elections in Japan, offers an explanation that happens also to fit almost exactly the case of America: "The fundamental reason for the high cost of campaigning in Japan is that every . . . politician must build and maintain his own political machine. He can rely neither on party organization, which hardly exists on the local level, nor on party loyalties among the electorate which, to the extent that they do exist, are effectively neutralized by an electoral system that forces candidates from the same party to compete with one another."[16] Partly as a consequence, corruption in Japan is rife.

Outright corruption is less rife in the United States than in Japan, partly because of America's strict ethics laws and the strong investigative traditions of the American press. Nevertheless, the consequences of the fact that in the United States candidates for public office at all levels have to raise the bulk of their own campaign funds—and of the additional fact that there are few effective limits on campaign spending—are well known. The American elections industry, referred to in the Introduction, is enriched. Serious questions are raised about the propriety of the relationships between individual congressmen and senators and the wealthy individuals, interest groups and ideologically motivated political action committees that provide them with the bulk of their campaign backing.

Yet another consequence is further to increase American politicians' electoral vulnerability. Not only must politicians in the United States spend a great deal of time, energy and other scarce resources in fund-raising; but they must also be constantly aware of their heavy dependence on those who make contributions to their campaigns. Campaign contributions may not "buy votes" in Congress in any straightforward sense; a good deal of evidence suggests they do not.[17] But the need for them is bound to color deeply a congressman's or senator's image of his political environment. Uncertainty about campaign finance is added to all the other uncertainties in his or her world. Certainly the sums involved are enormous. To take an example almost at random, in 1990 the *average* of contributions made to all House candidates—including nonincumbent challengers and total no-hopers—was $308,269; for Senate candidates the equivalent figure was no less than $2,661,559.[18] The two major parties' candidates for the U.S. Senate in California in 1994—Dianne Feinstein and Michael Huffington—between them spent roughly $40 million.

The total "vulnerability equation" that we have been implicitly developing thus reads: frequent general elections *plus* primaries *plus* lack of party cover *plus* the need to raise large amounts in campaign funds *equals* an unusually high degree of electoral exposure for American politicians compared with those in other countries. Table 1, which summarizes our argument so far, suggests that, if there were an International Index of Electoral Exposure, the United States would come out at or near the top. As the findings in the table suggest, only Japan is remotely in the same league.

The central point, however, is that American politicians are well aware that they are in this position. They may not be students of comparative politics, but everything in their personal experience brings home to them every day and every week how exposed they and their fellow politicians are, and how potentially precarious their political existence is. American politicians cannot, ever, afford to take it easy—and they know it.

The evidence that this is so is overwhelming. For the past quarter-century, the political scientist Richard F. Fenno, Jr., has immersed himself—as a sympathetic participant-observer—in the working political lives of some three dozen American congressmen, senators and House and Senate candidates. His dominant theme is the intimacy of the connection, in the United States, between the nation's capital and legislators' home districts and states—between governing on the one hand and campaigning on the other. House members operate, of course, on a very short cycle; Senate members, with six years at their disposal, can afford to operate on a somewhat more leisurely "campaigning-to-governing-to-campaigning" cycle. But both congressmen and senators continuously evince a consciousness of their home district or state and, remarkably frequently, a degree of unease about it.

Here are some of the things they have said to Fenno over the years:

> I remember when Charlie came up to me on the House floor in 1970. I had just gotten 72 percent in the election. He said, "It looks like you've got that district sewed up." I said, "It's the worst thing that could have happened to me. Everyone will think I'm safe and get complacent as hell. Then some son of a bitch will come along and defeat me."[19]

TABLE 1

Legislators' Electoral Vulnerability in Nine Countries

	Maximum legal life of largest house of national legislature (years)	Average actual life of largest house of national legislature 1960–94 (years)	Percent of years 1960–94 taken up by legislatures the lives of which lasted three and one-half years or more[1]	Level of use of primaries for selection of party candidates for national office	Level of candidate-centered, as distinct from party-centered, voting among electorate[2]	Level of member-centered, as distinct from party-centered, voting in national legislature[3]	Level of individual candidate's reliance on own fund-raising efforts[4]
Australia	3	2.3	0.0	Nonexistent	Low	Low	Low
Canada	5	2.9	72.3	Nonexistent	Low	Low	Low
France	5	3.5	76.7	Nonexistent	Low	Low	Low
Germany	4	3.2	83.3	Nonexistent	Low	Low	Low
Great Britain	5	3.3	94.3	Nonexistent	Low	Low	Low
Italy	5	3.2	85.6	Nonexistent	Low	Medium	Low
Japan	4	2.8	31.4	Nonexistent	Medium	Low	Medium
New Zealand	3	2.8	0.0	Nonexistent	Low	Low	Low
United States	2	2.0	0.0	High	High	High	High

NOTES to TABLE 1

[1]This column reports the proportion of the time between 1960 and 1994 during which the largest house of the national legislature in each of the nine countries lasted three and one-half years or longer. As such, it gives a better indication of the general length of a country's legislative terms than does the previous column, in which the average life of the legislatures is often affected by the occurrence of two or more elections very soon after one another. The percentages for each country are determined by adding together the length of all legislative terms lasting three and one-half years or more, including periods in the early 1960s that formed part of such terms as began in the late 1950s, and then calculating that figure as a percentage of 35 years, the total number of years under consideration. A caveat concerns the early 1990s. It was not always possible at the time of writing to determine whether a term that began, for example, in 1993 would last for three and one-half years or more, and should thus be included in the calculations for that country. This was the case with Canada (a new House of Commons was elected in October 1993), France (a new National Assembly in March 1993), Germany (a new Bundestag in October 1994) and Italy (a new Chamber of Deputies in March 1994). With these four countries, the period after those elections has been omitted from the calculations, so that their figures are a percentage of slightly less than 35 years. However, in the case of Great Britain, by the time of writing more than three and one-half years had passed since the April 1992 election; the percentage could therefore take in the whole 35 years. Equally, in the case of Japan, the elections in July 1995 meant that the whole period between the elections of July 1993 and the end of 1994 could be included in calculating the percentage.

[2]This column shows the extent to which voters consider the individual candidate, rather than the party, when voting. In most countries, the party label remains the main cue, although in Japan, until 1993, the single nontransferable vote system often required voters to choose between different candidates from the same party.

[3]This column considers the extent to which legislators tend to place their own political interests and those of their constituency above the requirements of party discipline when voting in the legislature. The fact that secret voting in the Chamber of Deputies was possible until 1990 made this easier in Italy than in most other countries (but, of course, makes it impossible to be certain how much member-centered voting went on).

[4]In most countries, the central party organization is the chief fund-raiser for election campaigns, spending for which is often fairly tightly regulated. An exception, until 1993, was the Japanese system that pitted candidates from the same party against each other, forcing individual candidates to develop their own fund-raising organizations that were distinct from the party.

SOURCES to TABLE 1

General: Thomas T. Mackie and Richard Rose, *The International Almanac of Electoral History*, 3rd ed. (London: Macmillan, 1991); *Electoral Studies, passim*; Alan Ware, *Political Parties and Party Systems* (New York: Oxford University Press, 1996); David Butler, Howard R. Penniman and Austin Ranney, eds., *Democracy at the Polls: A Comparative Study of Competitive National Elections* (Washington, D.C.: American Enterprise Institute, 1981).

Australia: Dean Jaensch, *The Australian Party System* (Sydney: George Allen & Unwin, 1983); Howard R. Penniman, ed., *Australia at the Polls: The National Elections of 1975* (Washington, D.C.: American Enterprise Institute, 1977); Howard R. Penniman, ed., *The Australian National Elections of 1977* (Washington, D.C.: American Enterprise Institute, 1979).

Canada: C. E. S. Franks, *The Parliament of Canada* (Toronto: University of Toronto Press, 1987); Howard R. Penniman, ed., *Canada at the Polls, 1979 and 1980: A Study of the General Elections* (Washington, D.C.: American Enterprise Institute, 1981); Alan Frizzell, John H. Pammett and Anthony Westell, *The Canadian General Election of 1988* (Ottawa: Carleton University Press, 1989).

France: Philip E. Converse and Roy Piece, *Political Representation in France* (Cambridge, Mass.: Belknap Press of Harvard University Press, 1986); Peter A. Hall, Jack Hayward and Howard Machin, eds., *Developments in French Politics*, rev. ed. (Basingstoke, Hants.: Macmillan, 1994); Howard R. Penniman, ed., *The French National Assembly Elections of 1978* (Washington, D.C.: American Enterprise Institute, 1980).

(continued)

SOURCES to TABLE 1 *(continued)*

Germany: Stephen Padgett and Tony Burkett, *Political Parties and Elections in West Germany: The Search for a New Stability* (New York: St. Martin's Press, 1986); Gordon Smith, William E. Paterson and Peter H. Merkl, eds., *Developments in West German Politics* (Durham, N.C.: Duke University Press, 1989); Christopher Anderson, Karl Kaltenthaler and Wolfgang Luthardt, *The Domestic Politics of German Unification* (Boulder, Colo.: Lynne Rienner, 1993).

Italy: David Hine, *Governing Italy: The Politics of Bargained Pluralism* (Oxford: Clarendon Press, 1993); Paul Furlong, *Modern Italy: Representation and Reform* (New York: Routledge, 1993); Howard R. Penniman, ed., *Italy at the Polls, 1983: A Study of the National Elections* (Durham, N.C.: Duke University Press, 1987).

Japan: Takeshi Ishida and Ellis S. Krauss, eds., *Democracy in Japan* (Pittsburgh, Penna.: University of Pittsburgh Press, 1989); Gerald L. Curtis, *The Japanese Way of Politics* (New York: Columbia University Press, 1988); Scott C. Flanagan et al., *The Japanese Voter* (New Haven: Yale University Press, 1991).

New Zealand: Martin Holland, ed., *Electoral Behaviour in New Zealand* (Auckland: Oxford University Press, 1992); Howard R. Penniman, ed., *New Zealand at the Polls: The General Election of 1978* (Washington D.C.: American Enterprise Institute, 1980).

It's important for me to show strength to keep the young state representatives and city councilmen away. If they have the feeling that I'm invincible they won't try. That reputation is very intangible. [But] your vote margin is part of it.[20]

If he [a potential primary opponent] ever runs against me, he'll give me fits. I'll need $100,000 and three months of campaigning. The first free ride he has is in 1980, and he may try then.[21]

I don't know where his support is. And that's what bothers me. Every time he makes a statement, I think the campaign is lost.[22]

He's out campaigning ten hours a day, seven days a week. He's well informed and articulate. It makes me nervous knowing there's a guy out there beating the bushes like that. You don't know whether he's making any sales, but he's sure making the calls.[23]

After I showed so much strength in the primary, I toyed with the idea of giving up my leadership of a local community caucus. . . . But I decided that if I disbanded [the caucus], a lot of people would think I'd weakened myself and might decide to run against me.[24]

My lack of confidence is still a pressure which brings me home.

This is my political base. I feel I have to come home to get nourished, to see for myself what's going on. It's my security blanket. . . . I had a rocky road getting here, and I'm going to do my damnedest to stay here.[25]

. . . I've learned a lot about politics in the past six years. And one thing I've learned is that you have to worry about how and what you do can be explained or twisted. I always thought if you did what was right, the explanation would take care of itself. But I find that you have to worry about the explanation of everything you do. That was a very new concept for me.[26]

I ran into a former Senate colleague in Washington a little while ago. He asked me how it was going, and I told him about the latest poll. He said that he had been ahead by 25 points, that his opposition had sneaked up on him, and by the time his supporters took it seriously it was too late and he lost. He said to me, "The best thing that could happen to you is to have the trouble come early enough so you can do something about it."[27]

In these remarks, and the dozens like them scattered throughout Fenno's reports of his interviews with politicians, words like "concern," "fear" and "worry" constantly recur. Campaigning is a never-ending activity. Even those members of Congress who positively enjoy it nevertheless usually admit to feeling twinges of apprehension about the outcome.

Political scientists in the United States, conscious of this fascinating and complex intertwining of governing and electioneering in America, have naturally chosen to focus a substantial scholarly effort on it. David R. Mayhew places "the electoral connection" at the center of his analysis. He conjures up "a vision of United States congressmen as single-minded seekers of reelection" in order to see what kinds of activity that goal implies, and he then speculates "about how congressmen so motivated are likely to go about building and sustaining legislative institutions and making policy." His substantive findings, he thinks, "fit political reality rather well."[28] His academic colleagues agree. Gary

Jacobson continually stresses the importance of electoral considerations in determining how congressmen and senators in Washington pursue their careers.[29]

What is striking, however, is that political scientists in other
countries, while they also write about both elections and governing, seldom feel the need to establish any intimate link between
the two. In most democratic countries other than the United
States, the holding of elections and the consequent need to elec-
tioneer are seen as occasional intrusions into an ongoing governmental process rather than as an integral and continuous part of
that process. Elections are important in other countries, of
course; but they are only intermittently so.

That said, there is an obvious objection to the line of argument that we have been pursuing so far—an objection that has
probably already formed in many readers' minds. If American
elective politicians are so electorally vulnerable, why are more of
them not defeated? In particular, why are more incumbent congressmen and senators not defeated? The analysis here would
seem to imply a very high rate of turnover among members of
the U.S. Congress; but in fact the rate of turnover—at least
among those incumbents seeking reelection—is notoriously low.
How can the argument of this chapter and the facts of congressional incumbents' electoral success be reconciled?

This objection has to be taken seriously, because the facts on
which it is based are substantially correct. The number of incumbent congressmen and senators defeated in either primary or
general elections *is* low. In the sixteen biennial elections to the
House between 1960 and 1990, there were only three in which
the proportion of incumbent congressmen who sought reelection
but were defeated rose above 10 percent; the average success rate
during that period was 93 percent.[30] Incumbent senators running for reelection were only slightly less successful. In the same
sixteen elections, the proportion of defeated senators rose on
only five occasions above 25 percent, and the average success rate
was nearly 80 percent.[31] Even in 1994, generally thought of as a
landslide year, a year of major change, 91 percent of all the in-

cumbent congressmen and 92 percent of all the incumbent senators who sought reelection succeeded in being returned.[32]

But to say that because incumbent members of Congress are
seldom defeated they are not really electorally vulnerable is to
miss two crucial points.

The first is that, precisely because they are vulnerable, they go
to prodigious lengths to protect themselves. Like workers in nuclear power stations, they take the most extreme safety precautions. The fact that the precautions are almost entirely successful
in both cases does not make them any the less essential. As David
Mayhew remarks of the American Congress in a frequently
quoted passage: "If a group of planners sat down and tried to design a pair of national assemblies with the goal of serving members' electoral needs year in and year out, they would be hard
pressed to improve on what exists."[33]

Members of Congress take advantage of the congressional
committee and subcommittee systems to specialize in areas that
will yield them electoral advantage. They pass legislation on a
"something for everyone" basis. When in doubt (as they often
are), they vote their district or state rather than their party. They
employ large staffs (in 1991 there was a total of 27,439 House
and Senate employees).[34] They visit their districts and states extremely frequently (often three or four times a month). They and
their staffs devote much of their time to constituency casework
(with roughly one third of members' staffs based in their home
district or state). They and their staffs make uncounted numbers
of free long-distance telephone calls. They avail themselves of
free facilities for making television and radio tapes. They seize
upon every available opportunity to appear on (and in) the local
media. They make extensive use of their franking privileges (in
1986 members of Congress dispatched 758,700,000 pieces of
free mail).[35]

No wonder that, if they run for reelection, they usually win:
they start with big advantages over their challengers (and also
over their would-be challengers, who are often discouraged from
running in the first place by the formidable obstacles that stand

in their way). There is in fact considerable debate among American political scientists about the precise extent to which incumbents' propaganda efforts and constituency service improve their chances of reelection; their importance can probably be exaggerated. But there seems no disposition anywhere to doubt that incumbents' constituency-oriented activities and their more or less continuous campaigning provide them with *some* advantage and that the advantage is probably quite considerable.

The second point is even more important. Congressmen and senators go to such inordinate lengths to secure their reelection because, although they may be objectively safe (in the view of journalists and academic political scientists), they do not *know* they are safe—and, even if they think they are, the risks to them of being wrong are enormous. John Maynard Keynes long ago distinguished between the probability of a specific event occurring and the personal stake that an individual or organization may have in whether or not it does in fact occur. To revert to our earlier example, the probability of anything going seriously wrong with nuclear power stations may approach zero, but they tend nevertheless not to be built near the centers of large cities. A congressman or senator may believe he is reasonably safe; but, if he wants to be sure of being reelected, he would be a fool to act on that belief.

For one thing, the figures relating to incumbents' success rates that we referred to a moment ago can be read another way. We reported that in only three House elections between 1960 and 1990 did the proportion of defeated House incumbents rise above 10 percent. But is it appropriate to use the word "only" in this context? A number of House members are defeated in every biennial election—and no one knows in advance which they will be. Moreover, there will always be elections in which more than 10 percent of members are defeated—and no one knows in advance which *they* will be. On the Senate side, matters are considerably worse. Incumbent senators' average success rate of nearly 80 percent conceals a number of elections—those of 1968, 1972, 1978 and 1980—in which more than one quarter of the senators running for reelection were defeated; and, in any case, to say that the average success rate of incumbents is as high as 80 percent is not much consolation for the 20 percent who lost (and who in most cases did not know in advance that they were going to lose).[36]

Unsurprisingly, there is an acute awareness among members of Congress of the fact that they endlessly face the possibility of electoral defeat. Apart from the freshmen, every member of both houses knows of a colleague, possibly a close friend or tennis partner, who has been beaten. In both houses there is a lore about the "dear departed" (although, as with the dead, they are not mentioned *too* frequently); "there but for the grace of God go I" is the rueful response of most members when they hear of yet another colleague's electoral demise. In other words, what matters is not political scientists' statistics concerning incumbents' electoral success rates, but congressmen's and senators' subjective awareness of how uncertain the world of politics is and of how much they personally stand to lose. Thomas E. Mann reported some years ago that, despite appearances, House seats were "unsafe at any margin."[37] The members themselves, however, did not need to be told. Mann's findings merely confirmed their worst suspicions.

American politicians thus run scared—and are right to do so. And they run more scared than the politicians of any other democratic country—and they are right to do that too. In later chapters we shall consider some of the implications of this further example of what has come to be known as "American exceptionalism"; but next, in Chapter 3, we consider the intellectual and historical sources of high-vulnerability, high-exposure politics in America. If America is exceptional in this regard (as in so many others), how did this come to be so?

3

HOW THEY CAME TO
BE VULNERABLE

The short answer to the question posed at the end of the last chapter—why are American politicians, more than the politicians of other countries, forced to run scared so much of the time?—is "Because the American people like it that way." The American people are, and have been for a very long time, the western world's "hyperdemocrats." They are keener on democracy than almost anyone else and are more determined that democratic norms and practices should pervade every aspect of national life. To explore the implications of this central fact about the United States, and to see how it came to be a fact, we need to begin by examining what different people—and different peoples—have in mind when they use the term "democracy."

In fact, there exist in democratic countries two differing conceptions of how a democratic political system should operate. These two conceptions have been discussed from time to time by political philosophers, but they have never been codified and they certainly cannot be found written down in constitutions or other formal statements of different countries' political principles.

Nevertheless, one or the other of the two conceptions underpins the political practice of every democratic country—even if, inevitably, the abstract conception and the day-to-day practice are never perfectly matched.

One conception of democracy might be labeled the "division of labor" conception. On this conception, there are in any democracy two classes of persons: the governors and the governed. The function of the governors is to govern, to take decisions on the basis of what they believe to be in the country's best interests and then to act on those decisions. If public opinion broadly supports the decisions that have been taken, that is a welcome bonus. If not, too bad. The views of the people at large are merely one datum among a large number of data that need to be considered. They are not accorded any special status. Politicians in countries that operate on this conception can frequently be heard using phases like "the need for strong leadership" and the "the need to take tough decisions." They stress "the importance of doing whatever is required in the national interest." There is no moral queasiness in such countries about defying public opinion. On the contrary, politicians often take a certain pride in doing what they believe to be right even if the opinion of the majority is opposed to it.

The function of the governed in such a system, if it really is a genuine democracy, is a very important function, but it is also a strictly limited one. It is not to determine public policy or to decide what "the right thing" is. Rather, it is to go to the polls from time to time to choose those who will determine public policy and decide what the right thing is: namely, the governors. On this conception, in the words of Joseph A. Schumpeter, "the democratic method is that institutional arrangement for arriving at political decisions in which individuals [i.e., politicians] acquire the power to decide by means of a competitive struggle for the people's vote."[1] The deciding of issues by the electorate is made secondary, in other words, to the election of those individuals who are to do the deciding. The analogy is with choosing a doctor. The patient certainly chooses which doctor to go and see, but he or she does not normally decide (or even try to decide) on the detailed course of treatment. There is an informal but clearly understood division of labor between the two.

It is probably fair to say that most of the world's major democracies—Great Britain, France, Germany, Japan—operate on this basis. The voters go to the polls every few years. In between times, it is up to the government of the day to get on with governing. The business of electing a government and the business of governing are two different businesses. Electioneering is, if anything, to be deplored if it gets in the way of governing.

This is a simplified picture, of course. In the first place, sheer prudence, if not any sense of moral obligation, forces politicians in all democracies, whatever theoretical conception they are based on, to govern to some extent in the light of public opinion. Democratically elected politicians are ultimately dependent on the electorate, and if at the end of the day the electorate does not like what they are doing, they are dead. In any democracy the ballot box is the final arbiter. In the second place, periodic national elections are not the only elections that take place and have to be taken into account; national-level politicians in countries like Great Britain, France, Germany and Japan are often acutely conscious of the importance to them and to their own standing of the frequent elections that occur at the regional, provincial and local levels (local and regional setbacks may seriously damage their own prestige). Finally, some countries that operate principally on a division-of-labor basis—notably France and Italy—also make provision for the holding of occasional national referendums, when the people themselves do decide policy directly. In recent years, for example, several European countries have held referendums on the future of the European Union.

Nevertheless, the central point remains. In those countries that operate their democracy on a division-of-labor basis, the great majority in the world, the process of government is regarded as a continuous process, though one punctuated, of course, by elections from time to time. There is no widespread feeling among the political elite that its members should pay any more attention to public opinion than they have to, and there is little pressure from below demanding that voters should be given a significantly greater say in determining the nation's policies than they already have. The existing division of political labor between governors and governed is broadly accepted.

The other conception of democracy might be called the "agency" conception, and it is of a wholly different character.[2] According to this conception, those who govern a country should function as no more than the agents of the mass of the people of that country. The job of the governors is not to act independently and to take—if need be, on their own initiative—whatever decisions they believe to be in the national interest. Their job, rather, is faithfully to reflect in all their actions the views of the majority of the people, whatever those views may be. Governors on this conception are not really governors at all; they are, rather, representatives, in the very narrow sense of being in office solely to represent the views of those who sent them there. Indeed, on this conception, the idea of governing as an activity in its own right—as a free-standing responsibility that may be exercised well or exercised badly—ceases to have any real meaning.

In this agency view, representative government of the kind common throughout the democratic world can be only a second-best. The ideal system would be one in which there were no politicians or middlemen of any kind but in which the people governed themselves directly; the political system would take the form of more or less continuous town meetings or referendums, perhaps conducted by means of interactive television. Meanwhile, given that direct democracy of this kind is impracticable, the citizens of an agency democracy are apt to complain that their system is "not sufficiently democratic," that their politicians are "out of touch" and that "the people's wishes" are constantly being frustrated. In the absence of direct democracy, an agency political culture is almost certain to be an anti-politician political culture.

It goes without saying that, while large numbers of division-of-labor democracies exist in the real world, there is no known case of a pure agency democracy (let alone of a pure direct democracy). Politicians in all countries have a good deal of autonomy, and there are always some institutions that, for one reason or another, have been allowed to escape from democratic control.

Nevertheless, the United States is almost unique in being a country that, at least since the middle of the nineteenth century, has refused to accept the notion of a clear-cut division of labor between governors and governed and has a remarkably pure version of agency democracy as its national ideal. The ideal is almost never spelled out in the abstract or argued for explicitly; if it were, its theoretical and practical disadvantages would soon become apparent. But on an imaginary continuum, with the division-of-labor version of democracy at one end and the pure agency version at the other, the United States, in terms of both its ideals and its practice, undoubtedly stands much nearer the agency end than any other democracy in the world except Switzerland. America has been a great political success story, but it distrusts politics. It has produced some of the greatest politicians the world has ever seen—George Washington, Abraham Lincoln and Franklin Roosevelt—but it deeply distrusts politicians. Despite the fact that the United States has a land mass of 3,536,341 square miles and a population of more than 250 million, most Americans still, at bottom, would like to see their country governed by a town meeting. They still want their politicians to be "more democratically accountable" and still resent it when they are not sufficiently accountable. The thought that their politicians—their governors—should be accorded more freedom of action, rather than less, seldom occurs to them.

A foreigner, Alexis de Tocqueville, observed the underlying tendency of American democratic thought and institutions as early as the 1840s:

> At the present day the principle of the sovereignty of the people has acquired in the United States all the practical development that the imagination can conceive. It is unencumbered by those fictions that are thrown over it in other countries, and it appears in every possible form, according to the exigency of the occasion.

Sometimes the laws are made by the people in a body, as at Athens; and sometimes its representatives, chosen by universal suffrage, transact business *in its name and under its immediate supervision.*

In some countries a power exists which, though it is a degree foreign to the social body, directs it, and forces it to pursue a certain track. In others the ruling force is divided, being partly within and partly without the ranks of the people. But nothing of the kind is to be seen in the United States; there society governs itself for itself. All power centers in its bosom, and scarcely an individual is to be met with who would venture to conceive or, still less, to express the idea of seeking it elsewhere. The nation participates in the making of its laws by the choice of its legislators, and in the execution of them by the choice of the agents of the executive government; it may almost be said to govern itself, so feeble and so restricted is the share left to the administration, *so little do the authorities forget their popular origin and the power from which they emanate.*[3] (Emphasis added.)

De Tocqueville was exaggerating in the 1840s, and to quote him now is to some extent to exaggerate today. But de Tocqueville was right, for both his day and ours, in identifying the central importance to the people of the United States of the idea of popular sovereignty (so clearly stated in the three passages italicized above). De Tocqueville could have been writing of no other country in the nineteenth century. His remarks could still be applied to no other country at the end of the twentieth.

The same abiding concern with democratic norms as almost the sole criterion by which a political system should be judged can still be found today in most textbooks written by Americans about the American system. Textbooks on most countries, written by citizens of those countries, tend either to be largely nonjudgmental, or to be Marxist in their coloration, or to assess the country's politics in terms of its success in producing certain outputs, such as national unity, economic growth or social welfare. Democracy as such seldom figures as a dominant theme. American textbooks, by contrast, are almost invariably preoccupied with the question of whether or not America has achieved, or could achieve, some ideal democratic state. Thus, Robert A. Dahl's textbook is entitled *Democracy in the United States: Promise and Performance,* and there is scarcely a single text in the United States that does not contain a chapter evaluating, favorably or unfavorably, America's democratic achievement.[4]

America is thus a country in which there is always a latent demand for more direct democratic participation and in which that demand is very hard to resist on theoretical (as distinct from purely practical) grounds. It is no accident that the practice of democracy in the United States embraces not merely representation, as in the U.S. Congress and the state legislatures, but also direct democracy, in the form of New England town meetings, popular referendums, available under the constitutions of twenty-three states, the popular initiative, available in twenty-four states, and the recall of legislators, available in fifteen states.[5] Several of these devices, notably the referendum, can be found elsewhere, but nowhere is the democratic "undergrowth," so to speak, as thick and luxuriant as it is in the United States. Indeed it is one of the striking anomalies of the American system that it does not provide for the holding of national referendums (for example, on constitutional amendments). The reverence in which the 1787 Constitution is held appears, for the time being at least, to be too great. (Most of the framers of the U.S. Constitution did, as it happens, believe in the division of labor that we referred to earlier, and it was no accident that the holding of popular referendums did not form part of their original design.)[6]

What are the origins of this peculiarly American predilection for agency democracy, in default of actual direct democracy? Rather surprisingly, the history of democratic thought and practice in the United States has not yet been written; but it is clear that the roots of American ideas about democracy lie buried deep in the past. By the time de Tocqueville wrote in the 1840s, it was already far too late for anyone to consider digging them up (even assuming anyone had wanted to).[7]

Two factors probably contributed most powerfully to the development of Americans' characteristic conception of democracy. The first was the fact that many of the original British colonies in America, especially in New England, were founded on a self-consciously anti-authoritarian basis. The colonists had come to the New World to get away from royal rule (that is, rule by others); they determinedly set about creating a new system of self-rule. Elsewhere in *Democracy in America* de Tocqueville describes how in New England the township was "completely and definitely constituted" as early as 1650:

> The independence of the township was the nucleus round which the local interests, passions, rights, and duties collected and clung. It gave scope to the activity of a real political life, thoroughly democratic and republican. . . .
>
> The towns named their own magistrates of every kind, assessed themselves, and levied their own taxes. In the New England town the law of representation was not adopted; but the affairs of the community were discussed, as at Athens, in the marketplace, by a general assembly of the citizens.[8]

A century later the American revolution reinforced the lessons the colonists had learned, since it was not merely a war of independence (colonies against the mother country) but also a war for political self-expression (the ruled against their rulers, on both sides of the Atlantic).

But the second factor was equally important and, perhaps because it is so obvious, may easily be overlooked. Agency democracy and the urge for direct democracy took root in America because, in the eighteenth and early nineteenth centuries, it was physically possible for them to do so. America was assuredly a vast continent, but settlement took place initially almost entirely along the eastern seaboard. There were thirteen colonies, not just one, so that political life was highly decentralized. The population initially was small and, far from being spread out evenly across thousands of square miles of forest and plain, tended to be concentrated in villages, townships and smallish cities (Philadelphia in 1787 had a population of only 44,000).[9] The physical setting for one or another version of face-to-face democracy was thus ideal. Swiss democracy today is probably able to function in the way it does because Switzerland is partitioned by its mountains into small, relatively self-contained communities, its cantonal system naturally reflecting its highly segmented geography.

Although most of the framers of the American Constitution believed in the traditional division of labor between governors and governed (and their views are reflected in such features of the Constitution as the electoral college and the six-year terms for senators), they were already in a minority in the 1780s; and by the time of Andrew Jackson, if not before, the notion that agency and direct democracy were the best forms of democracy—and that all other forms were to be regarded as only second-best approximations of them—was deeply implanted in the American mind. Division-of-labor democracy never again received a serious hearing. Indeed it was never really raised as a possibility.

Against this background, it is not difficult to explain most of the features of the modern American system—short terms, direct primaries and the weakness of political parties—that have led to the politics of vulnerability and high exposure.

When the Federal Constitutional Convention met in Philadelphia in 1787, all of the former British colonies had already adopted new state constitutions, and a large proportion of these constitutions provided that elections to the lower house of the state legislature should take place not every three or four years but *every* year. Voters were to be enabled to keep a *very* close eye on their representatives. Under the circumstances, the framers of the federal Constitution—in so far as they were prepared to countenance at all the idea of a popularly elected assembly as part of the new system of government (and most of them were)—really had little option but to decide that the assembly should be elected for a relatively short term. The only question was how short.

When the convention first considered the issue, on June 12, 1787, two members proposed that members of the "first branch" should be elected every year, one proposed that they should be elected every two years and another proposed that they should be elected every three years.[10] No one suggested a term of more than three years, and the debate soon settled down to one between the proponents of one year and the proponents of three. Those who favored annual elections made much of the fact that "the people were fond of frequent elections," one of them even insisting that annual elections were "the only defence of the people against tyranny."[11] Those who favored triennial elections thought that too frequent elections "rendered the people indifferent to them, and made the best men unwilling to engage in so precarious a service" and also claimed that in only one year representatives from one place would not have enough time to learn about the problems of other states and districts.[12]

But it was left to James Madison, a staunch triennialist, to raise in this context (he raised it in many others) the central issue of the nature of representation. During the convention's first debate on June 12, he deplored the idea that the opinions of the people should "be our guide," noting that no delegate to the convention knew what his constituents' opinions were at the moment, let alone what they would be if they were in possession of all the facts and had listened to all the arguments, or what they would be in six or twelve months' time; and when delegates returned to the subject on June 21, he warned that, if elections were too frequent, members of Congress would be tempted to neglect their duties at the seat of government and that those "from the most distant states [out of a fear of rival candidates] would travel backwards and forwards at least as often as the elections should be repeated."[13]

Madison's views attracted little support, however, and the proposal that members of the lower house should serve for as long as three years was struck out of the draft of the Constitution that was then under consideration by the vote of seven states to three, with one divided.[14] In the end, members of the convention agreed without a vote simply to split the difference between three years and one.[15] In this relatively casual way, but against the background of a popular demand for agency democracy ("the people are fond of frequent elections"), members of the U.S.

House of Representatives acquired the uniquely short two-year terms they still possess.

The decision that one third of the Senate should retire every two years, with the result that Senate elections are nowadays as frequent as House elections, appears to have been taken partly formally, partly informally. There were extensive debates in the full convention about the length of senators' terms, as there were about the length of representatives' terms, the various proposals in the case of the Senate ranging from three years to nine years or even life; but the idea that the Senate should be a continuing body, with its whole membership never being turned over simultaneously, appears to have arisen almost on the spur of the moment, as being "favorable to the wisdom and stability of the corps."[16] The decision that individual members of the Senate should serve for six years was, as in the case of the House, the result of an ad hoc compromise. In any event, the decisions concerning the Senate appeared less significant in 1787 than they do to us now, since the members of the Senate were initially to be chosen indirectly by the state legislatures rather than by the people. It was only with the passage of the Seventeenth Amendment providing for direct elections to the Senate in 1913 that congressmen and senators found themselves facing overlapping bodies of electors on the same biennial cycle.

The U.S. Constitution, as it emerged from the Philadelphia convention, thus represented a somewhat uneasy compromise between the views of the majority of delegates, who were not democrats and believed strongly in a governmental division of labor, and the minority of delegates, who were more democratically inclined themselves and were also more sensitive to the American people's increasingly insistent democratic demands. In hyperdemocratic America, the Constitution remains to this day, in some of its features, a strangely conservative, pre-democratic document.

The passage of the Seventeenth Amendment providing for the direct election of senators was one of the most significant political changes accomplished during the Progressive era at the turn of the twentieth century; but it was by no means the only one.

The years between 1880 and 1920 brought the secret ballot, the enfranchisement of women, the initiative, recall and referendum in many states and, not least, the direct primary for the selection of candidates for public office.

The story of the spread of the direct primary is a remarkable one.[17] On September 9, 1842, all the Democrats of Crawford county, Pennsylvania, who cared to do so were enabled to participate in the nomination of one of the party's candidates for local office. Neither legislative caucus nor nominating convention was to be allowed to stand in the way of the Crawford county Democrats' will. During most of the rest of the nineteenth century, the "Crawford county system," as it was still called, spread gradually in and around Pennsylvania; but it was not until the Progressive era at the end of the century that instituting the direct primary became a central plank in the reformers' platform. In the 1890s several states in the South and West adopted laws permitting the use of primaries, and in 1903 Wisconsin became the first state requiring their use for most local and statewide offices. At this stage, what had been a gradual development suddenly became an extremely rapid one, and by 1917 all but four states had made the direct primary compulsory for some or all statewide offices. The presidential primary for the choice of delegates to national nominating conventions followed later.

The almost universal adoption of the direct primary was a response to two political forces, one immediate, the other much longer-term. The more immediate in the 1890s and 1900s was the power of the organized political party, together with the abuse, as the reformers saw it, of the existing nominating process. In an era of strong party government, he who controlled the majority party's nominations controlled both party and government. Moreover, because state and local governments in many states and cities were taking on a wide range of additional responsibilities at the turn of the century, and because the spoils system meant that most nonelective as well as all elective offices fell into the victorious party's hands, the stakes were high. "Machines" and "bosses" emerged, with the control of their party's nominations as one of their central objectives. As the stakes were so high, the methods they employed were not always overscrupulous.

Two early historians of the primary movement described with evident distaste the lengths to which the leaders of the city machines were sometimes prepared to go:

> The abuses that arose under a system that staked the immense spoils of party victory on the throw of a caucus held without legal regulation of any sort were numerous and varied. They ranged from brutal violence and coarse fraud to the most refined and subtle cunning. . . . [The party nomination processes] were invaded and controlled by men of a different or of no political persuasion, and from other districts of the city. Sometimes this was done peaceably and with a show of decency and order; or . . . it was accompanied by violence and disorder of the most outrageous character. Both sneaks and sluggers were employed as the occasion dictated.[18]

If such abuses of the existing system were one of the forces leading to the introduction of direct primaries, the long-standing American preference for direct democracy was undoubtedly the other. In the eyes of turn-of-the-century Progressives, party machines and bosses were not merely self-interested and corrupt; they were an illegitimate barrier standing between the people and their elected representatives. The Progressives appealed to Americans to act to close the gap that had opened up between their national ideal of direct democracy and the domination of the powerful party machines.[19] "What the majority of Progressives hoped to do in the political field was to restore popular government as they imagined it to have existed in an earlier and purer age."[20]

The oratory of the Progressive age was suffused with direct-democratic rhetoric. William Jennings Bryan contended that the people were competent "to sit in judgment on every question which has arisen or which will arise, no matter how long our government will endure."[21] Woodrow Wilson asserted that the Democratic party intended "to set up a government in the world where the average man, the plain man, the common man, the ignorant man, the unaccomplished man, the poor man had a voice equal to the voice of anybody else in the settlement of the common affairs."[22] A candidate for the governorship of Iowa in 1910 declared that his great object was "to bring the individual voter into more prominence, and to diminish the influence of permanent organization in the ranks of the party."[23] The direct primary was thus to be one of a number of substitutes—the initiative, recall and referendum were to be others—for America's by now unattainable national town meeting.

What is striking about these developments is that they were, indeed, peculiar to America. They had no analogs in Europe, not even in those European countries, such as Great Britain, France, the Netherlands and Sweden, that were well on their way to becoming democracies by the time of the First World War. In Europe, progressive parties, factions and groups did not seek to dismantle the existing political machinery; they sought, on the contrary, to capture it, with a view to exploiting it for their own ends. European liberal and labor movements created, where necessary, their own political parties and pressed, increasingly successfully, for the extension of the franchise. But nowhere did they espouse—or even think of espousing—such direct-democratic devices as the initiative, recall, referendum or direct primary. Accepting division-of-labor democracy, they merely wanted to be on the right side of the division.

The succeeding era of electoral reform in the United States, following the Hubert Humphrey–Richard Nixon presidential election of 1968, took the process of direct democracy a stage further. As recently as 1960, only sixteen states held Democratic party primaries for the presidency; these chose only 38 percent of the delegates to that year's national nominating convention. On the Republican side, the figures were similar: only fifteen states and the same proportion, 38 percent, of the delegates.[24] In both parties, incumbent officeholders and leaders of state and local parties continued to have by far the largest say in determining who their party's presidential nominee would be. Primaries might influence the party leaders' judgment—they certainly did in John F. Kennedy's case in 1960—but, in themselves, they were not determinative.

The events of 1968, however, changed all that. Following the Democrats' tumultuous national convention in Chicago, with demonstrations and riots outside the convention hotels, the Democratic party felt the need to respond to charges that many rank-and-file Democrats had not been given a "full and timely" opportunity to participate in the process of selecting convention delegates. It accordingly changed its rules.[25] In particular, the "party caucus" method of delegate selection was made much more difficult to operate. The upshot was that many state Democratic leaders, unsure precisely what the new national rules meant and anxious not to fall foul of them, opted instead to introduce direct primaries. Primaries, at least, gave all Democrats a "full and timely" opportunity to participate. The Republican parties in many states followed suit.

Primaries burgeoned. By 1980, thirty-three states were holding Democratic presidential primaries, selecting no fewer than 71 percent of the Democrats' convention delegates (up from 38 per cent in 1960). In the same year, thirty-two states held Republican primaries, among them choosing 75 percent of the convention delegates (also up from 38 percent only two decades before).[26] The effect was to place the selection of presidential candidates in both major parties almost exclusively in the hands of primary electorates. Incumbent officeholders and state and local party leaders in both parties no longer played a significant role.

The important consequence from our point of view is that incumbent first-term presidents are now far more vulnerable than they were. Prior to the 1968 reforms, a first-term president, however unpopular he was and however remote his chances of reelection appeared to be, could nevertheless take his renomination for granted. State and local party leaders owed any incumbent president favors; it was inconceivable that they would want to repudiate their party's national standard-bearer. Between the turn of the century and the 1970s, not only was no incumbent president who declared that he wanted it ever denied renomination; none had ever seriously to fight to gain renomination. Herbert Hoover, even in the midst of the Great Depression in 1932, faced no challenge from within the Republican party. Harry Truman, doomed though he appeared to be in 1948, faced no challenge on the Democratic side.

The position of first-term presidents today is much less comfortable. Like senators and congressmen, they now have to be ready to jump not just one hurdle but two in order to secure re-election. A primary challenge is always a possibility—and governing has to take place in the light of that possibility. In the six presidential elections between 1972 and 1992, Nixon in 1972 and Ronald Reagan in 1984 were the only incumbent presidents who were never challenged in primaries and never looked like being challenged. Gerald Ford in 1976 had to take on Ronald Reagan. Jimmy Carter in 1980 was challenged by Edward Kennedy (who, like Reagan, took his challenge all the way to the convention). George Bush in 1992 was challenged by Pat Buchanan. The fact that all three incumbents eventually succeeded in being renominated is unlikely, however, to provide much solace to future presidents since all three, partly because of their fierce primary battles, went down to defeat in the ensuing November election.[27]

Moreover, the increased vulnerability of presidents brought about by the new primary-centered nomination system has been compounded in the mid 1990s by important alterations in the precise timing of the presidential election cycle. Once upon a time, presidential hopefuls announced their candidacies in the spring of an election year or, at the earliest, during the previous winter. The need to raise massive campaign funds, however, taken together with the fact that more of the big states are holding their primaries at earlier and earlier stages of the electoral cycle, means that presidential campaigns, if they are to have any chance of succeeding, now need to be launched not long after the beginning of the year *preceding* the election. Accordingly, all of the Republican hopefuls in 1996 had declared by the end of April 1995—note, not 1996 but 1995.

On the one hand, the new, greatly extended timetable reduces somewhat the chances of someone from an incumbent president's party declaring against him (such a person would have too much to do too soon and would be running grave political risks over a very prolonged period); but, on the other hand, the new arrangements ineluctably bring forward the date when all incumbent presidents have to start thinking about their electoral future. The Clinton economic adviser who complained in 1993 that the "campaign people act as if 1996 is tomorrow" had actually got the year wrong. He should have spoken of 1995—only twenty-four months away.[28]

It almost goes without saying that the widespread adoption of direct primaries—first for state and local offices, then for candidacies for the Congress and latterly for the presidency itself—has been a central factor in the weakening of American party organization, especially in the past twenty-five years with the adoption of presidential primaries. Party organizations have traditionally existed to nominate candidates for public office and then to secure their election. Largely deprived by primaries of their first function, that of nomination, they have proved less and less capable of performing their second, that of organizing for elections. Nominations and elections have become increasingly "candidate-centered" as political activists, fund-raisers, campaign donors, interest groups and the media have clustered round individual candidates and largely ignored the parties' formal organizations and structures.[29] As a result, state and local parties all over America—far more than in any other democratic country—have tended to atrophy. The Progressives set out to undermine the power of the party machine. They have largely succeeded, though the process has taken a little longer than they expected.

This combination of primary elections and the atrophying of state and local parties has gone far in depriving incumbent officeholders of what in the last chapter we called "party cover." Politicians no longer give voters cues that are primarily partisan; voters therefore no longer respond to politics and politicians primarily in partisan terms; politicians therefore have even less incentive than before to give the voters partisan cues. The process is reciprocal. Among voters, it leads to an increase in split-ticket and a decrease in party-line voting. Among officeholders, especially members of Congress, it leads to relatively low levels of party-line voting in legislative roll calls. Both of these sets of signals, passing in each direction, convey essentially the same message: that party is of little relevance. To the elective politician, as we remarked in the last chapter, they also convey the message that he is on his own, that he, personally, is vulnerable.

The same causes—primaries and the weakening of party organization—would probably have produced the same effects in any country; but in the United States they have been compounded by another feature of America's political culture that is unique to America: hostility to the very idea of political parties. The Progressives, with their preference for direct democracy, were hostile to political parties as organizations; but they were by no means the first to deplore the notion that political debate should be conducted along partisan lines or that voters should choose candidates on a partisan basis. As early as the 1790s, a contemporary of a prominent Virginia farmer, Edward Pendleton, said in praise of him:

> None of his opinions were drawn from personal views or party prejudices. He never had a connexion with any political party . . . so that his opinions were the result of his own judgment, and that judgment was rendered upon the best unbiased estimate he could make of the publick good.[30]

Two hundred years later—in a classic instance of ideals and institutions reinforcing one another—Americans are both enabled and encouraged to vote for the man or woman rather than the party and at the same time made to feel that it is their duty to do so. The encouragement comes from primary elections (where party cues are irrelevant), from the long ballot (which enables split-ticket voting) and from the fact that in almost every state the voter is legally entitled to enroll officially as a nonpartisan Independent (an opportunity for nonpartisan self-definition that is available only in the United States). The corresponding sense of duty comes from long-standing tradition. In the words of political scientist Martin P. Wattenberg, "Voting the man [or woman], not the party, has now become part of the American creed."[31] A survey in 1986 found 92 percent of American adults—an astonishingly high proportion—agreeing with the proposition "I always vote for the person who I think is best, regardless of what party they belong to."[32] The proportion of American voters who actually do just that is not nearly as high as 92 percent; but, by international standards, it is very high all the same.

The media have contributed significantly to this reciprocal anti- (or perhaps non-) party pattern of causation. Like the voters, the media receive fewer and fewer partisan cues from the politicians; they themselves therefore give the voters fewer and fewer partisan cues; the voters therefore vote less and less on partisan lines; the politicians therefore have less and less incentive to offer partisan cues to either the voters or the media. As Wattenberg, in his study of the decline of America's parties, has shown, American newspaper and magazine electoral coverage that links the names of candidates to the name of their party has declined precipitously since the early 1950s.[33] Moreover, American elective officeholders, on their own in so many other ways, are also largely on their own in having to cultivate the media, especially within their own state or district. In most countries, an individual politician's principal press agent is his party; in America, it is himself. The role of party is by no means nonexistent in the United States; it has tended to grow in recent years. But it remains secondary.

The same is true in connection with campaign finance. With the notable exception of Japan, the rule in most democratic countries is that the great bulk of political money is party money, raised by the parties, administered by them and spent by them. But yet again, the exception is the United States, where individual officeholders and candidates are their own principal fundraisers. In 1992, House incumbents running for reelection received on average a mere 3 percent of their total campaign funds from their party; challengers received 11 percent; candidates in open seats received only 5 percent. The average for all Senate candidates was only slightly higher: 13 percent.[34]

The scholar Paul S. Herrnson, who compiled these figures, comments on House incumbents' "fear of defeat" and their "need to raise large sums of money every two years." He adds that "incumbents routinely complain about the time, effort, and indignities associated with asking people for money."[35] The indignities involved and incumbents' lack of enthusiasm for fund-raising have led many of them to establish their own permanent fund-raising organizations. Senate candidates, who need to raise even more money, are even likelier to rely on professionals in their fund-raising efforts. They also need to start earlier. Herrnson observes: "They often meet with party officials, PAC [political action committee] managers, wealthy individuals, and other sources of money or fund-raising assistance three years before they plan to run."[36]

Efforts in the United States to reduce politicians' dependence on campaign funds by means of restricting total campaign expenditures have fallen foul of the First Amendment and the Supreme Court. Amendments in 1974 to the 1971 Federal Election Campaign Act sought, among other things, to impose limits on how much candidates for the presidency and Congress could spend on their election campaigns, even out of their own pockets, but these provisions were struck down by the Supreme Court in 1976 in *Buckley et al. v. Valeo.*[37] America remains virtually the only country without any legal limits on campaign expenditures. As American politicians know well, the price of unrestricted free speech is high.

From this analysis, there is one additional point that stands out. The American people have always exhibited a preference for direct democracy, and for that reason American politicians have always been more vulnerable than politicians in other countries. Their terms have been shorter in most cases; they have been subject in most cases to primary elections since the beginning of this century. But what is clear is that the vulnerability of American politicians has increased enormously over the past three decades. The spread of the direct primary into presidential races, the decline of parties, the rise of candidate-centered politics and the increased cost of campaigning in elections have all left incumbent officeholders today far more exposed than in previous generations.

The cumulative effect of these developments has been summarized by David S. Broder:

> Washington [today] is run by 536 individual political entrepreneurs—one president, 100 senators and 435 members of the House—each of whom got here essentially on his own. Each chooses the office he seeks, raises his own money, hires his own pollster and ad-maker and recruits his own volunteers. Each of them is scrambling to remain in office, no matter what.[38]

The analogy with business can be pressed further. Most individual entrepreneurs are financially vulnerable and live in constant fear of bankruptcy. Most individual congressmen and senators— and even presidents—in the United States are similarly vulnerable and live in constant fear for their political lives.

In this chapter, we have looked briefly at the causes of this uniquely high level of electoral vulnerability. In the next four chapters, we go on to explore some of its more important consequences.

4

WHY THEIR
VULNERABILITY MATTERS

The simplest, most central consequence of American politi- cians' electoral vulnerability—obvious, but requiring to be stated explicitly—is that most officeholders in the United States are extraordinarily sensitive to the opinions and demands of the men and women upon whom their political futures depend: the voters in their state or district or in the nation at large. Not only are they extraordinarily sensitive; they are continuously sensitive. The pressures of electoral politics in America are incessant. Only if an elected official has decided not to run for office again—or has both a highly exalted opinion of his status as an elected rep- resentative and an extremely thick skin—are the pressures signif- icantly relieved.

Finding themselves inhabiting this turbulent and torrid politi- cal environment, most American elective officials respond as might be expected: in an almost Darwinian way. They adapt their behavior—their roll-call votes, their introduction of bills, their committee assignments, their phone calls, their direct-mail shots, their speeches, their press releases, their sound bites, who

73

they see, how they spend their time, their trips abroad, their trips back home and frequently their private and family lives—to their environment: that is, to their primary and overriding need for electoral survival. It goes without saying that the effects are felt not only on the lives of individual officeholders and their staffs but on America's political institutions as a whole and the shape and content of American public policy.

It all begins with officeholders' immediate physical environment: with bricks, mortar, leather and wood paneling. The number of congressional buildings, and the size of congressional staffs, have ballooned over recent decades. A generation ago, most members of the House of Representatives contented themselves with a small inner office and a larger outer office, to accommodate their three- or four-strong staffs; and senators' office suites were not significantly larger. Apart from the Capitol itself, Congress was reasonably comfortably housed in four buildings, known to Washington taxi drivers as the "Old" and "New" House and Senate office buildings. The designations "Old" and "New" cannot be used any longer, however, because there are now so many congressional buildings that are even newer than the old new ones. To the four original buildings have been added the Rayburn House Office Building, which took ten years to build and turned out to be larger than the Capitol itself, and the Hart Senate Office Building, which accommodates half the Senate. In addition, the House has taken over a former hotel and a large FBI warehouse to gain extra space, and the Senate has also sprouted a number of annexes around the Hill.

Congressional staffs have grown at roughly the same rate (the buildings being built mainly to house the staffs). In the late 1950s the total number of persons employed by members of the House and Senate in their individual capacities was 3,556. By the early 1990s that figure had grown to 11,572—a more than threefold increase within the political lifetime of many long-serving members.[1] In the mid 1990s the total number of persons employed by Congress in all capacities, including committee staffs and the staffs of support agencies such as the Congressional Research Service, was between 25,000 and 30,000, making Congress "by far the most heavily staffed legislative branch in the world."[2]

Much of the growth of staff in recent decades has been in response to the growth of national government, to Congress's insistence on enhancing its policy-making role in the aftermath of Vietnam and Watergate and to decentralization within Congress, which has led to subcommittee chairmen and the subcommittees themselves acquiring their own staffs; but there is, in addition, no doubt that a large proportion of the increase is owing to the response of congressional incumbents to their ever-increasing electoral exposure. Because of their increased exposure, Congress itself has become an integral part of the American elections industry.

One useful measure of the changes that have taken place in recent decades—and also an important consequence of the changes—is the increased proportion of staff and staff time devoted to constituency service. As recently as 1972 only 1,189 House employees—22.5 percent of House members' personal staffs—were based in district offices. By 1992 the absolute number had more than doubled, to 3,128, and the proportion had also more than doubled, to 42.1 percent. On the Senate side, a total of only 303 state-based staffers in 1972—12.5 per cent of senators' personal staffs—had more than quadrupled by 1992 to 1,368—fully 31.6 percent of the total.[3] As a significant proportion of the time of Washington-based congressional staffs is also devoted to constituency service, it is probably a fair guess that more than half of the time of all congressmen's and senators' personal staffs is now given over to nursing the district or state rather than to legislation and policy-making.

Much constituency service is undoubtedly altruistic, inspired by politicians' sense of duty (and constituents' understandable frustrations with an unresponsive bureaucracy); but at the same time nobody doubts that a large proportion of it is largely aimed at securing incumbents' reelection. The statistics on members of Congress's outgoing mail, and their use of the franking privilege, point in the same direction. Despite new restrictions on franking introduced in the 1990s (largely in response to mounting voter outrage), congressional mailings have nearly trebled, from roughly 100 million in the early 1960s to nearly 300 million today. (In 1984 the total of franked mail reached a spectacular 924.6 million items—nearly five pieces of congressional mail for every adult in America.) Not surprisingly, the volume of mail emanating from both houses of Congress is invariably higher in election years.[4]

The monetary costs of these increases in voter-oriented congressional activities are high (the American Congress, in addition to being the most heavily staffed legislative branch in the world, is also the most expensive); but there is another, nonmonetary cost: the staffs themselves become another of the representative's or senator's constituencies, requiring to be managed, taking up his time and always tempted to go into business for themselves. In particular, American scholars who have studied the burgeoning of congressional staffs express concern about their cumulative impact on Congress as a deliberative body, a body in which face-to-face communication between members and their constituents, and between members and each other, facilitates both mutual understanding and an understanding of the issues. Largely in response to the requirements of electioneering, more and more congressional business is conducted through networks of intermediaries.

The Harvard political scientist Morris P. Fiorina expresses the widespread concern in these words:

> Members rush from committee meeting to committee meeting and flit back and forth between Washington and their districts. Meanwhile, the staffs deliberate, and understanding is not the goal—credit is. All too often members talk to their staffs, who talk to other members' staffs, who talk to their members, who talk back to their staff, and so on and so forth up and down the chain. Members themselves complain that they have insufficient chance to get to know one another and express appreciation for opportunities to get together sans staff.[5]

Such are the unremitting pressures of electioneering that, even when they do get together sans staff, their conversation is likely to turn, as Senator Moynihan complained, to the latest opinion polls rather than the substance of issues.[6]

Not only is much of the time of congressional staffers taken up with trying to enhance the reelection prospects of their politician-employers; but the exigencies of America's never-ending election campaign also have measurable effects on the way members of Congress use their own time. American public officials have always been assiduous campaigners; they have become even more so over the past few decades.

James Madison in 1787 was worried that, if elections were too frequent, members of Congress would neglect their duties in the capital and "would travel backwards and forwards [to their home state] at least as often as the elections should be repeated." He was right to suspect that they would—and he reckoned without the jet airplane. There used to be a minority of congressmen and senators, mainly from the East Coast, who were notorious among their colleagues for shirking their legislative duties by traveling home to their district or state every weekend. They were known as the "Tuesday-to-Thursday club." That term is now seldom used because almost the entire Congress has joined the club.[7] In the early 1960s members of both houses were allowed a mere three government-paid trips home per year. By the late 1970s members of the House were allowed thirty-three trips and members of the Senate more than forty. One researcher discovered that, whereas in 1970 members of the House spent roughly fifteen weeks of each year in their congressional districts, by 1976 that figure had risen to twenty-two weeks. In more recent years, congressmen seem to have been visiting their home districts rather less often, but staying longer when they get there.[8] The total time consumed is enormous, not least because the United States is an enormous country; but then the electoral incentives are powerful.

Even when in Washington, members of Congress are concerned to ensure that the lines of communication between them and their constituents are always open—and are at least as concerned with the style and content of the messages they communicate. American politicians have no need to "hit the campaign trail." Psychologically they never leave it.

Evidence abounds of the extent to which incumbent members of Congress—not to mention incumbent presidents—skew their political activities toward self-advertisement, credit claiming and often meretricious position taking.[9] Suzanne Garment, in her exhaustive study of American political scandals, notes that in the early 1970s Sam Ervin's Watergate committee consisted of only seven members; but by 1986 "when Iran-contra exploded, Watergate had already shown politicians what great benefits they could glean from serving on an investigating committee in a blockbuster scandal. A congressman would have the chance to appear before his constituents—indeed, the nation—early and often. . . ."[10] The Iran-Contra committee in the House accordingly had twenty-six members. Garment goes further and attributes the spate of recent U.S. political scandals, in part at least, to a combination of the media's hunger for salacious news and the fact that "because of . . . the demands of modern election campaigns, congressmen thirst with special intensity for media exposure."[11]

The skewing process extends even to more routine congressional hearings. A study of committee hearings which compared the 1970s with the 1950s found that, whereas in the 1950s members of Congress frequently interacted with one another and joined forces in questioning witnesses, by the 1970s the great majority of members insisted on operating as lone wolves, jealously guarding their right to examine witnesses uninterrupted. What, the author of the study asks, is the explanation?

> The answer, it seems, is that hearings have increasingly come to fulfill another function [that is, other than exploring policy issues]: self-display. Congressmen come to hearings to publicize themselves, to take stands, to win points with particular constituencies, to make a record, to boost their image as hardworking, concerned legislators. This orientation leads them to exclude each other from

the floor. . . . Interpositions and interruptions represent attempts to steal the limelight. Hence they are resisted.[12]

Certainly members of both houses go to considerable lengths to publicize themselves in other ways. Almost all senators and more than three-quarters of congressmen employ full-time press secretaries (sometimes more than one); there are even professional associations of Capitol Hill press secretaries.[13] In addition, both the Senate and the House, and all four congressional parties (two in each house), provide heavily subsidized state-of-the-art radio and television studios, equipped with satellite links, so that members can communicate directly, and frequently, with constituents. The studios are heavily used.[14] Undoubtedly some of the members' desire for self-publicity is purely self-gratifying ("I am on TV, therefore I am"); but most of it is more instrumental.[15] Its primary purpose, as any member of Congress will freely confess, is electoral.

Do members of Congress actually thrive in the electoral hothouse—with the temperature seldom less than ninety degrees—in which they are forced to live? Do they like the self-publicizing and electioneering which, even more than in the past, have become a central part of their lot? It goes without saying that many of them do not thrive and do not like it. For them, winning elections (and piling up sufficiently large margins to deter challengers) is not an end in itself, something to be enjoyed for its own sake; it is merely a necessary—but a *very* necessary—condition of their being able to do what they really want to do, which is to influence public policy, participate in the government of their country and perhaps play some part in determining their country's destiny.

In the mid 1980s a Washington-based organization called the Center for Responsive Politics conducted a survey of members of Congress to find out how much time they actually devoted to various political activities, but also to find out how much time, in an ideal world, they would like to devote to each of them.[16] The members' responses, set out in a simplified form in Table 2, provide a measure of the tensions that exist in many congressmen's and senators' minds (and probably their psyches) between their personal priorities and the exigencies of their job. As is evident from the table, the pattern is consistent. Significant numbers of members would rather spend less time on those aspects of their job that involve them in constituency service and electioneering and more time on studying and discussing pending legislation and attending or watching floor debates. The table fairly breathes frustration.

It stands to reason that this degree of frustration might be ex-

TABLE 2

Ideal and Actual Activites of Members of Congress

Activity	% who actually spend a great deal of time	% who would like to spend a great deal of time	Difference
Meet on legislative issues with constituents, lobbyists, officials	61	23	+38
Attend committee hearings, markups, other meetings	74	58	+16
Work back in the state	52	42	+10
Raise funds for the next campaign	10	2	+8
Do nonlegislative work for constituents in Washington	13	9	+4
Attend floor debate or follow it on television	13	25	-12
Study pending legislation, talk about it with members, staff	24	63	-39

SOURCE
Adapted from Roger H. Davidson and Walter J. Oleszek, *Congress and Its Members*, 4th edn. (Washington, D.C.: CQ Press, 1994), Table 5-2, p. 132.

pected to have two effects: to deter many otherwise well-equipped and able men and women from seeking public office in the first place (especially since the sources of the frustration are so visible and so well-advertised) and also to cause some incumbent officeholders to retire in disgust (or at least out of a sense that they were not fulfilling themselves). In other words, America's never-ending election campaign may be affecting, adversely, the size and quality of the political profession in America.

Political scientists unfortunately know little about America's (or any other country's) pool of "potential politicians," the group of men and women who are interested in politics and who, if the circumstances were right, might be attracted into running for office, especially national office.[17] But what seems clear is that, controlling for sense of civic duty and personal ambition, a key factor is sheer enjoyment: the pleasure people expect to derive from running for office, the pleasure they expect to derive from actually holding office. No anticipated enjoyment, no decision to run.

Hard evidence on the point is lacking, but many writers on U.S. politics give the impression that they think the pool of available candidates for national office in America may be shrinking and that one factor causing it to shrink may be not merely negative campaigning, Congress's diminished reputation or the intrusiveness of the modern media but the fact that congressmen and senators cannot any longer settle in to governing but have to contemplate fighting the next election campaign before they have even finished the last. In the words of Alan Ehrenhalt, writing in *The United States of Ambition:*

> There are thousands of politicians around the country who decide every year that a career in Congress is not for them. But they do not make that decision after two years or four years in office. They make it in advance, knowing what is involved. Congressional burnout still exists. But it isn't a midcareer problem anymore. It happens at the starting gate.[18]

The possibility that large numbers of able men and women may be ruling themselves out of national-level politics at the starting gate, or even before, is lent support by the large numbers of voluntary retirements among those already elected to Congress.

Voluntary retirements from Congress, especially from the House, having remained static at relatively low levels for most of the postwar period, soared in the 1970s. They then fell back somewhat during the 1980s, only to rise sharply again in the early 1990s. Many of the increased retirements can be explained by factors that have little or nothing to do with job satisfaction: the inevitable surges in retirement rates that occur after they have been at low levels for many years; the watering-down of the seniority rule in the 1970s (leading to the early retirement of many long-serving members); improved congressional pensions (which triggered an exodus in 1972); a never-to-be-repeated opportunity for retiring members to convert unspent campaign funds to their own use (which helped trigger another exodus in 1992); and, not least, such fortuitous circumstances as the 1992 House banking scandal.[19]

Nevertheless, in recent years lack of job satisfaction does appear to have been a factor—sometimes probably the decisive factor—in prompting considerable numbers of incumbent representatives and senators to stand down.[20] It may seldom have been the only factor; but in many cases it undoubtedly made a contribution to the final decision. At least that is what many of the retirees say, and there seems no reason to disbelieve them. Lack of job satisfaction, lack of sheer enjoyment, in turn have many causes, but one certainly seems to be the demands of the neverending election campaign and, in the case of the House, the job insecurity that is an inevitable concomitant of the two-year term.

One recently retired congressman told an inquiring political scientist in the late 1970s:

> Every time you turn around there is another election coming up. It makes things more intense and nerve-wracking. You are always running, and I suspect this is why members of the House seem to burn out more quickly than senators. I suppose I would still be there if I didn't have to run for re-election every two years.[21]

In the 1990s another congressman who was about to retire remarked: "To have to go back and fight for your life is not something I want to do every two years."[22]

Al Swift, a Washington Democrat, who quit in 1994 after twenty-five years in the House, put the blame on the demands of incessant campaigning and the never-ending need to raise funds:

> What you have to do to get the job is something I'm just not willing to do anymore. Campaigns get more mechanistic. Money has virtually divorced campaigning from people. Money has allowed us to professionalize campaigns, when they should be an amateur sport.
>
> I did negative research the last time. I'm appalled at what you can find out about people, all legally. I'm appalled. And I'm not sure it contributes anything to the process.

Swift then added, for emphasis: "It's not the job; it's the campaign. I'm so elated at not having to campaign."[23]

Dislike of fund-raising, in particular, is a constant theme. A congressman who retired in 1978 maintained: "If I could put my finger on one thing that drove me out of office, it would be fund-raising."[24] Another, who left the House relatively young, said:

> The amount of money needed for a viable campaign in this day and age is outrageous. You have to raise money constantly, and this is a big nuisance, especially for the old members because they are not used to it. But even if you are young, fundraising is nothing but hard work. I don't know anyone who enjoys it. By the way [he went on], I still owe from my last campaign. If you have some loose change. . . .[25]

Another retiree was said to have "flinched" as he recalled the amount of fund-raising he had had to undertake to defeat a millionaire opponent.[26]

To insecurity and incessant fund-raising and campaigning are added, in some retirees' minds, the frustrations of the job and the tensions—unearthed in the Center for Responsive Politics survey—between the demands of governing and the demands of campaigning and constituency service. In the 1970s James Hastings, a New York Republican who was about to stand down, complained to the *Washington Post* about his constituents' lack of interest in his legislative accomplishments:

> In the minds of many people those things don't count. Number one they are not aware of them. And number two, what's important is what I can do for them on a personal basis. . . .
>
> All a member of Congress needs to do to win reelection is run a good public relations operation and answer his constituents' mail promptly.
>
> What kind of whore am I?[27]

Their vulnerability and the demands of the never-ending election campaign thus drive some national officeholders out of politics; but of course the great majority wish to remain and to survive, and for them the activity of seeking reelection is time-consuming, attention-demanding and incessant. It colors everything they do. Its cumulative effects on the U.S. system are tremendous.

One set of effects—those on the internal organization of Congress—are well known and have frequently been described. As a result of members' preoccupation with securing reelection, the procedures of Congress are still biased toward the norms of individualism and decentralization. The more benefits individual members can deliver to their constituents and campaign donors, the more attention they can draw to themselves and the more credit they can claim, as individuals, for whatever they do and say. Hence the relative weakness of the congressional parties (with great pressure on members to "vote the district").[28] Hence, too, a congressional budgetary process that facilitates spending. "That's the beauty of the budget process," said one congressman. "You can vote for all your favorite programs, and then vote against [the] deficit." It is the programs that come first.[29]

But to most American citizens the effects of the never-ending election campaign that really matter are not its effects on the internal organization of Congress but its effects on the outputs of government—the effects, in other words, on public policy. What might these effects be expected to be? It would be surprising, to say the least of it, if vulnerable politicians did not produce policies—and nonpolicies—that bore all the hallmarks of their vulnerability.

Five possible policy effects can be singled out. Two of them are familiar and well documented. The other three are less familiar and less well documented, but deserve to be more so.

One of the familiar effects of officeholders' vulnerability, often discussed in the textbooks, is particularism: the disposition of the American political system to generate policies deliberately designed to target specific benefits for specific individuals and groups in the population—a disposition that extends to "framing laws to give a particularistic cast to matters that do not obviously require it" (or indeed that obviously require the opposite).[30]

The specific benefits include everything from tariffs, subsidies and tax breaks for specific industries through rivers and harbors projects to the building of local post offices and veterans hospitals. These last are known as "pork," and one of Congress's unwritten rules is that every member gets a slice. The instances of general laws being given "a particularistic cast" are innumerable. R. Douglas Arnold lists some of them:

> The idea behind model cities (1966) was to create a demonstration program pouring massive federal funds into a handful of troubled cities. Congress transformed it completely by providing for 150 cities, making small cities eligible, and limiting any state's share to 15 percent of the total funds. Bureaucrats then selected the cities strategically for maximum political effect, spreading the benefits among as many of the program's congressional supporters as possible, even selecting a handful of villages with populations under 5,000. Similarly, a water and sewer program (1965) conceived to help rapidly growing areas was transformed so that all areas were eligible. The Appalachian regional development program (and most other economic development programs) have been broadened to include less distressed areas. The poverty program (1964),

conceived as an experiment that would concentrate funds in pockets of poverty, evolved into a program with benefits spread thinly
across the country. The list could go on.[31]

In every case, the purpose of the original program was blunted;
the waste was enormous.

The other familiar effect of American politicians' vulnerability
is the power it accords to lobbyists and special interest groups, especially those that can muster large numbers of votes or have
large amounts of money to spend on campaigns. Members of the
U.S. Congress "walk the electoral world alone"; they can be
picked off one by one; they know it; they adjust their behavior
accordingly.[32] The influence of the American Association of Retired Persons, the National Rifle Association, the banking industry and the various veterans lobbies is well known. The power of
organizations like these derives partly from their routine contributions to campaign funds and the quality of their lobbying activities in Washington, but it derives far more from the votes that
the organizations may be able to deliver and from congressmen's
and senators' calculations of how the positions they take in the
present may affect their chances of reelection in the future—a future that usually is not at all distant. Might a future challenger
use that speech against me? Might I be targeted for defeat by one
of the powerful lobbying groups? Most politicians are intensely
risk-averse when it comes to elections. "A few instances where
such [lobby] groups have helped to defeat seemingly entrenched
incumbents are sufficient to keep most members from taking
them on."[33]

The three less familiar effects of U.S. politicians' high degree
of electoral exposure will be explored in detail in the next three
chapters; but they can be outlined briefly here.

The first is that, under intense electoral pressure, American
politicians are even more likely than other people's politicians to
engage in symbolic politics: the politics of words masquerading
as deeds, of actions that purport to be instrumental but are in
fact purely rhetorical.[34] A problem exists; the American people

demand that it be solved; the politicians cannot solve it; more-over they know they cannot solve it; they nevertheless engage in an elaborate pretense of trying to solve it, often at great expense to the American taxpayer and almost invariably at a high cost in terms of both the truth and the politicians' own long-term repu-tations for integrity and effectiveness. The politicians lie, not be-cause in most cases they are liars or approve of lying, but because the potential electoral costs—to them, as individuals—of not lying are too great.

At one extreme, symbolic politics consists of speech making and public position taking in the absence of any real action or any real intention of taking action; casting the right vote is more important than achieving the right outcome (American politics is especially rich in bullshit).[35] At the other extreme, symbolic politics consists of whole government programs that are ostensi-bly designed to achieve one set of objectives but are actually de-signed to achieve other objectives (or in some cases no objectives at all beyond the reelection of the politicians who can claim credit for them). The 1960s model cities program has already been mentioned. Other examples would include much federal action in the fields of housing, education, pollution and business regulation. Prohibition in the 1920s was an almost pure exam-ple. Some would argue that Star Wars in the 1980s was too.[36]

At any given moment, a useful clue to the fact that symbolic politics, rather than genuine problem-solving politics, is proba-bly being engaged in is the language used to describe both the problems and any proposed solutions. The punchier the slogan, the less thought has probably gone into matching the proposed policy to reality; indeed the real match that is being made is probably not between policy and reality at all but between the slogan and politicians' electoral needs. As David Mayhew has pointed out, Congress has a "penchant for blunt, simple ac-tion"—and the blunt, simple action is usually couched in blunt, simple language.[37] In the mid 1990s, for example, American pol-itics was awash with blunt, simple language and with quick-fix proposals ranging from lifting the United Nations arms embargo on the Bosnian Muslims ("leveling the playing field") through putting an American on Mars ("because Americans must pioneer tomorrow's frontier") to "three strikes and you're out" as a method, most unlikely to prove successful, of trying to reduce violent crime. In each case, it seemed most unlikely that all the politicians who publicly backed these proposals actually believed that they were good public policy. But they sounded good—and opposing what sounds good, or even being indifferent toward it, can be electorally dangerous.

The second less familiar effect of American politicians' electoral vulnerability is the systematic foreshortening of their personal political time horizons—and therefore of the time horizons of the American governmental system as a whole. Again, the foreshortening is in no way American politicians' fault. It is an inevitable consequence of a system in which elections are so frequent and make such continuous and heavy demands on those who fight them. Who can afford to think of the next decade or the next millennium when the next electoral contest is probably only a year or two away? Samuel Johnson famously said that "when a man knows he is going to be hanged in a fortnight, it concentrates his mind wonderfully."[38] American politicians' minds are always concentrated—and, alas, their thoughts are seldom of all eternity (or even, so far as one can make out, of their own place in history).

Many American officeholders are themselves aware that short-termism is an occupational disease from which they all suffer. John Danforth, a Republican senator from Missouri, complained during his first reelection campaign: "The Senate is on a hair-trigger. There's an absence of a long view. People are running for reelection the day they arrive."[39] Dale Bumpers, one of Danforth's Senate colleagues, complained in almost identical terms:

> The Founding Fathers gave senators six-year terms so they could be statesmen for at least four years and not respond to every whim and caprice. Now a senator in his first year knows any vote could beat him five years later. So senators behave like House members. They are running constantly.[40]

If the Senate, with among the longest legislative terms in the democratic world, suffers from chronic short-termism, it need hardly be said that the same disease in the House is more acute—and even more virulent.

The third less familiar effect of American politicians' extreme vulnerability is that it makes it even harder for American politicians than for democratically elected politicians in other countries to take tough decisions: to court unpopularity, to ask for sacrifices, to impose losses, to fly in the face of the conventional wisdom, in short, to take decisions in what they believe to be their constituents' interest and the national interest rather than in what their constituents believe to be in their own interest. Timothy J. Penny, another congressional retiree, a Democrat who left the House of Representatives in 1994, put the point starkly, perhaps even too harshly:

> Voters routinely punish lawmakers who try to do unpopular things, who challenge them to face unpleasant truths about the budget, crime, Social Security, or tax policy. Similarly, voters reward politicians for giving them what they want—more spending for popular programs—even if it means wounding the nation in the long run by creating more debt.

"Consequently," he says, "a Culture of Hypocrisy thrives in Washington." And it is not just the voters' fault: "Incumbents of both parties use it and reinforce it."[41]

This culture of hypocrisy—the difficulty that the American system as a whole has in facing up to tough decisions—will be discussed in detail in the ensuing chapters, so there is no need to elaborate the idea further here; but a particular feature of the ongoing debate about the quality of American democracy does perhaps need to be mentioned at this point because it bears on the central argument of this book.

Ask any U.S. citizen to say what is wrong with the functioning of present-day American democracy and he or she will almost certainly mention special interest groups, corruption on Capitol Hill, the budget deficit, high taxation, waste in government, the nation's "army of bureaucrats," the uninspiring quality of presidential leadership and a host of other factors; but, in addition, he or she is almost certain to insist, sooner or later, that the modern American system is not sufficiently democratic, that the nation's lawmakers and administrators are not sufficiently responsive to the American people's wishes.

As readers must already be aware, the argument of this book is precisely the opposite: that the U.S. system, as it has developed in recent decades, is too responsive, that many of the ills about which Americans complain so frequently are the results, not of politicians being too remote from the voters, but, on the contrary, of their being altogether too close to them. America suffers, not from an insufficiency of democracy but from a surfeit of it. Less of what Americans think of as democracy—meaning direct and continuous citizen control over politicians and the government—might produce results with which Americans themselves were better satisfied. Less democracy, as will be argued later, might well mean better democracy—and better government.

With these considerations in mind, it is interesting to note that doubts about the degree to which the American system is overresponsive to voter concerns, rather than not being responsive enough, are already creeping into the recent writings of some commentators on the American system. The commentators in question are seldom vehement, and they seldom spell out their arguments in any detail; but they are clearly worried. The political scientist Gary C. Jacobson refers to "responsiveness without responsibility," and a former Democratic congressman, David E. Price, is concerned, not about "governance in disregard of the popular will" but about "a *failure* of governance, based on an exaggerated sensitivity to the anticipated campaign use of difficult policy decisions."[42]

Alan Ehrenhalt makes the same general concern one of his principal themes in *The United States of Ambition*. He describes the American system as one "in which the elected representatives are, if anything, hyper-responsive."[43] Senators and representatives have, he says, "become magnificent responders":

The flights that bring them home on weekends guarantee them a full array of constituent problems, complaints, and suggestions. Those same flights bring constituents to the Capitol, precluding any real insulation from constituent pressure even within the halls of Congress. It is sometimes written that members of Congress, blessed as they are with a variety of free privileges and perquisites denied to the rest of us, have lost touch with ordinary experiences. In fact, the opposite is true. Congressmen may not have to pay the full cost of an airplane flight or a restaurant meal, but when it comes to hearing constituent complaints, they are tuned in fifty-two weeks a year.[44]

It is with the consequences, and the desirability, of this degree of responsiveness that the rest of this book is largely concerned. We begin with a case study of a specific policy consequence of American politicians' electoral fears.

5

A CASE OF FRIGHT

The First Oil Shock

M ore than two decades ago, in 1973, the Organization of
Petroleum Exporting Countries (OPEC) took advantage
of its dominant position among the world's oil producers—and
its newly won cohesion as a cartel—to raise world oil prices first
by 6 percent, then by another 6 percent, then, following the out-
break of an Arab-Israeli war in October, by fully 70 percent.[1] In
October 1973, because the United States appeared to be siding
with Israel in the Middle Eastern conflict, the Arab OPEC countries went even further and imposed a total embargo on the ex-
port of Arab oil to the United States. The United States suddenly
found itself having to cope with both the unexpected rises in the
price of oil and the even more unexpected shortages of petroleum
products, including gasoline, brought about by the embargo.
American politicians began to speak for the first time of a national "energy crisis."

Although no one knew it, or could have known it at the time,
the "first oil shock" of 1973 ushered in what amounted to a new
political era throughout the democratic world. The new era was

an era of belt-tightening, of hard choices, of loss imposition, and it was to impose heavy strains on the holders of elective office everywhere.

During the years of the long postwar boom, from the late 1940s until the early 1970s, democratic politicians in North America and Europe were in the happy position of being able to provide ever-expanding public services and welfare benefits without at the same time having to impose unduly heavy tax burdens and also without having to disadvantage some social groups for the benefit of others. High rates of economic growth during this period funded both unprecedentedly high levels of private consumption and also a vast expansion, in almost all countries, of the welfare state. Because the economic cake was steadily growing, everyone—and almost every interest group—could have a larger slice, or at any rate not a smaller one. Democratic politicians could play Santa Claus.

This happy state of affairs effectively came to an end in 1973. The upward surge in world oil prices led to more than two decades of relative economic stagnation in most of the advanced industrial countries—to lower rates of economic growth, higher unemployment and persistent inflationary pressures. At the same time, profound demographic changes meant that in many countries the productive work force was declining in size while the proportion of the economically dependent—not least the elderly—was rising. Falling tax revenues, largely resulting from the recession, thus coincided with ever-increasing demands on the resources of the welfare state. Democratic governments, once the distributors of largesse, now found themselves—not always or everywhere, but frequently—having to impose losses and having to disappoint expectations that had been built up during the preceding period. Santa Claus began to look a little like Scrooge.

It goes without saying, however, that holders of elective office in democracies do not like imposing losses and are not terribly good at it. The reason is simple. They are afraid that the citizens upon whom they impose the losses will vote them out of office. They are likely to be especially afraid when they believe that the voters will be able easily to identify the culprits—when they reckon the voters know who to blame. And they are likely to be still more afraid when what they are contemplating is imposing specific losses on specific individuals in the present—but only in the interests of achieving diffuse benefits that will allegedly accrue to all citizens at some unspecified time in the future. Politicians reckon that when voters go to the polls they trade off the future against the present and their own interests against those of the country as a whole. The presumption, in the classic American phrase, is that "everybody's interest is nobody's interest." In addition, elective politicians have a shrewd suspicion that voters punish those who do them harm more than they reward those who do them good.[2]

Elective politicians make these same calculations in all countries, and everywhere they arrive at the same conclusions; they certainly did so from the early 1970s onwards. But there was an additional and separate factor operating in the United States. Completely by accident, the era of belt-tightening politics in the democratic world as a whole coincided, in the United States, with an era when American politicians, having always been electorally vulnerable, suddenly became more so. The political parties became weaker from the late 1960s onwards. Primary elections became more numerous. Election campaigns became vastly more expensive. As a consequence, members of Congress were even more out on their own than they had been in the past. It followed that, as compared with politicians in other countries, they were peculiarly badly placed to impose losses on the electorate just at the moment when the objective need to do so was becoming increasingly pressing. The results were evident in the case of the 1973 oil shock. Although, at that time, politicians did not know that a belt-tightening era had begun, they certainly knew they faced an immediate belt-tightening lack of oil.

When the first oil shock hit the United States, two relevant pieces of policy were already in place. Both, as it happens, were already the product of politicians' responses to electoral concerns.[3] In the first place, the United States had recently adopted what amounted to a policy of free trade in oil. Import quotas—sometimes voluntary, sometimes mandatory—had been the hallmark of American policy since the time of President Eisenhower, the aim being to protect domestic American producers, whose prices were far higher than world market prices; but in the early 1970s dwindling domestic reserves together with temporary shortages of heating oil caused widespread voter unrest and led the Nixon administration gradually to abandon import quotas, a process that was complete by April 1973. Quotas or no quotas, however, imported oil was accounting for an ever-increasing proportion of total American oil consumption. That was why the 1973 oil shock—and the second one in 1979—hit so hard.

In the second place, the president of the United States by 1973 possessed the power to control the prices of petroleum products, including gasoline, on the U.S. domestic market. Whatever the price levels of oil on world markets, America's president had the legislative authority to maintain prices in the United States at substantially lower levels. The story was a curious one. In 1970 members of the Democrat-controlled Congress, responding to accelerating inflation and anxious to avoid defeat in that year's congressional elections, provided President Nixon with powers to freeze wages and prices. Nixon, safe in office for another two years, disdained to use them. A year later, however, Nixon was beginning to contemplate his own reelection and, fearing the voters would blame him for inflation, used the powers Congress had given him to impose a temporary across-the-board freeze on all wages and prices. Even after the temporary freeze lapsed three months later, an elaborate array of compulsory wage and price controls was allowed to remain. Or, rather, it was allowed to remain until after Nixon had been safely reelected, when the whole of it was scrapped. Scrapping the controls led, however, to a sharp increase in the price of oil, notably heating oil, in the winter of 1972–73; and in March 1973, under intense congressional pressure (and with the next congressional elections only twenty months away), Nixon again reversed himself and imposed mandatory price controls, but this time only on oil.

Thus, at the time of the first oil shock the United States exhibited a strange mixture of policies: free trade abroad but strict price controls at home. If OPEC was defying free-market principles by using its muscle as a cartel to force up world prices and by imposing an oil embargo on the United States, the U.S. was defying free-market forces by seeking to rig the price of oil in the domestic market. This insistence on domestic price rigging had three consequences, all perverse and all utterly predictable. By keeping the price of oil artificially low, it encouraged consumption just at the moment when the nation's need was for energy saving and conservation. By reducing the financial return to domestic producers, it discouraged domestic production just at the moment when increased domestic supplies were urgently needed. Not least, by encouraging demand while discouraging supply, it ensured that shortages of oil would soon appear—which they duly did, with heating oil hard to obtain and long lines forming at the nation's filling stations. So in the name of reducing pain—or, better, for the sake of appearing to reduce pain—Nixon considerably increased it.

Moreover, the initial response of Congress to the OPEC-induced crisis of October 1973 was to make the position, if anything, even more bizarre. Congress passed, and President Nixon signed, the Emergency Petroleum Allocation Act, which kept the existing price controls in place and, in addition, sought to deal with the developing oil shortages by requiring that "the president establish and administer a mandatory system for allocating all petroleum and petroleum products among regions, refiners, and retailers so that no one would suffer disproportionately."[4] By these means, the United States, even though it could not control (or even affect) the worldwide price of oil, and even though U.S. consumers were left free to consume as much oil as they wanted, acquired a mechanism for controlling the prices and allocation of oil products that was worthy of the former Soviet Union.

There was no mystery from 1973 onwards about U.S. policymakers' objectives. They wanted to increase domestic oil production (and the domestic production of other forms of energy);

they wanted to reduce America's dependence on imported oil; they wanted to eliminate shortages; and they wanted, on environmental as well as economic grounds, to encourage conservation. And, just as there was no mystery about the desired objectives, there was, or should have been, no mystery about how they could best be achieved. The most efficacious policy—and also the cheapest and simplest to administer—would be one that, first, allowed U.S. domestic oil prices to rise more or less immediately to world market levels and that, secondly, imposed higher taxes on petroleum products with a view to reducing consumption (and also possibly encouraging the exploitation of alternative energy sources).[5]

This was the line of policy pursued throughout western Europe and in Japan.[6] The price mechanism in those countries was the central, though not necessarily the sole, instrument of policy. This line of policy was not, however, pursued in the United States until the very end of the decade. Instead the approach adopted, from the Emergency Petroleum Allocation Act onwards, was one of regulation and control. At the beginning of 1975, Nixon's successor in the White House, President Ford, proposed measures for the gradual phasing out of the price controls on natural gas as well as oil. "Without these measures," he said, "we face a future of shortages and dependency which the nation cannot tolerate and the American people will not accept."[7] Although the existing law gave the president the power to propose such decontrol measures, it also gave Congress the power to veto them. This power the House of Representatives proceeded to exercise. The president's initial proposals, calling for a thirty-month phasing-out period, were defeated in the House by 262 votes to 167. A further set of proposals, allowing for an even more gradual phasing out of controls, similarly went down by 228 votes to 189.[8] President Ford himself failed to take advantage of a short-lived opportunity later in the year to abolish the controls by presidential fiat.

In 1976, fully three years after the first oil shock, Congress went even further. Far from decontrolling prices, it insisted that the existing controls be retained and, moreover, that they be extended to so-called "new" oil—that is, domestic production that had come on stream since 1972. The combined effect of the overall price controls, plus the controls that were now put in place on new oil as well as old, was further to encourage consumption and discourage production. On top of all that, Congress decreed that oil prices to consumers should actually be cut by as much as 12 percent. America in 1976, writes R. Douglas Arnold, was truly marching to the beat of a different drum: "While the world price of oil was soaring, Congress was voting to *reduce* oil prices in the United States."[9] Having been merely perverse, U.S. policy was now patently absurd.

In January 1977 President Carter succeeded President Ford, and it was now his turn to try. More than either Nixon or Ford, Carter felt strongly about the issue, and in an address to the nation in the early weeks of his presidency he maintained that the energy crisis facing the nation should be seen as the "moral equivalent of war."[10] He was offended, even embarrassed, by the fact that, four years after the OPEC embargo, foreign oil's share of total American consumption, far from having declined, had actually risen from 35 percent to nearly 50 percent and that the United States remained the world's only developed country without what could reasonably be called an energy policy. And during the next two years he succeeded in persuading Congress, often with great difficulty, to adopt a wide range of energy-saving and other energy-related measures: penalties on the production of gas-guzzling cars, improved home insulation and more efficient home appliances, tax incentives for car pooling, encouragement for solar power, increased coal production (along with pollution-control devices) and a phased decontrol of natural-gas prices.

But missing from the package was any provision either for decontrolling domestic oil prices or for raising taxes on the use of oil. Carter had included a tax on oil consumption in his original 1977 National Energy Plan, but this had immediately run into a solid wall of opposition in Congress and had been abandoned. Frustrated, Carter had to wait until after the second oil shock—

the renewed surge in world oil prices that followed the January 1979 revolution in Iran—before taking action. Under the 1975 Energy Policy and Conservation Act the existing mandatory controls on oil prices in the United States were due to lapse, and to become discretionary, in June 1979. Carter was determined to seize the initiative, and several weeks ahead of time, in early April 1979, he announced that he intended to use his new discretion to phase out the controls on domestic oil prices gradually between June of that year and October 1981. He proposed at the same time that Congress impose a special tax on the oil companies, which would otherwise stand to make enormous windfall profits as a result of decontrol.

Even at this late stage, and even though Carter was taking the responsibility for decontrol entirely on his own shoulders, many in Congress still balked. The Democratic caucus in the House— the caucus of the president's own party—sought to distance itself from the president's action, voting by a margin of 137 votes to 69 in favor of maintaining controls.[11] "The Congress," Carter noted in his diary, "is disgusting on this particular subject."[12] Collectively, however, Congress turned out to lack the will to reimpose controls. Proponents of renewed controls would have required two-thirds majorities in both houses to overcome a probable presidential veto, and such majorities seemed unlikely to be forthcoming. Many in both houses who had hitherto backed controls were beginning, after six years, to have doubts about their wisdom; and the fact that they could now support Carter's proposed windfall profits tax meant that they could be seen to be siding with the general public against the oil industry's increasingly unpopular "moguls." In the event, controls were not reimposed, and Carter's successor, President Reagan, eventually brought forward total decontrol to February 1981, rather more than seven years after the first oil shock had been felt. Even so, an eventual willingness on the part of Congress to accept decontrol in 1979–81 was still not matched by any willingness on its part to impose increased gasoline taxes, even though such taxes would have promoted fuel conservation and helped reduce American dependence on oil imports, both of which were allegedly among the major policy objectives of the time. Between 1975 and 1980 Congress debated a number of proposals to raise taxes on gasoline but rejected all of them. In five roll-call votes in the House on the issue, an average of 79 percent of all the House members voted against any proposed tax increase, however small.[13]

What accounts for this strange pattern of policy, for this persistent pattern of inaction, which President Carter, not normally a man to use strong language, called "disgusting"?

One possible explanation can be ruled out straightaway. Some of those who write about American politics are apt to attribute every policy failure or malfunctioning of the system to the influence of "special interests" or "big business" or, in this case, "the oil industry." The difficulty with this theory, in this instance, is that what it might possibly be able to explain never actually happened. The oil industry wanted price decontrol from the moment in 1973 when OPEC forced up the price of oil on world markets. Given the gap between world market prices and domestic American prices, price decontrol for American producers and distributors would mean significantly higher profits. But the oil industry did not get decontrol. On the contrary, it got, initially, a regime of controls even stricter than before. When decontrol was finally accepted in principle in 1979, it was accompanied, to the oil companies' great chagrin, by President Carter's windfall profits tax. The oil companies did not dictate the terms of the decontrol debate. Their preferences cannot explain how policy developed (or, more precisely, failed to develop).

Some students of the organization of Congress have drawn attention to another feature of U.S. energy politics during the 1970s and since then: the almost byzantine complexity of the committee and subcommittee structures that dealt with energy issues:

> By 1981 Congress had divided up authority over energy policy among forty-three subcommittees, more than double the number of a decade before. This increased by 100 percent the number of

senators and representatives with some authority over the energy agencies and increased by at least that amount the number of interests to which the agencies were expected to respond.[14]

It also increased, almost exponentially, the number of veto points in the system and therefore the number of opportunities for delay. President Carter confessed in his memoirs that he was "shocked" by the size and complexity of the obstacle course through which his initial energy proposals would have to pass.[15]

The complexity of the legislative arrangements—and the fact that on many energy issues there were competing regions of the country as well as competing interests—undoubtedly meant that U.S. policy was developed more slowly than it would otherwise have been and was marked by innumerable compromises, some of them unsatisfactory. But, in the specific cases of price decontrol and increases in gasoline taxes, the degree of complexity was largely irrelevant to the outcomes. Decontrol did not occur until 1979–81, and sharply increased gasoline taxes did not occur at all, not because of complexity and delays but because large majorities in both houses of Congress did not want them to occur. They were able to vote on both. They did. They voted them down. Why?

Part of the answer undoubtedly lies in matters of principle and genuine policy conviction. Decontrol and higher taxes would lead to higher gasoline and other oil prices and would thus give a further upward ratchet to inflation, which was already seen as a serious national problem. By imposing higher costs on both consumers and industry, any combination of price and tax rises might also have the effect of triggering a serious recession. In either case, those who would suffer most would be the poor and those, notably in suburban and rural areas, who were most heavily dependent on the motor car. The workings of market forces seemed to dictate that gasoline and other oil prices should go up; but many in both houses, mainly on the Democratic side, were not overly enamored of free-market economics—especially as in this case the market was manifestly not free but had been rigged by the OPEC cartel. In the back of almost everyone's mind was the thought—or at least the hope—that the problem might turn out to be strictly temporary and might, given time, simply go away.

One late convert to the cause of decontrol was Representative John Dingell, a Michigan Democrat who chaired the House Commerce Committee's influential Subcommittee on Energy and Power. Dingell changed sides in 1979 and in an interview a year later explained why:

> It was my view that we ought to hold prices down. Then all of a sudden I realized that a lot of the conservation was coming from cost increases. Now I don't like that, but it has provided a far stronger stimulus than anything I have been able to do through the passage of legislation. [Asked if anything in particular had changed his mind, he admitted that personal experience had been a factor.] I moved into a little town-house and it costs me $70 a month to heat it. Then I insulated and caulked to beat hell and double glazed the windows, and all of a sudden it's costing me $40.[16]

Others were similarly persuaded. In addition, it was fairly clear by 1979 that the problem was, after all, not going to prove temporary and that more drastic action was now necessary.

Part of the answer thus does lie in genuine conviction; some members of Congress voted just as they would have done in the absence of any external pressures. But there seems little doubt that America's dilatoriness in responding to the new post-embargo oil situation owed far more to the existence of massive external pressures—specifically, electoral pressures.

Ordinary Americans by the early 1970s had gotten used to cheap fuel; they had come to regard it as natural, almost as a right. Moreover, to a very large extent they had become reliant on it. Millions of Americans lived in sprawling residential neighborhoods, with poor public transportation facilities, rather than in the relatively compact cities of Europe or Japan. Unlike most European countries and Japan, America still had a large rural population. Americans drove around in large gasoline-thirsty automobiles, "landgoing battleships." They lived in poorly insulated houses and turned on the central heating or (increasingly) the air-conditioning at the slightest provocation. From all of this it followed that the great majority of Americans, as individuals, had a large personal stake in keeping gasoline and other fuel prices low—especially at a time, as in the 1970s, of relatively high inflation.

All the same, ordinary Americans might have accepted sharply higher oil prices if they had been persuaded of the need for them. But most of them were not. Two of the most striking features of American public opinion in the aftermath of the first oil shock were, first, American citizens' reluctance to accept that the shock was indeed shocking (a serious matter requiring serious attention) and, secondly, the apparent refusal of many of them to accept that this unwelcome new development was not something that the United States on its own could do anything about. Americans in the 1970s were still used to their nation being a superpower. They found it hard to believe that the country could have significant economic damage inflicted upon it by a force entirely beyond its control. President Carter comments at several points in his memoirs on how difficult it was to arouse the U.S. public on the issue and on how frustrating he often found this. "It was like pulling teeth," he writes, "to convince the people of America that we had a serious problem . . . or that they should be willing to make some sacrifices or change their habits to meet a challenge which, for the moment, was not evident."[17]

Underlying the American public's skepticism about the energy crisis was almost certainly a diffuse cynicism directed at those in power in the United States following the twin (and tragic) debacles of Vietnam and Watergate. Contemporary opinion polls point to a feeling that, if something were wrong with America's energy supplies, "they," the people in Washington, not the American people as a whole, should do something about it. The public's cynicism was directed, not least, at the oil companies, which, like withholders of corn in the Middle Ages, were accused of keeping back supplies in order to be able to sell them at higher prices. Asked in mid 1979, soon after the second oil shock, who was to blame for the gas crisis, only 13 percent of a Gallup sample blamed the real culprits, OPEC, the Arab oil-producing countries and Iran; 23 percent blamed the U.S. government and another 15 percent either President Carter or Congress; but by far the largest single group, 42 percent, blamed the oil companies (and a further 4 percent "big business").[18] In the same survey, respondents were asked to say how much effort the oil companies were putting into solving the country's energy problems. The replies attested to the public's hatred of the industry: a great deal, 4 percent; some, 16 percent; not much, 37 percent; none at all, 41 percent.[19]

Whatever the precise sources of the public's dubiety about the reality and seriousness of the oil crisis—and about who was to blame for it—the bottom line so far as price and tax increases were concerned was that the public did not believe they were necessary and gave the distinct impression that they would not put up with them. The Gallup Poll asked in the survey already quoted: "Some people think we should increase the price of gas so that there will be more money to dig new wells; others say we have a big enough supply now without having to increase prices. Which do you agree with?" The responses could have been more lopsided, but not much: should increase the price of gas, 16 percent; should not, 70 percent. The findings of all the polls pointed in the same direction.

American politicians in the 1970s thus found themselves in a position that would have been self-defining for the politicians of any democratic country. A large majority of voters did not believe price or tax rises were necessary. They did not want them. Moreover, if such price and tax rises were imposed, they themselves would suffer immediate, tangible and in many cases large-scale losses—losses that would not be offset by comparable gains elsewhere but would instead be suffered for the alleged purpose of dealing with some abstract, remote and quite possibly nonexistent entity called "the energy crisis." As though this were not enough, voters would know precisely who to blame for any price or tax rises that took place: the politicians in Washington who voted for them. The decision to raise prices or taxes would be—every elected politician's worst fear—"traceable."[20] Members of Congress had no difficulty drawing the correct inference. They knew a red light when they saw one. They stopped dead in their tracks, declining to act even though in many cases they undoubtedly believed that action on either prices or taxes would be right. It was left to President Carter, six years on, to incur the political odium of decontrolling prices on his own.

Fear of the electoral consequences might have been expected to act as a deterrent to allowing prices and taxes to rise in all democratic countries; but, as we have seen, it did not. In most countries, prices and taxes rose sharply in the immediate aftermath of the 1973 oil shock. They probably did so for a number of reasons. The citizens of countries without indigenous oil supplies were probably quicker than most U.S. citizens to grasp the enormity as well as the reality of what had occurred. They also, in most cases, drove smaller cars shorter distances and were less reliant on petroleum products in other ways. Moreover, in most of the other countries the prices of gasoline and oil—and the taxes on them—were already high, so that adjusting to still higher prices was not so difficult. Most other countries were also blessed with not having had price controls already in place when the first shock struck. Politicians in those countries did not have to take positive action; they just had to let events take their course. Members of Congress should have been so lucky.

But there was another factor bearing on American politicians that was not present throughout the rest of the industrial world: the sheer frequency of elections in the United States. In the five years following the first oil shock, Great Britain had two national elections (but both in the same year), and West Germany, Italy and Japan had one each. By contrast, the United States had three: the off-year congressional elections of 1974, the presidential and congressional elections of 1976 and the off-year congressional elections of 1978.[21] Every year without exception was either a pre-election year or an election year. There was no intermission, no period during which America's politicians could contemplate the national interest without having simultaneously to contemplate their own electoral interests.

Even this hectic schedule of elections was punctuated by primaries—and the fear of primaries. President Ford was challenged for the Republican nomination by Ronald Reagan, who launched his campaign in November 1975, fully twelve months before the 1976 general election and scarcely more than a year after Ford had taken office. President Carter knew early on that he might be challenged for the Democratic nomination by Edward Kennedy, as he eventually was. In 1974, 151 congressional incumbents had to fight contested primaries. In 1976, the total was 135, and in 1978, 134. Many other incumbent senators and congressmen did not have to fight primaries but must have feared at some stage that they might have to. The electoral pressure was unremitting.

It is not surprising, therefore, that political scientists and others who have studied America's political response to the first oil shock almost invariably place electoral considerations somewhere near the center of their analysis and several of them refer specifically to the unusually compressed quality of America's electoral cycle. These scholars' testimony is the more eloquent for being largely unself-conscious. None of them is seeking to argue a case about American politicians' peculiar vulnerability.

For example, R. Douglas Arnold in *The Logic of Congressional Action* makes constant reference to electoral imperatives as they were experienced by U.S. political leaders in the 1970s. America, he says, acquired strict controls on petroleum prices and allocation almost by accident:

> Elected politicians were attempting to solve several small problems, not to erect a vast regulatory apparatus. In 1970 the problem was that Democratic legislators wanted to transfer to the president any blame for inflation [on the eve of the congressional elections of that year]. In 1972 the problem was that the president needed to make inflation disappear until after the election. In 1973 the problem was the oil embargo, and legislators sought to ensure that no segment of society would suffer unduly.[22]

Two years later there was a brief period during which President Ford had complete authority to decontrol all oil prices instantly; but the president declined the opportunity: "He much preferred sharing the blame with Congress, for he, too, was up for reelection in 1976."[23]

With regard to Congress's parallel reluctance to enact meaningful gasoline taxes in order to encourage conservation, Arnold writes:

> Such taxes would have imposed immediate and direct costs on all motorists, with all costs traceable to legislators' actions, while offering only modest and distant general benefits, as decreased consumption reduced the nation's demand for foreign oil. Proposals that contain immediate group and geographic costs and only distant general benefits are inherently unattractive to legislators who face the electorate biennially.[24]

In an even more pessimistic vein, Alan Ehrenhalt remarks: "It is not that Congress tried the wrong solution to the energy problems of the 1970s; it tried no solution. Years of intense debate and legislative effort produced no consistent policy, no conservation or strict price controls or reliance on market forces."[25] Seeking to explain Congress's paralysis, Ehrenhalt suggests that "Congress became the victim of all the important institutional changes that were taking place within it." These included "individualism" and the "hyper-responsiveness" of members and leaders to the electorate.[26] Harvey Feigenbaum and his colleagues, in their comparative analysis of energy policy in the 1970s and 1980s, similarly refer to the extent to which U.S. politicians were motivated after the first oil shock "by short-term electoral considerations (especially crises and swings in public moods) rather than by long-term policy considerations."[27]

That said, Congress did manage to pass one important energy-saving measure in the 1970s; and it did so with great expedition as early as December 1973. By threatening to withdraw federal funds from state highway programs, it effectively imposed a 55 mph speed limit throughout the United States. In this case, the public did not object. The same sacrifice was being demanded of everyone. By reducing fuel bills, the move would actually save motorists money. It would also save lives. It probably helped passage, too, that Americans were already among the slowest drivers in the world.

Still, the 55 mph speed limit was an exception to the general rule on energy policy making in the 1970s; and the political system's difficulties in dealing with the energy crisis of that decade did not augur well for what would happen when successive presidents and the Congress confronted the comparable, but even more serious, crisis of the 1980s and 1990s: the burgeoning federal budget deficit. If energy policy in the 1970s was a disturbing case of elective politicians' fear of those who elected them, the budget deficit in the 1980s and 1990s was an even more disturbing case of the paralysis that that fear can help to induce.

6

A CASE OF PARALYSIS

The Budget Deficit

The phenomenon of high-exposure politics—of the extreme vulnerability of American politicians—has scarcely been noticed in the United States largely because most Americans take their never-ending election campaign for granted. It is a "given" of American politics, no more to be questioned (or thought remarkable in any way) than the three-strikes rule in baseball or the predominance of Hollywood in American movie-making. It is regarded as so natural and normal that no one bothers to talk about it.

One consequence is that it seldom occurs to anyone in the United States to factor American politicians' vulnerability into their discussions of whatever features of the American political system puzzle or disturb them. It does not occur to politicians to do so; and even among political scientists and journalists vulnerability is largely a "missing variable." We saw one example in the last chapter in the case of the poor handling of the first oil shock, which tended to be put down to such factors as the complexity of the committee organization in Congress. The American system's failure to deal adequately with the budget deficits of the 1980s and 1990s provides us with another example of the vulnerability factor's tendency to be overlooked. How serious America's budget deficits actually were (and are) is open to debate. What cannot be debated is that most American politicians believed them to be extremely serious.

The first oil shock did indeed come as a shock, to Washington policymakers if not to the American people at large. The issue of the budget deficit crept up on them far more slowly. During the 1950s the federal government's annual revenues, compared with its expenditures, frequently showed a surplus, and during the 1960s the government's deficits, though persistent, were seldom large. In only a single year during the two decades from 1950 to 1969 did the federal government's deficit exceed $10 billion. Beginning in the 1970s, however, the annual deficit figures began to edge upward—to an extent that did not seem alarming at the time but that appears significant in retrospect. The deficit reached $23 billion in 1971, rose as high as $74 billion in 1975 and then, after 1977, never fell below $40 billion. In the early 1980s it again rose above $70 billion.[1]

What was causing the deficits to rise, albeit slowly and as yet in a nontroubling way? The answer is that two factors were combining to create blades of a scissors, cutting away at the budget surpluses of the previous era. One was massively increased social spending following the Great Society programs of the 1960s, notably Medicare and Medicaid, and the substantial increases in pensions and other Social Security benefits that took place in the early 1970s under Presidents Nixon and Ford. Not only were Social Security benefits paid out at increased rates: they were paid out to more and more people, as the number of over-sixty-fives in the American population increased sharply. Moreover, after 1972 Social Security benefits, together with other federal pensions, were indexed to the rate of inflation, which was high. The cumulative effect of all these developments on total federal spending was, as can be imagined, immense.

The other blade of the scissors was the failure of the American economy—partly as a result of the first oil shock—to grow as rapidly as had been expected. Policymakers during the 1960s and at the beginning of the 1970s had tended to assume that gross national product would grow at an annual rate of roughly 4 percent. Instead it grew during the 1970s at an annual rate of less than 3 percent, reducing substantially the federal government's revenues. Sharply increased spending thus combined with sharply reduced revenues to produce deficits in the late 1970s, which were made worse by an increase in defense spending toward the end of the Carter administration. Ronald Reagan as a result inherited a deficit problem when he took office in January 1981; he was by no means the author of it.

He did, however, make it worse. In the first place, as one of the first acts of his administration in 1981, he persuaded Congress to cut taxes sharply, the hope being that reduced taxes would help kick-start a sluggish economy and also ease inflationary pressures; personal income taxes, in particular, were cut by 5 percent in the first year and by 10 percent in each of the two succeeding years. In the second place, Reagan persuaded Congress to agree to massive increases in defense expenditure, which rose by more than 50 percent in real terms in the course of the 1980s. Reagan, however, was not able to persuade Congress to cut domestic spending by more than relatively small amounts.

Many in Congress were worried from the start that this combination of tax cuts and increased defense spending would—in the absence of compensating spending cuts elsewhere—lead to ballooning budget deficits; but it was only in the late summer of 1981 that worry began to turn to panic, including among some in the administration. David A. Stockman, Reagan's budget director, has described in vivid detail how he alerted the president and other senior White House officials to the scale of the problem at a meeting on August 3, 1981. "We are," he told the meeting, "heading for a crash landing on the budget. We're facing potential deficit numbers so big that they could *wreck* the President's entire economic program."[2] The already existing structural deficit was being driven still further into a seemingly bottomless pit by the onset of a deep economic recession. Unless remedial action were taken, and taken quickly, Stockman fore-told multibillion-dollar budget deficits for the foreseeable fu-ture—and they would tend to increase over time.

The problem of the federal budget deficit has been high on the agenda of American politics ever since, not least because Stock-man's direst predictions turned out to be true. The annual deficit rose, as Stockman had said it would, to more than $100 billion in 1982, in the depths of the "Reagan recession," and to more than $200 billion in the following year. In the years since 1983 it has only once fallen below $150 billion and in most years has ex-ceeded $200 billion, usually by wide margins.[3] Interest payments on the debt have risen correspondingly and by 1990 accounted for fully 14.7 percent of federal spending (more than half as much as the total defense budget).[4] By the end of fiscal 1994 the accu-mulated national debt—i.e., the gross debt of the federal govern-ment—had risen to the prodigious sum of $4,643,711,000,000.[5]

Initially the problem of the deficit was seen as a purely eco-nomic problem. Large-scale government borrowing would fuel inflation. It would drive up interest rates, as the federal govern-ment competed with private investors in the financial markets. High interest rates in turn would depress investment. They would also tend to strengthen the dollar in relation to foreign currencies, with the result that a budget deficit would inevitably be accompanied by a trade deficit, as the United States sucked in imported goods and could no longer sell its own goods at com-petitive prices. All of these forces would tend, in the long term if not the short, to cause the American economy to grow at less than its optimal rate and to be liable to persistent, and recurring, economic downturns.

These economic worries persisted throughout the 1980s. They persist to this day. But, in addition, as time went on the deficit took on an increasingly salient moral dimension. In the eyes of many Americans, the budget deficit was not merely eco-nomically deleterious; it was positively wicked, an evil in itself quite apart from any questions of its adverse economic impact.

Americans had always believed in frugality, in the importance of everyone paying his or her own way; they had likewise always believed in balanced budgets.[6] Now they were forced to contemplate the spectacle of the federal government, the nation itself writ large, failing to be frugal, failing to pay its way. They did not like what they saw. They also saw America's foreign creditors, notably the Japanese, buying up American property and well-known landmarks—and they did not like that either. Worse, many Americans felt increasingly guilty at the thought of the burden of debt they were bequeathing to future generations. "Buy now, pay later" they could just live with. "Buy now, but your children will have to pay later" left them feeling extremely uneasy. By the end of the 1980s, the deficit had become more than a problem to be solved: it had become, in the eyes of many, a sin to be rooted out.

Among those on whom the economic and moral burdens of the deficit weighed most heavily were the politicians themselves. A survey in the mid 1980s found that nearly two thirds of congressmen and senators believed that the budget deficit was having a strong (and adverse) influence on the economy at that time, and roughly 80 percent thought it was a "major problem area of the economy." The latter figure far exceeded the proportions citing interest rates, productivity growth, unemployment and inflation. The only dissenters were a small number of left-liberal Democrats at one end of the political spectrum and an equally small number of "supply-side" Republicans at the other.[7]

Feeling strongly about the deficit, and feeling that something should be done about it, the great majority of national-level politicians came quite rapidly—and wholly commendably—to the conclusion that to do something about it was their responsibility. America was not yet a direct democracy. They were the nation's elected representatives. It was therefore their duty to act. Failures on their part they felt keenly—and more so as time went on. Joseph White and Aaron Wildavsky, the historians of budgetary politics in the 1980s, probably exaggerate only a little when they write:

The whole complex of moral notions surrounding the deficit—household management, trusteeship, care for future generations, good government—spoke to the self-worth of the nation's governors. . . . The politics of responsibility was self-imposed by many of our leaders upon their visions of themselves.

White and Wildavsky add that the deficit in time became a symbol of order and legitimacy inside the political household:

Both its persistence and [the high] level of budgetary strife convinced politicians that they were failing to govern the nation. Thus, the failure to solve the problem became the problem: the deficit mattered because it proved the politicians were too inept to handle it.[8]

Whatever politicians' precise motives, and however serious the deficit problem was "objectively," the great majority of America's political elite—from the time of Ronald Reagan to the time of Ross Perot and Bill Clinton—thought it was serious and set their hands to trying to solve it. The media and the opinion formers expected no less. As White and Wildavsky point out, the budget deficit dominated the politics of the 1980s and 1990s in the way that slavery dominated pre–Civil War politics and the Great Depression dominated the politics of the 1930s. In connection with every issue and every policy proposal, the question arose: "But how would that affect the deficit?"[9]

The deficit was thus high on the agenda. It could not have been higher. Yet little was done. Unless we fully understand this gap between aspiration and action, between promise and performance, we cannot really understand American politics and its discontents today. The deficit lies at the heart of the story.

A certain amount, it must be said, *was* done to try to reduce the deficit, or at least to prevent it from running out of control. A succession of small tax increases—the Republicans liked to call them "revenue enhancements"—were introduced at intervals throughout the 1980s; and payroll taxes, in particular, rose sharply as part of a package of Social Security reforms introduced in 1983. In terms of the revenue they raised, the new, higher payroll taxes substantially offset the losses resulting from the successive income tax cuts that were taking place at about the same time. On the expenditure side, substantial savings were made over the years, mainly by tightening up social spending in such fields as food stamps, housing, Medicare, Medicaid and financial assistance to students. The total savings achieved in the very first year, 1981, were estimated at more than $30 billion.[10]

Despite such efforts, however, the deficit continued to grow, and at intervals in the 1980s and 1990s the president and Congress sought to mount major assaults on it. In 1986, under President Reagan, a planned reduction in the federal tax on cigarettes was indefinitely postponed, curbs were placed on reimbursements to health care providers under Medicare and Medicaid, and means tests were applied for the first time to the medical care provided at Veterans Administration hospitals. In 1990, under President Bush, personal income taxes were raised, as were the taxes on gasoline, tobacco, alcohol and a variety of luxury items; defense spending and spending on farm price supports were cut, and health care providers were further squeezed. In 1993, under President Clinton, personal income taxes and corporate taxes were both increased, the gasoline tax went up again, and Medicare spending was squeezed still further.

These recurrent attempts to deal with the deficit undoubtedly prevented it from rising to truly astronomical proportions. They also, it must be said, required political courage. President Bush's personal ratings plummeted as he reversed his "Read my lips, no new taxes" pledge in 1990; and his efforts in that year to reduce the deficit, working with the Democrats, almost certainly played a part in his defeat when he ran for reelection in 1992. A year later Marjorie Margolies-Mezvinsky, a freshman Democrat from a traditionally Republican district in Pennsylvania, cast the deciding vote in the House in favor of President Clinton's deficit-reduction package. As she signed her crucial green voting card, Republicans chanted, "Goodbye, Marjorie." She duly lost in 1994.[11]

Yet, although the growth of the deficit had been effectively

curbed by the mid 1990s, it had not even begun to be eliminated. Huge deficits by historical standards could be seen rolling
far away into the distance. Balanced budgets—of the kind that
Ronald Reagan promised in 1980 could be achieved by 1983 "if
not earlier"—remained a chimera.[12] Reducing the deficit naturally remained at the top of the agenda. This failure to eliminate
the deficit, or to reduce it very substantially, clearly represents a
serious failure of the political system. Views might differ about
how serious a problem the deficit really was; a few economists
pooh-poohed its importance. The point is that almost the whole
of America's political elite *thought* it was important. *They* believed the deficit should be cut. *They* failed to do so on a scale
that *they themselves* were satisfied with. In other words, the system failed in its own terms.

Moreover, the continuing deficits, although they may not have
proved as damaging economically as was originally feared, have
certainly had damaging political effects. The deficits mean that,
in terms of economic and social policy, the U.S. government is
effectively locked in: it cannot undertake any major new policy
initiatives that involve substantially increased federal spending
(on, for example, health care or workfare programs). Partly because it is so tightly locked in, it is increasingly disposed, since it
cannot impose new burdens on itself, to impose them on others.
John H. Makin and Norman J. Ornstein point out in *Debt and
Taxes* that a major, and unexpected, consequence of the continuing deficits has been increased government regulation:

> Government, in essence, has three tools with which to shape pub-
> lic policy: spending, the tax system, and regulation. Spending
> more money is not an attractive option now, nor is raising taxes.
> But when public demands for government action are urgent, the
> easiest way to do something, but to avoid directly worsening the
> deficit or raising taxes, is to require somebody else to do it. Thus,
> we have seen in recent years a buildup of political pressure to man-
> date that business provide more benefits to workers, make fringe
> benefits portable, and clean up the environment, among other
> things. These expensive mandates, some of which amount to a ris-

ing tax on hiring American workers and all of which reduce the international competitiveness of the American companies, now constitute a serious negative by-product of the unwillingness of the federal government [to reduce the imbalance between its own expenditures and revenues].[13]

The federal government has likewise been requiring the fifty states to do more while paying them less.

In addition to locking the government in and forcing it to rely more and more heavily on regulation, the problem of the deficit has led U.S. politicians to indulge in a veritable orgy of symbolic politics. They claim to be solving the problem of the deficit even when, patently, they are not. Someone early in the Reagan administration used the phrase "smoke and mirrors" to describe the subterfuges that Reagan and his people were employing to disguise the truth underlying their own budget numbers. Deficit politics has largely been a case of smoke and mirrors ever since.

Although admittedly somewhat extreme, the Balanced Budget and Emergency Deficit Control Act of 1985—otherwise known as Gramm-Rudman-Hollings or "GRH"—was typical. The act, passed in a great hurry after President Reagan and Congress failed to agree on a budget for fiscal 1986, sought to eliminate the budget deficit entirely by 1991 (though this was later extended to 1993). The mechanism for doing this was to be both simple and automatic. GRH required that, if the president and Congress failed in any year to agree on a budget that met the act's deficit-reduction targets, the amounts necessary to do so would be automatically "sequestered"—that is, legally eliminated—from federal spending. A few of the senators and congressmen who supported the act, including its principal sponsor, Senator Phil Gramm of Texas, actually did want across-the-board cuts in spending to take place; but the great majority hoped that the mere threat of the cuts would coerce the president and Congress into reaching agreement on a budget package that was better conceived but that would still, in time, cause the deficit to disappear.

To the 332 members of both houses of Congress who voted for it, the political attractions of Gramm-Rudman-Hollings were enormous—and also obvious. They could be seen to be voting for deficit reduction in the abstract without actually having to vote in favor of reducing any specific government program. Better still, any spending cuts that took place as a result of the act would take place at some time in the future; they would certainly not take place until after the 1986 congressional elections.[14] Not least, if the GRH sequesters ever had to be enforced, the politicians doing the enforcing would be able to claim that in raising taxes, cutting spending or both, they were not really doing what they wanted to do: they were merely doing what a previous act of Congress mandated them to do. GRH could be made—and was in 1985 made—to look like biting the bullet.

In fact, it was biting blancmange. If the political costs of enforcing rigorous budget discipline were so great that politicians could not increase taxes drastically or else make substantial cuts in federal programs in 1985, why should they be any less in some future year? Those who voted for GRH were voting to bequeath problems to their successors; but why should their successors be any more eager to embrace such an inheritance? Senator Mark Hatfield of Oregon put his finger on the problem at the time: "Our current predicament lies not so much with the present congressional budget process as with our will to make it work, and no new system, no matter how cleverly contrived, will work unless we summon the will and courage to make it work."[15]

Some will and courage were forthcoming, but not nearly enough; and, although the existence of GRH undoubtedly exerted some downward pressure on the deficit, the cynics were right to think that, confronted with real (and hard) choices, people both in the administration and on Capitol Hill would go to great lengths to be seen to be adhering to the terms of Gramm-Rudman-Hollings without actually adhering to them. More smoke, more mirrors—until GRH was inevitably superseded by later developments.

The wheezes used to circumvent GRH—no sequester was ever imposed—did not have to be especially ingenious. One was to make a given year's deficit-reduction target appear easier to achieve by the simple expedient of forecasting a high-growth, booming economy (and therefore augmented federal revenues and reduced entitlement payments). This device, often employed, was known in the early Reagan days as Rosy Scenario. Another was to appear to reduce spending in the next fiscal year by pretending that money had already been spent in the current year. Thus, in 1989 a substantial portion of the cost of rescuing the savings-and-loan industry was added to the current year's spending total (to which, of course, GRH did not apply). Or the opposite could easily be arranged: spending due in the next year could be offloaded onto the year after that. Or, alternatively, embarrassing items could be removed entirely from the GRH totals by being placed "off-budget" (as happened to much of the money required for the savings-and-loan bailout). "In an era of extended budget conflict," wrote Allen Schick, a leading student of the budgetary process, "the two branches [of government] managed to agree principally on one thing: that it is better to lie about the budget than to take the bitter medicine of deficit reduction."[16] Under Gramm-Rudman-Hollings the budget deficit was supposed to have disappeared completely by, at the latest, 1993. In 1993, far from having disappeared, it totalled $255 billion—almost exactly the same, in real terms, as it was in the year GRH was passed.[17]

The trouble with smoke, mirrors and mendacity is that first the politicians notice it (because they are doing it) and then the people do (because they are having it done to them). Perhaps the most important political consequence of deficit politics in the 1980s and 1990s was that it induced intense frustration among many politicians and widespread cynicism among the general public.

It is hard to be sure, but all the signs suggest that the morale and collective self-esteem of America's political class took a considerable knock as a result of its collective failure to deal adequately with the deficit problem (and despite its far more important success in winning the Cold War). On one occasion, Dan Rostenkowski, the chairman of the House Ways and Means

Committee, admitted ruefully that "word of our impotence will precede us."[18] On another, one of the co-authors of GRH, Senator Warren Rudman of New Hampshire, described himself and his colleagues as "a bunch of turkeys" for failing to deal with the deficit.[19] In 1986, when Congress adopted yet another of its innumerable GRH-evading expedients, one that would have the effect of making the 1987 deficit figures look better only by making the 1988 figures look even worse, Rudman exploded: "If Congress were covered by the criminal law, it should be indicted."[20] Such self-contempt gave many American politicians a somewhat hangdog appearance during the 1980s and 1990s. It may well have contributed to some of the premature retirements from Congress described in Chapter 4.[21]

And politicians' self-disgust was more than matched by the general public's contempt for politicians. As Makin and Ornstein point out in their history of American fiscal politics, the public's dismay at the politicians' failure to deal with the deficit—which would have existed in any case, in view of the emphasis that the politicians themselves laid upon it—was compounded by the fact that every move in the deficit-reduction game, every pointing of the finger of blame, every retreat from a previously stated position, was played out in full view of the public. The new openness in America's political processes precluded any alternative. "The result of such unprecedented scrutiny," they conclude, "has been public disgust."[22] The public's disgust with politicians' failure to deal with the budget deficit has undoubtedly fueled a more generalized alienation from politics and the political process as a whole.

What, then, explains the persistent failure? The answer is a complicated one, containing a number of disparate elements.

The extended periods of divided government that have marked the politics of the deficit era, with the presidency and Congress in the hands of opposing parties, have certainly made the problem somewhat harder to tackle than it would otherwise have been; but probably more important has been the absence among the political elite of anything approaching a consensus on the practical steps that should be taken (and on the priority that should be accorded reducing the deficit as compared to other desirable objectives such as full employment, a strong national defense and fiscal fairness).[23] Broadly, fiscal conservatives in both political parties have agreed that the deficit should be reduced by some combination of tax increases and spending cuts, but they have disagreed about what the precise ratio of tax increases to spending cuts should be and also about where the heaviest cuts in spending should fall (whether on defense, Social Security or other domestic programs). Liberals have tended to give deficit reduction a lower priority in any case and have adamantly resisted large increases in taxes, except on the rich, and large cuts in spending, except on defense. The upshot has always been that it has been easier to find a coalition ready to oppose any suggested deficit-reduction package than to find a coalition prepared to vote in favor of it. Faced with difficult and unpalatable choices, members of Congress over the years have usually, and naturally, simply voted "no."

Voting "no" has been made easier by the sheer robustness of the American economy. David Stockman was quite right to predict that, unless drastic remedial action were taken, the U.S. government would run massive budget deficits into the indefinite future; but he was wrong to suppose that such deficits would quickly—in a few years, rather than in decades or centuries—inflict terrible damage on the nation's economy.[24] The deficits have persisted, but the economy has continued to grow; and, largely because it has continued to grow, the deficits as a proportion of gross domestic product have tended to fall. In the 1980s the deficit as a proportion of GDP exceeded 5 percent on four separate occasions. During the 1990s it will probably never exceed 5 percent and in the latter part of the decade is expected to fall below 3 percent.[25] The economic apocalypse confidently predicted during Reagan's first term has conspicuously failed to materialize; and apocalypse now would have been a sharper goad to action than apocalypse, maybe, and at some distant time in the future. It is largely because the economic skies have not fallen that the budget deficit's moral dimension has loomed so much larger in recent years.

The failure of the economic skies to fall has certainly influenced policymakers and politicians; it has greatly eased the pressure on them. But it has probably had an even greater impact on the American people. It has made them even more reluctant than they already were to make immediate and real sacrifices in the interests of long-term and purely conjectural gains. The deficit is, in most people's minds, immoral and therefore to be deplored; but fiscal rectitude, however worthy, has little if anything to do with paying the rent or feeding the family.

There is, needless to say, no unanimity among the American electorate on fiscal issues any more than there is on other issues. People differ. Nevertheless, most people in the United States broadly agreed about the main issues relating to the deficit during the 1980s and 1990s. Their views changed relatively little over time, and the differences among them tended to be at the margin. They certainly did not affect the broad message that politicians were receiving. The majority view can easily be summarized:

> Is the budget deficit a bad thing?—Yes.
> Should the politicians do something about it?—Yes, definitely.
> Is it something you personally are very worried about?—No, not really.
> Are you willing to pay higher taxes to cut the deficit?—No.
> Should programs like Social Security, Medicare and Medicaid be cut?—No.
> Should other domestic programs be cut?—Yes, but only so long as the cuts don't affect me or my community.
> Should spending on defense be cut?—Yes, definitely.

In other words, most voters thought the deficit was important in the abstract but not in the concrete; and, while they thought the politicians in Washington should do something about it, they showed little inclination to do anything about it themselves. The only big-ticket item they were prepared to see cut was defense (though other evidence suggested that their enthusiasm even for defense cuts tended to diminish if the cuts seemed likely to affect their own industry or community).[26]

Lest the above be dismissed as a caricature, consider a Gallup survey conducted in April 1985. It is typical of the whole era. Respondents were asked: "In your opinion, is the current federal budget deficit a very serious problem for the country, a fairly serious problem, not a serious problem, or is this something you haven't thought much about?" Fully 58 percent of those interviewed thought the deficit was a very serious problem, and a further 23 percent thought it was a fairly serious problem. A mere 5 percent thought it was not serious. Given that most (81 percent) thought it was serious, what were they prepared to do about? The short answer is: precious little. Although respondents were informed that the deficit was running at the rate of over $200 billion per year and that there were only a few ways in which it could be reduced, a mere 18 percent said they approved of raising income taxes, only 39 percent approved of "making cuts in government spending for social programs," and a minuscule 9 percent were in favor of cutting entitlement programs like Social Security and Medicaid. Only defense stood out: 66 percent were in favor of cutting that.[27]

For their part, the politicians in Washington read the polls, they talked to the folks back home, and they knew they were in a bind. On the one hand, voters took the deficit seriously (or said they did) and wanted something done about it; on the other, it looked as though they would punish any legislators who were so bold as actually to try to do something about it. Cutting defense would be relatively easy (apart from immediate constituency concerns); but successive presidents and many members of Congress passionately believed in a strong national defense, and in any case after the end of the Cold War in 1989–90 defense spending fell more or less naturally, thereby reducing the deficit but by no means eliminating it.

The deficit was thus a high-risk issue for elective officeholders, and the great majority of incumbents were well aware on which side of the issue the risks lay. As a former member of the House put it, "I can't think of anybody on my watch that I've observed who's lost because they were not sufficiently concerned about the deficit, but I can think of people that probably lost because they didn't bring home the bacon."[28] Moreover, as time went on the pile of "deficit scalps" inexorably grew. Walter Mondale, Reagan's Democratic opponent in 1984, was thought to have lost partly because he acknowledged the need for tax rises. A number of incumbent senators were thought to have lost in 1986 because they had voted to rein in social security spending. President Bush's defeat in 1992 was put down in large part to his involvement in the 1990 deficit-reduction package (including its new taxes). Every member of Congress will long remember the fate of Marjorie Margolies-Mezvinsky.

Faced with this classic dilemma—between doing what they thought should be done in the national interest and doing only as much as they thought their constituents would let them get away with—most of America's elective politicians naturally opted for prudence: the deficits, to their own dismay, remained high. And it would seem that any full explanation of why they opted for prudence—and why they did so so consistently and over such a long period of time—has to give considerable weight to their extreme, and continuous, vulnerability. Many of them voted as they did, not out of conviction, but because they believed that if they voted in any other way they would be out—and sooner rather than later. A senior British politician once admitted that electoral politics forced him "to be immoral one year in five."[29] The modern U.S. system puts American politicians under intense pressure to be immoral one year in one. The wonder is not that they succumb so frequently to the pressure but that from time to time some of them, like Marjorie Margolies-Mezvinsky, bravely resist it.

Because the fact of continuous electoral pressure is so completely taken for granted in the United States, none of the published accounts of American deficit politics in the 1980s and 1990s reflects any need to include electoral vulnerability as a separate factor in whatever overall analysis is being offered. All the same, vulnerability runs like a colored thread throughout the history of the period. Four episodes spanning the decade from 1981 to 1990 can stand for others like them.

The first two both featured in the politics of 1981, the first year of Ronald Reagan's presidency. The Republicans in 1981 controlled the Senate as well as the White House; but they did not control the House of Representatives. If, therefore, the new president's radical tax and spending proposals were to pass the House, the Republicans in that chamber had to stand shoulder to shoulder, and they also had to attract to their side the support of a considerable number of House Democrats. A total of about thirty Democrats were needed. Fortunately for the Republicans, there already existed in the House a group of about fifty conservative Democrats, who were organized in the Conservative Democratic Forum. As they all came from the South, they were known collectively as the Boll Weevils.

Most of the Boll Weevils liked the general thrust of Reagan's program, with its emphasis on high defense spending, cuts in many domestic programs and substantial tax cuts, but it was far from certain that they would go so far as to support his program with their votes. Many of them were senior members of the Democratic party in the House, by virtue of which they chaired influential House committees and subcommittees. Many of them also had doubts about the details of the program. They wanted domestic programs to be cut, but not *their* programs. On a more philosophical level, none of them believed in supply-side economics—the belief that sufficiently large tax cuts would soon pay for themselves by boosting the economy and generating increased revenues—and, being traditional fiscal conservatives, they were worried, rightly as it turned out, that tax cuts on the scale Reagan was proposing would lead to unacceptable budget deficits in the future. In the end, a considerable minority of the conservative southerners stuck with the Democrats and voted for the Democratic leadership's compromise budget proposals; but a core group of twenty-nine defected on a key vote in June 1981 and provided the Republican minority with its margin of victory.

Given the doubts of many of those who supported Reagan, and given their concerns about their leadership positions in the House, what prompted so many Democrats to rebel? A number of them seem to have been straightforwardly bought off. One loyal Democrat complained that just prior to one of the key votes "the Democratic cloakroom had all the earmarks of a tobacco auction."[30] In addition to all manner of tax breaks, the White House conceded an extra $400 million for veterans hospitals (one of the Boll Weevils was chairman of the House Veterans Affairs Committee), continued funding for the Clinch River Breeder Reactor project in Tennessee and a promise of administration backing for higher sugar support prices.[31] Needless to say, the combination of tax breaks and concessions on the administration's proposed spending reductions had the effect of increasing the probability of a serious deficit.

But, although the tobacco auction probably tipped the balance in the case of some Boll Weevils, electoral considerations were almost certainly crucial in more cases—and therefore in enabling the full Reagan program to pass the House. The Boll Weevils represented mainly conservative districts. Their own voters had voted overwhelmingly for Reagan only six or eight months before. Reagan, especially after the March 1981 assassination attempt, was personally extremely popular. If the Boll Weevils voted for all or most of his tax and spending package, they would be doing what their constituents wanted them to do. If they opposed it and the economy failed to recover (the act cutting taxes was actually entitled the Economic Recovery Tax Act), they personally would be blamed; they might face primary opposition; their financial backers might turn against them; they might go down to defeat in 1982.

The evidence suggesting that these were indeed their calculations, although anecdotal, is powerful. Kent Hance, a second-term Democratic congressman from Texas, who had been given a coveted place on the House Ways and Means Committee, was wavering. Along with the other Boll Weevils, he was summoned to the White House where Reagan told them over breakfast that, while he could not prevent Republican opposition in their districts, he personally would not campaign against them if they voted for his tax cuts.[32] Hance had said earlier: "Reagan got 72 percent of the votes in my district. If a person is going to vote for something other than the President's plan, it could cause him some real problems." Now he added, for emphasis: "The president is very popular with the American people."[33] He voted for the cuts. Another southern waverer, Carroll Hubbard, Jr., of Kentucky, feared that the spending cuts in Reagan's program would cause hardship in his district and elsewhere; but he was aware that his people were having serious doubts about the Democrats in 1981: "They think the Republicans are more serious about fiscal restraint and balancing the Federal budget." "I have solid citizens," Hubbard told the *New York Times,* "calling me up and saying, 'We've tried everything else, let's try something new, vote with the President.' "[34]

It was at doubtful Democrats like Hubbard that a television address to the nation by President Reagan on July 27, 1981, was aimed. The results were spectacular:

> What the Speaker [Tip O'Neill] called "a telephone blitz like this nation has never seen" set switchboards ablaze on Capitol Hill. Offices were flooded with calls, according to one estimate, favoring Reagan by about six to one. On Gramm-Latta I [an earlier Reaganite spending measure], Carroll Hubbard had resisted the blandishments of a state dinner and the president's appeal, but on the tax bill his office received 500 calls, 480 of them siding with the White House. "It is obvious that the president's tax cut has overwhelming support in western Kentucky," said this previously loyal moderate who then voted [with the president]. Beverly Byron had not been convinced by the Camp David barbecue, but 1,000 phone calls won her over to the president's side. Bo Ginn of Georgia received a call from Jimmy Carter urging him to hold fast, but, though Carter was Ginn's 405th caller, he was only the fifth to back the Democrats. Ginn also defected. "The constituents broke the doors down," he explained. "It wasn't very subtle."[35]

The doors were broken down because the waverers could see the writing on the wall.

More systematic evidence comes from a study conducted by Darrell M. West. He found evidence of intense activist pressure on the Boll Weevils emanating from their constituencies. For example, whereas 65 percent of the district mail received by Reagan's opponents on the July tax cuts favored the cuts, and 88 percent of that received by Reagan's Republican supporters did the same, the corresponding figure for the Boll Weevils was fully 91 percent.[36] Despite their conservative ideological commitments, the Boll Weevils were also unusually late in making up their minds on how to vote on the tax cut—further evidence that they were torn between their loyalty to their party and the views of their constituents.[37] West concludes about the Boll Weevils that "this critical swing group of southern Democrats . . . took cues from their district activists and voted in favor of Reagan's policies."[38]

What is remarkable about these findings is not the fact of electoral pressure as such—democratic politicians everywhere are subject to electoral pressure—but that it was being exerted on this scale considerably less than a year after Reagan and the Boll Weevils had originally been elected. The 1982 congressional elections were already, in the summer of 1981, casting their shadow before them. The organizational weakness of the House Democratic party was also evidenced by the fact that none of the Boll Weevils, even though they had defied their party on one of the most crucial votes of the 1981 legislative session, had any sanctions imposed upon them. Kent Hance remained on Ways and Means.

The other 1981 episode also bore witness to the consciousness of their electoral vulnerability shown by members of Congress—and did still more damage to the cause of a balanced budget.

By the middle of that summer, David Stockman and others in the White House had realized that, because of the tax cuts and the deepening recession and because the cuts in domestic spending had not been sufficiently drastic, the budget numbers on which he had lavished so much care were going seriously awry. It was on August 3 that Stockman warned Reagan that his entire economic program could be wrecked: "every single number in the budget," he said, "is going in the wrong direction."[39] Stockman's response was to recommend a "September offensive," for purposes of which Stockman was prepared to envisage almost anything that would make the budget numbers go in the right direction: tax increases (despite the earlier cuts), reductions in defense spending (despite Reagan's promises to increase it) and draconian cuts in social programs, including Social Security.

But by this time the mood on Capitol Hill had changed. Members of the Senate and House were receiving new—and different—signals from their constituents. In what Howard Baker, the Senate majority leader, later dubbed "the shock of August," members of Congress returned home for the recess to discover that their constituents, far from applauding what they had done, were extremely restive.[40] They thought in many cases that the tax cuts had gone too far. They were beginning to have doubts about some of the spending cuts. They were worried about what they read in the papers about the budget numbers. They were equally worried about rising interest rates. Above all, they noted with alarm that the economy, far from recovering, appeared to be (as indeed it was) sliding into even deeper recession. As tax rises and further spending cuts would cause the economy to slide still further into recession, most voters were adamantly opposed to both.

The shock of August effectively put an end to hopes of a September offensive. Reagan and his defense secretary, Caspar Weinberger, were not prepared to envisage cuts in defense spending. Most members of Congress were not prepared to envisage cuts in anything else—and certainly not tax rises. Stockman, the angry chronicler of the Reagan administration's budget woes, describes Republican reaction to the suggestion of further domestic spending cuts:

> Minority Leader Bob Michel had met the day before with a large group of House Republicans who had returned from the recess hustings paranoid on the subject of further domestic spending cuts. Their constituencies were now organized, mobilized—and

mad. The President's decision only to nick defense hadn't helped. There was a revolution going on all right—among the House GOP rank and file.[41]

In case Stockman had not gotten the message, Trent Lott, another House Republican, told him a few days later that Social Security cuts were "dead in the water": "That's like in: No way! Period! End of discussion! Not a prayer!"[42] Richard Cheney, hitherto a staunch supporter, warned: "This isn't the right time to launch a new bloodletting. . . . You can't go back to the well over and over. People are shell-shocked and antsy."[43] Any lingering suggestion that a serious September offensive might be possible was finally killed by Senator Pete Domenici, the chairman of the Senate Budget Committee, who phoned Stockman to say: "You can forget Social Security and the COLAs [cost of living adjustments]. Your spineless House Republican friends have poisoned the well. Nobody over here is going to fall on their swords if they're going to cut and run in the House."[44]

As we now know, the failure of the Reagan-Stockman September offensive, before it had even been launched, set the pattern for deficit politics in the United States for more than a decade and a half. But Domenici was being much too harsh. His "spineless House Republicans" well knew what he had perhaps forgotten: that they, all of them, had to face the voters in only fourteen months' time. Even as it was, the Republicans lost twenty-six seats in the House in the 1982 midterm elections—the worst defeat for any party two years after it had regained the White House since the time of Warren G. Harding.[45] The politicians' vulnerability in this case was practical, not just theoretical.

Although Senator Domenici was being somewhat unfair to the House Republicans when he described them as spineless in 1981, he himself certainly had political backbone. He was the hero—if the ultimately unsuccessful hero—of the third episode illustrating the effects on the budget deficit of America's high-exposure politics: the effort made in the spring and summer of 1985 to do something about runaway Social Security expenditure.

As the new Congress assembled in January 1985 following the 1984 presidential and congressional elections, the budget deficit was still running at the rate of more than $200 billion each year, and politicians were agreed that reducing it must be their top priority in the new session. "No doubt," said House Speaker Tip O'Neill, "the public will judge the success of this Congress by our willingness to take the tough decisions to get our financial house in order."[46] Senator Thad Cochran of Mississippi remarked: "It's a little depressing when you realize the votes we'll have to cast to reduce spending. That's the reverse of what politicians like to do. They like to curry favor with their constituents, and we'll really be irritating a lot of people by cutting popular programs."[47]

President Reagan, despite his comfortable reelection, had lost interest in opposing the budget deficit by this time (the deficit effectively prevented the Democrats from passing social legislation); his own deficit-reduction plan failed to meet the targets he himself had set; and it was clear, not least to themselves, that if a serious effort were to be made to reduce the deficit, the Senate Republicans would have to take the lead. Little could be expected from the White House, nothing could be expected from the Democratic House, and Senate Republicans felt more keenly than almost anyone in Washington (apart from David Stockman) that the deficit was a national disgrace and a potential economic disaster and that something must be done about it. They, at least, were not going to be invertebrate.

In fact, what they achieved over the next few months was remarkable. Led by a determined Pete Domenici and also by the new Senate majority leader, Bob Dole, they all but unanimously agreed on a package that, if implemented, would reduce the deficit in fiscal 1986 by $50–60 billion. Funding for thirteen separate federal programs was axed completely. Defense spending was to be frozen in real terms. Most significant of all, there was to be no 1986 Social Security cost of living adjustment; Social Security spending was, at last, to be brought under control. The final vote on the Senate floor, on May 10, 1985, was dramatic.

Everyone knew it would be close. Senator Pete Wilson, a Republican from California, was wheeled in, still attached to an intravenous drip, from Bethesda Naval Hospital where he was supposed to be recovering from a ruptured appendix operation. His vote made the tally 49–48 in favor. A Democratic senator's "no" produced a 49–49 tie, which Vice-President George Bush then broke by voting with Dole and Domenici. The day was Domenici's.[48] "We have done," he exulted, "what many thought was impossible—significant deficit reduction."[49]

Well, not quite. May 10, 1985 was the climax. The rest was anticlimax. The Senate deficit-reduction package—with its crucial freezing of the 1986 Social Security COLA—got no further than the Senate. What emerged to stop it?

The conventional view is that it was stopped when President Reagan and Speaker O'Neill met a few weeks later and reached what became known as the "oak tree agreement." Reagan indicated that he would no longer support (insofar as he ever had) any freezing of Social Security COLAs. That pleased Tip O'Neill. O'Neill for his part announced that he would no longer press for major tax increases to be included in any deficit-reduction package. That pleased Ronald Reagan, whose enthusiasm for low taxes far exceeded his enthusiasm for low deficits and who was more sympathetic to Social Security and its beneficiaries than many in his party. The President's defection pulled the rug out from under Dole, Domenici and the majority of Senate Republicans (and naturally infuriated many of them) as there was no way the House of Representatives would accept the Domenici plan without the President's active approval. Without that approval, it also seemed very unlikely that even an overall majority in the Senate—where the two parties were very finely balanced—would want to move forward.

Reagan's apostasy undoubtedly killed the Domenici plan; but would it have survived and been adopted even if the president had instead given it his all-out support? That is what most commentators seem to suggest; but it seems unlikely. Such a scenario reckons without both the Democratic majority in the House, most of whom were ideologically opposed to Social Security cuts, and also, crucially, the 1986 midterm elections (which would be held just as the proposed COLA freeze was coming into effect).

The truth is that the Senate Republicans—especially the sixteen freshman senators up for reelection in 1986—had taken an awful electoral risk when they voted for the Domenici plan on May 10, 1985; they knew it—and they admitted as much once the plan was dead. "People," said Senator Rudman bitterly, "felt they flew a kamikaze mission and ended up in flames and got nothing for it."[50] Senator Alan Simpson of Wyoming said of the Reagan-O'Neill bargain: "that was not an agreement by the fifty guys who jumped off a cliff over here."[51] Others spoke of Republican senators as having "walked the plank"; and Speaker O'Neill, admittedly a partisan in this matter as in others, maintained that "if the Senate were to take another vote on the COLAs, they'd run so fast from it they'd trample all over themselves."[52]

But there was no need for them to do that because, even without President Reagan's intervention, it seems extremely doubtful whether the House of Representatives would ever have voted for anything like the Senate budget resolution. As early as May, House Republicans were saying they would gladly vote to restore the Senate's COLA cut, and toward the end of that month the House voted by 372 votes to 56 in opposition to a COLA freeze.[53] Timothy J. Penny, a former Democratic congressman (who was in the House at the time), describes in *Common Cents* the aftermath in the House of the crucial Senate vote:

> On the other side of the Capitol, House Republicans are thinking the Senate Republicans are crazy. They don't see the benefits of lower deficits. All they see is the danger of cutting Social Security. House Republicans lost twenty-six seats in 1982 after Reagan *proposed* cuts in Social Security, and they are not going to take any more chances. . . .
>
> "I remember getting calls right after the Senate vote," recalled Rep. Bill Gray, Pennsylvania Democrat, who was then the chairman of the House Budget Committee. "Republicans said, 'Bill, if

you don't accept the Senate version, we can help you in the House.' They'd already given the signal. House Republicans were already backpedaling."[54]

Reagan or no Reagan, the Senate budget resolution was almost certainly dead on arrival in the House. It undoubtedly expired before the end of the year. The death of the Domenici plan—killed, not least, by immediate reelection fears—led directly to the largely vacuous symbolism of Gramm-Rudman-Hollings.[55]

Our fourth episode actually took place during an election year (the chances of that happening in the United States are of course fifty–fifty). The year was 1990, when yet another frontal assault on the budget problem was launched. Its fate is instructive.

Early in the year, Reagan's successor as president, George Bush, and his budget director, Richard Darman, concluded that the coming year's budget numbers were almost too frightening to contemplate. The forecast deficits for 1991 were running at $120–160 billion compared with the Gramm-Rudman-Hollings target of $64 billion. Within a few months the estimate had soared to $290 billion. Tax revenues were turning out to be substantially less than forecast, and the necessity of dealing with the aftermath of the collapse of much of the savings-and-loan industry was tending to push up federal spending at the same time. With interest rates edging up worldwide, Bush and Darman were especially worried that an extra-large U.S. budget deficit would further force up interest rates in the United States, possibly precipitating a major recession.

Accordingly, leaders of the administration spent much of 1990, well away from the limelight, seeking to negotiate an agreed deficit-reduction package with the leaders of both parties in both houses of Congress. The aim in a midterm election year was to ensure that all sides, presidential and congressional, Democratic and Republican, would provide political cover for all the others—or that, as someone put it, reviving Alan Simpson's metaphor of five years earlier, they would "all jump off the cliff together." After five months of negotiations, some of them in the seclusion of Andrews Air Force Base, President Bush and representatives of both sides in Congress were finally able, at the end of September 1990, to announce a package of measures. It was a tough one. As previously mentioned, it included a further squeeze on federal payments to health care providers and sharply increased taxes on gasoline, alcoholic beverages, cigarettes and a range of luxury items including private airplanes and yachts. If accepted, the package would cut $40 billion from the revised deficit in the first year and $500 billion over the next five years. The president pronounced the package "balanced" and "fair," adding: "In my view it is what the United States needs at this point in our history."[56] Two days later Bush commended the deal to the American people on television.[57]

The deal did not, however, commend itself to Congress. Despite public pleas for its passage from Alan Greenspan, the chairman of the Federal Reserve Board, and from three former Republican presidents, Nixon, Ford and Reagan, as well as President Bush, the proposed package was roundly defeated in the House of Representatives by 254 votes to 197. The leaderships of both parties in the House were firmly disowned.

As usual, there was no single reason why the bipartisan package was rejected. Genuine differences of opinion undoubtedly played an important part. Conservatives disliked the proposed tax increases and complained that "big government" was still too big; liberals insisted that under the plan the ordinary man and woman would be hit far too hard while the rich would get off lightly. Even in the absence of the forthcoming elections, these fundamental ideological differences might well have prevented the plan from being adopted. That said, however, it is hard to escape the conclusion that the imminence of the midterm elections—they were only a month away when the House voted—probably played a crucial role in many members' calculations. "Everybody wants to see this pass," a Utah Democrat told the *Wall Street Journal*. "But nobody wants to vote for it."[58]

Members of Congress did not want to vote for it for two related reasons. In the first place, they feared that the voters might quite straightforwardly take their revenge. Republican members, having in most cases won their seats as tax-cutters, did not fancy losing them as tax-hikers. Democrats did not relish being seen to vote for new taxes that would fall mainly on the middle classes. Everyone in Congress was well aware that almost everyone in the electorate would be adversely affected. David Price, a North Carolina Democrat, though he finally voted for the plan, could see the risks to members on both sides of the aisle:

> One reason for the skittishness in both parties was the chorus of protest that came from affected constituencies, prompted in large part by the tendency of the media, especially television, to cover the budget agreement by focusing on its supposed "victims." I knew we [those who wanted to reduce the deficit] were in trouble when I saw the network news coverage immediately after the agreement was announced: motorists at the gas pump, frail nursing home residents . . . and others bewailing their victimization.[59]

One Iowa Republican reported that in the days after the agreement he personally "dropped fifteen points in the tracking polls."[60]

The second reason many in Congress did not want to vote for the plan was that their bipartisan cover had been blown. The intention of Bush and the Senate and House negotiators had been, in effect, that the entire political elite, in both parties, would present a collective front to the electorate. None could be blamed for what happened because all would be. That tactic, however, failed to take into account—perhaps because there was no way in which it could have—the determination of some in both parties to disown the agreement on purely ideological grounds. Most notably, Newt Gingrich, the House Republican whip, made it clear as soon as the deal was announced that he would lead the fight against it. As soon as Gingrich and some liberal Democrats came out against the deal, they were bound to be joined by many others. If all members of Congress were not going to jump off the cliff together, many were not going to jump at all. Members did not want, as individuals, to be thus electorally exposed.

In the event, all was not lost. A compromise deal was cobbled together and passed both houses on October 27, less than two weeks before election day. It passed largely because most of those who were retiring from Congress, or who were unopposed, or who faced weak opponents felt safe enough to vote for it.[61] But the compromise deal provided for considerably smaller reductions in the deficit than the original bipartisan package, and for the first half of the 1990s the deficit continued to run at more than $200 billion annually (though, it did gradually fall as a proportion of GDP).

There is, in the end, no way of proving that the electoral vulnerability of America's politicians delayed and made substantially more difficult the implementation of tough deficit-reducing measures during the 1980s and 1990s; but the record of those two decades suggests that it probably played a part, and it may well have played a very substantial part, in prolonging the deficit agony.[62] If at any stage the political class had had a respite of, say, two or three years from America's never-ending election campaign, more might have been accomplished. As it was, almost everyone in the system, including the voters, felt let down. Somehow democracy did not seem to be serving its own best interests.

7

A CASE OF FRAUD

The Wars on Crime

Electoral vulnerability helps explain America's halting response to the first oil shock. It also helps explain the slow, almost imperceptible progress that has so far been made in tackling the federal budget deficit. It helps, in addition, to explain some of the stranger features of the U.S. government's innumerable and well-publicized wars on crime.

The phrase "wars on crime" should in itself give the wary citizen pause. Real wars are fought between rival states and rival armies. They usually have known causes. They almost always have discernible beginnings and ends. Periods of war are punctuated by periods of peace. At the ends of most wars, it is possible to identify victors and vanquished. But crime is not like that at all. There always has been crime. There always will be. Its causes are multifarious and obscure. In seeking to prevent it and to punish its perpetrators, governments of whatever political stripe are not confronting organized armies (let alone some generalized abstraction called "crime"); they are dealing as best they can with a bewildering complex of crimes and criminals, from sophisticated white-collar fraudsters and international drug dealers to murderers, muggers, wife-batterers and car thieves. Because the war against crime is not a war and, sadly, can never be won, it is fraudulent to call it a war. To do so is to raise false expectations and hold out false hopes. Those who speak of "wars on crime" and "wars on drugs" have chosen to enter the fantasy world of symbolic politics.[1]

Three facts about the politics of crime in the United States over the past quarter-century stand out. The first is that, contrary to widespread belief, crime rates in the United States have *not* increased dramatically in recent years. On the contrary, and despite inevitable short-term fluctuations, the incidence of most crimes changed very little between the early 1970s and the early 1990s, and in the 1990s the overall incidence of crime actually showed signs of diminishing. According to the National Crime Victimization Survey, the proportion of American households experiencing crime fell sharply from 32.1 percent in 1975 to only 22.6 percent in 1992; the proportion experiencing violent crime (rape, robbery or assault) fell over the same period from 5.6 percent to 5.0 percent. The rates of household theft, personal theft and burglary also declined. Only the theft of motor vehicles showed a slight increase.[2] The myth of an American crime wave in the 1980s and 1990s is precisely that: a myth. There is, however, one exception to this overall picture. The number of homicides perpetrated by young men, especially young men using firearms, did increase sharply from 1985 onwards. Moreover, the victims of these homicides were often—in one-third or more of cases—total strangers to their killers.[3]

This sharp increase in the incidence of seemingly random stranger-to-stranger crimes, perpetrated mainly by the young and often involving the use of guns, undoubtedly helps to account for the second fact: a sharp increase, beginning in the mid 1980s, in American citizens' concerns about crime. As recently as 1980, only 3 percent of the respondents to the U.S. National Election Study volunteered crime as one of the three "most important problems facing this country." By 1994 that figure had risen to 52 percent—from fewer than one respondent in thirty to more than one in two in less than fifteen years.[4] Although crime as a whole was static or down, fear of it was up. "People are not responding to the statistics," the criminologist James Q. Wilson told the *New York Times,* "but to what they hear reported." He added: "It's the stranger-to-stranger nature of the crime, the youth of the offenders and the level at which they're armed which alarms people." Notwithstanding the statistics, he concluded, "it's rational to be scared."[5]

The third fact about the American politics of crime was that no one who was both honest and well-informed really knew what to do about it. Some advocated attacking the "root causes of crime"; but no one really knew what the root causes of crime were, and even those who claimed to know had few practical (and affordable) prescriptions to offer. Others, reverting to the language of war, insisted that crime could only be "fought" by means of stiffer penalties and vastly increased numbers of prison cells and police; but both the history of crime and the current criminal statistics seemed to suggest that extra vanloads of police and expanded prisons could indeed accomplish something, but not much. Expert criminologists put forward a variety of specific suggestions—such as community policing, the intensive policing of criminal "hot spots" and new technology to identify individuals carrying concealed weapons—but their suggestions did not, and could not, add up to a "solution" to the nation's crime "problem."[6]

It is under these circumstances—when few if any practicable solutions are to hand but when politicians are nevertheless under intense pressure to respond to voters' anxieties—that symbolic politics, the politics of the grand but empty gesture, is liable to come to the fore. The electoral syllogism of the 1990s with regard to crime was straightforward. In the words of a former congressman:

Lawmakers in Washington feared reprisals if they didn't persuade voters they were in touch with their fears of violent crime and prepared to do something about it.

Simply put, voters were afraid of criminals, and politicians were afraid of the voters.[7]

Some of the politicians' responses were sensible; most criminologists would probably agree that the previous "social work"
regime (to the extent that it existed) had not worked and that incarceration turned out to be the most effective way of preventing
violent and repeat offenders from committing new crimes. But
some of the results of the politicians' fears, had they not been so
serious, would have been comic.

One important manifestation of their fear of the voters in this
connection was the enactment, beginning in the mid 1980s, of
large numbers of mandatory minimum sentences—that is, terms
of imprisonment that the judge presiding in a given case could
add to but not subtract from. Legislatures, in other words, increasingly took over the role of determining sentencing policy.
Judges were denied the discretion they had previously enjoyed.

In the case of the federal government, most of the mandatory
sentences were directed at violent and drug-related crime. The
penalties were draconian and, especially in relation to drugs offenses, were often intended to be imposed on first-time and relatively petty offenders. For example, the possession by anyone of
more than five grams of crack cocaine with intent to distribute
attracted a mandatory minimum sentence of five years. Moreover, the statutory minimums were meant to be just that: there
were no grounds on which prisoners subjected to the minimum
sentences could be paroled. Between 1986 and the early 1990s,
the appetite of Congress for mandatory sentences grew by what it
fed on, and by 1995 it was estimated that there were some one
hundred federal crimes for which minimum sentences had,
under the law, to be handed down.

The purposes of these new mandatory minimum—and very
severe—sentences were straightforward. More criminals who were
a menace to society would be kept off the streets. The certainty of
long sentences would act as a deterrent, not least to those who had
already done time in prison. The fact that the sentences were
mandatory would mean greater uniformity in sentencing among
judges; and it would also mean that the sentences actually meant
what they said. Five years would mean five years, not two years

and four months, with time off for good behavior. "Truth in sentencing"—a catchphrase of the 1980s—would thus be achieved.

The logic seemed impeccable. It soon became clear, however, that the mandatory minimum sentences enacted by Congress were having all kinds of perverse and unintended consequences. They led to manifest injustices and a near-rebellion on the part of the judiciary. Moreover, not only did they not reduce crime; there is reason to think they may actually have increased it (and by the mid 1990s many in both Congress and the executive branch were having second thoughts).

It was not surprising that federal judges disliked being deprived of their discretion; most of them regarded sentencing as being one of their key responsibilities, and they resented having to impose mandatory sentences, determined by someone else, regardless of the circumstances of specific cases. They protested that they were sentencing crimes instead of criminals. More serious were the gross injustices that they believed were resulting. One classic case—there were many—concerned Nicole Richardson, an eighteen-year-old Alabama high school senior, whose boyfriend was a drug dealer. Posing as a buyer, a federal undercover agent phoned her and asked her where her boyfriend was so that he could pay for some drugs. Both Richardson and the boyfriend were arrested. Because the boyfriend, the real criminal, had useful information to share with the authorities, he was able to plead guilty and received a sentence of five years. However, Richardson, whose role was wholly peripheral, had no such information and was sentenced to a mandatory minimum of ten years. The presiding judge, Alexander Howard, irate, said that in all his experience of federal guidelines and statutory minimums, "this case represents to me the top miscarriage of justice."[8]

Howard was not alone in his anger. A survey conducted by the Gallup Organization for the *American Bar Association Journal* found that 90 percent of federal judges thought that mandatory minimum sentences for federal drug offenses were a bad idea. A mere 8 percent approved of them. One in five of the judges said they had given thought to taking "serious action" to protest the sentencing policies that they were forced to follow. Six percent said they had even considered resigning from the federal bench.[9] Judge A. Leon Higginbotham, Jr., of the U.S. Court of Appeals for the Third Circuit wrote: "Judges and legislators must always remember that ultimately we are not sentencing widgets or robots, but human beings." He added that "convicted defendants should be sentenced within the spectrum of what most able judges would consider fair and reasonable both for our society and for the sentenced defendant."[10] No less a figure than the chief justice of the U.S. Supreme Court, William Rehnquist, indicated in 1993 that he, too, had doubts. He referred to mandatory sentences for drug crimes as "perhaps a good example of the law of unintended consequences" and added: "There is a respectable body of opinion which believes that these mandatory minimums impose unduly harsh punishment for first-time offenders, particularly for mules who play only a minor role in a drug distribution scheme."[11] A California state judge, Carol J. Fieldhouse, was more forthright: "I refuse to dispense injustice," she said. "I wasn't put here to annihilate people because some politically hungry morons wanted [me] to."[12]

The unhappiness of the judges could perhaps be dismissed on the grounds that mandatory sentences merely offended their professional pride and *amour propre*: but it was harder to dismiss the charge that mandatory minimum sentences were introducing major unintended and unwanted distortions into the whole U.S. criminal justice system; and it was harder still to dismiss the charge that they might well be leading, perversely, to an actual *increase* in criminal activity.

The distortions, like the injustices, were not hard to identify. The mandatory minimum sentences were intended to take discretion away from judges; but, in doing that, they did not eliminate discretion: they merely handed it over to prosecutors instead. Public discretion by judges, over sentencing, in practice gave way to private discretion by prosecutors, over charging— and prosecutors often had their own reasons for seeking to flout the spirit of the mandatory-minimum laws. Predictably, many prosecutors, faced with a choice between pressing charges that carried severe mandatory sentences and pressing charges carrying lesser penalties, frequently opted for the latter. A survey of forty-six prosecutors conducted by the federal U.S. Sentencing Commission found that twenty-six of them sometimes declined to charge a defendant with a crime that carried a mandatory sentence if the defendant was cooperative or if they thought that the defendant, if convicted, would be sentenced too harshly.[13]

In some cases, prosecutors by this backstairs method achieved the flexibility in sentencing of which Congress and state legislators sought to deprive the judiciary, thereby also achieving a modicum of justice. But in other cases prosecutorial discretion favored only those, like Nicole Richardson's informative boyfriend, who were of use to prosecutors.

Cases like that of Richardson and her boyfriend were numerous and gave rise to the phenomenon that came to be known as the "cooperative paradox."[14] A report published by the Federal Judicial Center explained the nature of the paradox:

> The transfer of discretion from neutral judges to adversarial prosecutors tilts the sentencing system toward prosecution priorities, sometimes at the expense of other sentencing goals. For example, the government relies on assistance and cooperation from some defendants—perhaps as confidential informants or witnesses at trial—to make cases against others. Sentencing incentives for those who cooperate are viewed as an important component of law enforcement. The problem is that offenders who are more involved in the drug network and have more valuable information to provide are in a better position to receive a reduced sentence than are less culpable offenders who are less informed. Consequently, more culpable offenders may get *shorter* sentences than the low-level offenders who participated in the same conspiracy.[15]

In general, the scope of plea bargaining was considerably reduced by mandatory sentencing. Some prosecutors deliberately chose to charge defendants with crimes carrying minimum penalties; others believed that they had no option. In cases where plea bargaining did not take place, the burden on the courts was greatly—and unexpectedly—increased. Confronted with the prospect of a long custodial sentence without the possibility of parole, many defendants who would once have pleaded guilty now pleaded not guilty. What had they to lose? They might get off. Large amounts of court time were taken up with such cases.[16] Moreover, many observers believed that, even when cases did finally come to court, mandatory minimum sentences made convictions harder to obtain. The more severe (and seemingly unjust) the sentence in prospect, the greater the reluctance of juries to convict.[17]

A further distortion was introduced by the fact that almost all of the mandatory minimum sentences, certainly in the federal courts, focused on the nature of the crime committed rather than on the character and previous record of the criminal who committed it. Under many federal statutes, if two men were convicted of identical crimes, they received identical sentences, even if one of them was a teenage first-time offender while the other was a hardened villain who had spent most of the previous decades behind bars. The case for incarcerating the former might be negligible while the case for incarcerating the latter might be overwhelming. No matter: both were treated the same. A federal judge in California, on having to impose a ten-year mandatory sentence on a first-time offender, complained that "it could make no difference if the day before making this one slip in an otherwise unblemished life, defendant had rescued fifteen children from a burning building, or had won the Congressional Medal of Honor while defending his country."[18] Again, convictions for relatively minor offenses were thereby made harder to obtain.

Most of the federal statutes requiring mandatory minimum sentences were concerned with drugs and the drug trade. They were meant to help "stamp out" drug trafficking as part of the federal "war on drugs." They certainly had the effect of putting more drug dealers behind bars and putting them there for longer. According to the Federal Bureau of Prisons, 34 percent of all federal prisoners were in prison on drugs charges in 1985, the year before Congress adopted the 1986 Anti-Drug Abuse Act, which provided for a wide range of mandatory penalties. Three years later the proportion was 45 percent. Two years after that it was 52 percent, and by 1992 the figure had reached 60 percent.[19]

This startling increase in the size of the drugs-related federal prison population did not, however, have any discernible effect on the number of drugs-related offenses that were committed or on the incidence of actual drug abuse among American youngsters.[20] Quite apart from the criminal justice system's limited ability to deal with pathologies of social and individual psychology such as drug abuse, the problem was that, under mandatory minimum sentencing, the wrong people were being put away: thousands of unsuspecting minnows, but almost no big fish. Of the offenders convicted under the federal mandatory minimum statutes in fiscal year 1992, for example, only 5 percent were the organizers or leaders of extensive drug operations. More than 85 percent did not manage or supervise trafficking activity; a large proportion of them were merely low-level couriers or "mules."[21] A 1994 Department of Justice study similarly found that first-time offenders comprised 28.8 percent of all federal drug offenders and 16.6 percent of all the offenders in the federal prison system.[22] The utility of incarcerating large numbers of these low-level offenders for long periods was negligible. All the evidence made it clear that, if they were not on the streets distributing and selling illegal drugs, others certainly would be. The sheer profitability of the drugs industry would—and did—see to that.[23]

The fact that large numbers of relatively petty drug offenders were being imprisoned under mandatory-minimum-sentence laws might not have mattered much (except, of course, to those in prison) had it not been for the further fact that the policy introduced yet another serious distortion into the system. The ultimate irony of mandatory minimums is that, far from reducing the incidence of crime, there is good reason to think that they may actually have increased it. To the "cooperative paradox" referred to earlier, in connection with plea bargaining, there needs to be added an "opportunity cost paradox."

Every prison cell occupied by one person is at the same time a cell not occupied by some other person. If the aim is to prevent crime, each prison cell should, therefore, ideally be occupied by the person who, if free, would be most likely to commit crimes and, in particular, the most serious crimes. The federal policy of mandatory minimum sentences achieves, however, the opposite effect. Because the number of cells in federal prisons is limited, the incarceration of large numbers of minor and usually nonviolent drug offenders means that other offenders have to be released (or never incarcerated in the first place) in order to make room for them. In practice, the offenders who are released (or never incarcerated in the first place) include a considerable number of dangerous, violent and repeat offenders who happen not to have been given mandatory minimum sentences. The relatively harmless remain in prison; those who are truly a menace to society may go free.

The perversity of this outcome is widely recognized by those who study the U.S. criminal justice system. David B. Kopel of the Washington-based Cato Institute favors long sentences for violent offenders but, precisely for that reason, opposes most mandatory minimum sentences, which have the effect of forcing the early release of violent offenders to make room for nonviolent drug offenders. In a 1994 article, Kopel pointed to the case of Kenneth McDuff, paroled after twenty-three years in prison. McDuff killed again within three days of leaving prison and murdered at least two more people in the year before he was caught. The irony was that McDuff was released early because Texas, the state in which he committed his crimes, revised its parole rules to relieve the overcrowding caused by a quadrupling of incarcerated drug offenders.[24] Two Harvard criminologists, one a former Justice Department official, assert baldly that "the result of long mandatory sentences for minor drug offenders is to increase crime."[25]

It was obvious by the early 1990s that mandatory minimum sentences were a failure. They not only offended the judiciary: they were extremely costly to administer, they did little or nothing to reduce crime, and they may even have increased it. None of that, however, stopped many individual states, and in 1994 the federal government, from embarking on a new variant on the theme of mandatory sentences: the policy of "three strikes and you're out." Baseball, in the characteristically simpleminded style of symbolic politics, was to come to the aid of penology.

Like the case for mandatory minimum sentences, the case for "three strikes and you're out" was quite straightforward, especially when it was applied, as it was in most states and by the federal government, only to violent offenders. A person who had committed three major crimes of violence was clearly, by virtue of that fact alone, a dangerous person, someone who was likely to commit more such crimes. With luck, "three strikes and you're out" might deter some violent offenders from reoffending; but, even if it did not do that, it would still ensure that those with records of violence would be locked up and no longer constitute a menace to society. Almost all the relevant laws provided that third-time violent offenders should serve life "where life meant life." An additional attraction of the policy was the likelihood that those unlucky enough to have been caught three times would probably, in fact, have committed more than three crimes. "Three strikes and you're out" would therefore help clear the streets of some of the most persistent offenders.

The case for "three strikes and you're out," at least for violent offenders, was considerably stronger than the case for mandatory sentences for mules and other petty drugs offenders. The criminals in question *were* violent; they *did* have previous convictions; getting them off the streets *was* likely to have some effect in reducing violent crime. In other words, "three strikes and you're out" was more than just symbolic.

Even so, the element of pure symbolism surrounding it was still very large. The federal penal code and the penal codes of most states already provided for long prison sentences for repeat violent offenders, and the judges showed themselves willing to hand down such sentences, so that the main purpose of "three strikes and you're out" was already being served. In addition, three-strikes sentences tended to affect men who, because they had already done time for previous violent offenses, were in any case coming to the end of their criminal careers. The author of a RAND study commented acidly on the foolishness of locking up large numbers of "old felons who no longer pose much threat to society but who are going to spend the rest of their lives in prison getting geriatric care at the state's expense."[26]

Apart from being largely redundant, "three strikes" laws had other disadvantages. Once again, they handed discretion over to prosecutors. With so much at stake, they deterred defendants from pleading guilty to charges that would now count as "strikes." In doing that, they clogged up the courts, thereby delaying the hearing of large numbers of other cases.[27] In jurisdictions such as California, where the "three strikes" law covered nonviolent as well as violent offenders, they also caused manifest injustices (the case of a man jailed for life for stealing a child's pizza became notorious) and put intense strains on the prisons. In California an independent report predicting that the cost of building new prisons and incarcerating large numbers of additional prisoners under "three strikes" would come to approximately $5.5 billion a year was headlined in one newspaper: "Three strikes and we're broke."[28] There was also the possibility, raised by a case in the state of Washington, that convicted offenders who already had two strikes against them might try to shoot their way out of trouble rather than face going to prison for life on a third-strike charge.[29]

The criminologist James Q. Wilson pointed out that third-strike laws in general suffer from an inherent contradiction:

> If they are carefully drawn so as to target only the most serious offenders they will probably have a minimal impact on the crime rate [because the most serious offenders are subject already to long sentences], but if they are broadly drawn so as to make a big impact on the crime rate they will catch many petty repeat offenders who few of us think really deserve life imprisonment.[30]

The director of corrections for Washington state was a good deal more blunt. Asserting that "three strikes and you're out" laws were not really dealing with violence on the streets, he admitted: "I felt that we're sort of pulling one over on the public."[31] In other words, the laws were largely symbolic, designed more to make a good impression on the general public than to make a real impression on actual crime.

But the element of symbolism in the various three-strikes laws reached its acme in connection with the federal legislation in the field. In 1994 Congress enacted its own version of "three strikes and you're out," providing that a person who was convicted in a court of the United States of a serious violent felony should be sentenced to life imprisonment if he or she had already been convicted in either a federal or state court of two serious violent felonies or one serious violent felony plus a serious drugs offense.

The catch lay in the phrase "in a court of the United States," because, as is well known, the vast majority of crimes, including serious violent crimes, are prosecuted in the United States not through the federal courts but through the state courts. Hence the reference to the state courts in the federal act. In fact, the 1994 act covered only federal crimes and, despite its impressive-sounding provisions, applied only to serious violent felonies committed in somewhat unusual surroundings: notably in national parks, on army, navy and air force bases and on some, but not all, Indian reservations. On the basis of official data that were already available, John J. DiIulio, Jr., and his colleagues calculated that in 1991 only 1,871 of those committed to federal prisons were persons whose sole or most serious offense was a violent offense: "If as many as one-tenth of these convictions were for a third violent felony—a high estimate given the recidivism profile of federal prisoners—then a federal three-strikes law, [had one been] in effect in 1991, would have affected only 187 persons, or about one-half of 1 percent of all persons sent to federal prisons in that year."[32] In other words, the gap between the politicians' rhetoric and the law's probable impact on crime could hardly have been wider. The federal courts, it seems, seldom play baseball.

Federal three-strikes laws are bad enough—or, more precisely, irrelevant enough; but the pinnacle, the summit, the veritable zenith of symbolic politics, of the politics of fraud in connection with Congress's self-proclaimed wars on crime relates to capital punishment. Congress growls, rears itself up on its hind legs and bares its fangs—but nothing happens.

The story of capital punishment in the federal judicial system is a curious one. A number of federal statutes provided for the death penalty until 1972, when the U.S. Supreme Court in *Furman vs. Georgia* struck down all existing capital-punishment statutes, both state and federal, on the grounds that they operated in a wholly arbitrary and discriminatory way (as one of the justices put it, they smacked "of little more than a lottery").[33] A large number of states quickly responded, however, by rewriting their death-penalty statutes to try to make them less arbitrary in their effect; and in 1976 the Supreme Court, by now differently constituted, ruled in *Gregg vs. Georgia* that capital punishment was constitutionally permissible provided that it was administered in a nonarbitrary, nondiscriminatory fashion.

Unlike the majority of states, however, it took Congress several years to get round to responding to the Court's tacit invitation to produce a new set of capital-punishment laws. The problem did not seem pressing. The House Judiciary Committee, in particular, was opposed. But then, beginning in the late 1980s, the mood changed. Death-penalty provisions began to find their way into bills and statutes relating to crime, and by 1990 there were some thirty federal crimes that were punishable, in principle, by death. Warming to its task, Congress in 1994 added some fifty new crimes to the federal tally, bringing the total of such crimes to more than eighty. The new list included such offenses as the smuggling of aliens where death resulted and the murder of a person guarded under the federal witness protection program. The aim was to deter and, failing that, to punish.[34]

The only trouble with this formidable array of death-dealing weaponry was that it was aimed (though the general public probably did not know it) at a target that, for all practical purposes, did not exist. Once again, the great majority of violent offenses are prosecuted not through the federal courts but through the state courts. Federal offenders are more likely to be the perpetrators of elaborate white-collar crimes or the drug offenders referred to earlier. A simple measure of the death penalty's sheer irrelevance to the federal government's war on crime is easily provided. The last federal offender to be put to death, Victor H. Feguer, a convicted kidnapper, was hanged in March 1963. As of the end of 1995, no federal offender had been executed for more than thirty years, and hardly any federal offenders were awaiting execution on death row. The ferocious-seeming federal statutes were almost entirely for show.

This symbolic character of the federal government's war on crime extends to many other fields. The much-touted proposal in 1994 to put an additional 100,000 policemen on the beat would have had little effect, even if it had been implemented in full and in its original form.[35] Similarly, although the famous "Brady bill," named after President Reagan's press secretary who was badly wounded in the 1981 assassination attempt on Reagan, did seek to provide a limited measure of federal gun control, it was doomed to fail—and it was obvious in advance that it was doomed to fail—in a country where roughly two hundred million firearms, including sixty million handguns, are already at large. America's leading student of the politics of gun control noted laconically in 1995 that "in policy terms, the Brady law's consequences were expected to be modest."[36] Quite so.

Thus, American policymakers across the board in the 1980s and 1990s passed anti-drug and anti-crime legislation much of which was, at best, useless and, at worst, wholly pernicious in its effects, leading to manifest injustices and possibly even to an actual increase in the amount of crime committed. Why did U.S. policymakers, including presidents Bush and Clinton, choose to behave in this perverse fashion?

There appear to be two reasons. The first is undoubtedly that many in Congress and in and around the White House genuinely believed that measures such as harsh mandatory minimum sentences, "three strikes and you're out" laws and extending the death penalty to more and more federal offenses would actually constitute an effective attack on crime, that they really would deter some criminals and, by incarcerating others, remove them from the streets. There is no reason to doubt the word of (for example) Senator Phil Gramm of Texas, a leading proponent of mandatory minimum sentences who argued consistently over the years that such sentences would deter potential criminals, because they would know with certainty beforehand what the penalty would be if they transgressed.[37] Few elective politicians and their aides are criminologists. Few have time to do their homework. A large proportion are attracted, like ordinary citizens, by simple slogans and plausible-sounding theories of criminal behavior. Most lawmakers are not experts or specialists. Their views mirror those of the general public.

But genuine conviction is certainly not the whole story. The second reason why Washington politicians chose to "get tough on crime" in the 1980s and 1990s was undoubtedly, as the former congressman quoted earlier said, because the "voters were afraid of criminals, and politicians were afraid of the voters."[38] Republicans exploited voters' fears to beat up on Democrats; Democrats in turn were desperate not to be branded "soft on crime." The ways in which the wars on crime and drugs were fought cannot be understood without taking into account the incessant pressure that elected officeholders felt they were under from their electorates. Voters wanted tougher laws, and there is seldom a moment when any American elective politician is not running for election or reelection.[39]

The role that electoral pressures may have played in the wars on crime and drugs is—how shall we say?—hinted at in Table 3. A total of fourteen years elapsed between 1981 and 1994. Seven of those years were election years. Seven were not. During those fourteen years, the U.S. Congress passed no fewer than seven major crime bills. Of those seven, six were passed in election years (usually, as the table shows, late in those years). Only one was passed in a nonelection year. Looking at the matter the other way round, there was only one election year in which a major crime bill was *not* passed, and there was only one nonelection

TABLE 3

Major Crime Legislation Passed by Congress Since 1980

1981	No legislation
1982 (October)	Anti-crime bill passed by Congress but vetoed by President Reagan
1983	No legislation
1984 (October)	Comprehensive Crime Control Act of 1984
1985	No legislation
1986 (October)	Anti-Drug Abuse Act of 1986
1987	No legislation
1988 (October)	Anti-Drug Abuse Act of 1988
1989	No legislation
1990 (October)	Crime Control Act of 1990
1991	No legislation
1992	No legislation
1993 (November)	Brady Handgun Violence Prevention Act
1994 (August)	Violent Crime Control and Law Enforcement Act of 1994

SOURCE
Congressional Quarterly Almanacs.

year in which a major crime bill *was* passed. The correlation between election years and crime bills is almost perfect. The table in and of itself, of course, proves nothing; the seeming pattern it presents may simply result from coincidence or from the fact that American elective politicians just happen, for some extraneous reason, to turn their legislative attention to crime only in even-numbered years. All the same, one does not have to be unduly cynical to have one's suspicions aroused.

More direct evidence bearing on the same point comes from the politicians themselves. No one has ever studied what David

Mayhew calls "the electoral connection" with regard to crime; but it is striking that, when American politicians talk in an un-self-conscious way about policymaking in the fields of drugs and crime, they repeatedly refer to the electoral pressures that they believe they and their colleagues are under.[40]

Here, chosen almost at random, is a sample of the sorts of things they say:

Rep. Pat Schroeder on the 1986 Anti-Drug Abuse Act: "In football there's a thing called piling on. I think we're seeing political piling on right before the election."[41]

Rep. Don Edwards, chair of the House of Representatives Subcommittee on Civil and Constitutional Rights, on the 1988 Anti-Drug Abuse Act: "Drug legislation plus election-year posturing equals an assault on the Constitution."[42]

Rep. Tim Hughes on death-penalty amendments to the 1990 Crime Control Act: "I hope we never, ever bring up a crime bill again a month before an election."[43]

Rep. Charles Schumer on a 1991 vote to delete gun-control provisions from a pending crime bill: "I think the bill came at an inauspicious time when members felt under political assault. We're close to an election year and a presidential election year."[44]

Senator Joseph Biden on amendments to increase the range of penalties in a 1993 crime bill: "I think they are essentially worthless. There is a mood here that if someone came to the floor and said we should barb wire the ankles of anyone who jaywalks, I suspect it would pass, considering the mood we are in today."[45]

Senator Orrin Hatch on the same occasion: "There is no use kidding ourselves, some of these tough-on-crime amendments may not have tremendous effect because we do not have that many crimes that are handled by the Federal laws. On the other hand, they will make a difference because these amendments are sending a message across this country that the Congress has finally awakened. . . . "[46]

Rep. Barney Frank on mandatory minimum sentences applied to low-level drug offenders: "There's a perception that you pay a big price for being soft on drugs. People are afraid of the 30-second spot."[47]

Senator Orrin Hatch on mandatory minimums: "Mandatory minimums are a political response to violent crime. Let's be honest about it. It's awfully difficult for politicians to vote against them."[48]

Senator Bill Bradley on the 1994 crime bill: "In a way it reminds me of what a group of anxious citizens would do if they threw furniture and household goods onto a barricade to stop the invading hordes."[49]

Incessant electoral pressure—the great constant of American politics—thus gave rise to bad public policy. More to the point, it gave rise to policy that many of those who voted in favor of it knew to be bad. They felt that they had no choice. Perhaps the most telling of the quotations above is Congressman Schumer's comment that a particular vote on the 1991 crime bill "came at an inauspicious time when members felt under political assault": they were "close to an election year." Indeed they were. But it was also true that Schumer and his fellow congressmen and women had been sworn in only ten months before. Elections in America know no rest.

8

MORE DEMOCRACY,
MORE DISSATISFACTION

It should be evident from all that has been said so far that the costs of America's never-ending election campaign—of rendering American politicians so vulnerable to the electorate—are high. The peculiarly American combination of short terms, primary elections, weak parties and prodigiously high campaign costs exacts a heavy toll.

As we have seen, the politics of high electoral exposure is expensive in terms not only of campaign costs but of congressional buildings and staff. It takes up inordinate amounts of legislators' time and energy. It distorts the organization and internal processes of Congress, bending them toward credit-claiming and constituency service and away from deliberation and debate. Not least, it drives considerable numbers of able people out of politics and undoubtedly deters even more from coming in in the first place. General Colin Powell, in declining to run for the 1996 Republican presidential nomination, spoke of "this test of fire" and "the political treadmill."[1]

American politicians' vulnerability also affects the way they make policy—and the policies they make. Short-termism rules. Tough decisions are deferred, as in the case of the first oil shock and the budget deficit. Symbolic politics takes over from empirical politics, as in the case of the "wars" on crime and drugs. The power of the lobby groups, with their access to both campaign funds and disciplined blocks of voters, is substantially increased. In addition, policies designed to be targeted on specific social and economic problems are warped so that, instead, they serve the widest possible spread of individual legislators' electoral needs, as in the case, referred to in Chapter 4, of the model cities program.

It goes without saying that the instances of gross policy malfunction described in detail in the last three chapters constitute only a fraction of the instances that could have been chosen.

Perhaps the most spectacular single instance of American politicians' electoral vulnerability adversely affecting the content of a specific government policy concerns the now largely forgotten Medicare Catastrophic Coverage Act of 1988. The act was intended to provide all elderly Americans with substantially expanded coverage under Medicare, including assistance with paying for acute hospital care, skilled nursing facilities and expensive prescription drugs. It was fiscally responsible, providing for a substantial element of fiscal "front-loading" so that during the program's first few years receipts from increased Social Security premiums would considerably exceed its outgoings. It had the backing of President Reagan and bipartisan majorities in both houses of Congress. It passed the House of Representatives by 328 votes to 72 and the Senate by 86 votes to 11.

But a year later, in 1989, the act and the whole program were repealed—by even larger congressional majorities. Why? The long answer is that the act failed to provide for long-term care for the elderly (the cost of which was in fact most older Americans' principal personal concern) and that it also imposed considerable financial burdens on the elderly (who were expected, by themselves, to meet the program's cost). In consequence, both a number of the pressure groups claiming to speak for the elderly and also majorities of the elderly themselves, as demonstrated by the opinion polls, came out against the act. But the short answer, as so often, is that members of Congress were running scared. The elderly were up in arms; they had votes; experience suggested that they were prepared to use them. Congress backed off. As the historian of the act remarks, "Congress emerged from the episode with a renewed awareness of and heightened sensitivity to the perceived political power of the elderly."[2] It certainly did.

Whatever the explanation, by the 1990s millions of Americans had become profoundly dissatisfied with the way in which their political system was working. A cloud of public anger and despair seemed to hang over the whole of U.S. public life. Although the existence of the anger and the despair is well known, it is worth pausing to consider their depth and extent. Opinion surveys taken over the past four decades tell one version of the story. The figures relating to voter turnout in national elections tell another.

Take the opinion surveys first. Ever since the early 1950s the American National Election Study (NES), based at the University of Michigan, has used a variety of survey questions to monitor American voters' feelings about the current state of American democracy. In every case, and despite short-term fluctuations, the trend has been downward. For example, in 1952 a healthy 68 percent of the study's respondents actively disagreed with the statement: "People like me don't have any say about what the government does." The level of satisfaction with the system was high. By 1990, however, that 1952 figure of 68 percent had fallen by half to only 34 percent. In that year, well over half the total NES sample, 54 percent, took the gloomy view that people like themselves have no say in what the government does.[3]

Similarly, people were asked in the early 1950s and again in the early 1990s (as well as at intervals in between) whether they agreed or disagreed with the statement: "I don't think public officials care much what people like me think." At the beginning of the 1950s only 35 percent of the NES sample agreed with the statement, with 63 percent disagreeing. By the early 1990s, however, the proportions had been reversed. By that time, 64 percent of Americans reckoned that public officials did not care much about what people like them thought, and only 23 percent said they believed that their views still counted.[4] In the case of both questions, the proportions of the almost equally gloomy citizens who replied "don't know," low in 1952 (1 and 2 percent respectively), had grown considerably by 1990 (to 11 and 12 percent). On both measures, the proportions of Americans feeling disconnected from their government had more or less doubled over the forty-year period.

A great deal of other polling evidence points in the same direction. None points in the opposite. To take another example, various polling organizations, including the NES, have asked since the mid 1960s: "How much of the time do you think you can trust the government in Washington to do what is right?" According to the NES, the proportion replying "most of the time" in 1964 stood at 63 percent. By 1976 it had fallen to 31 percent. During the 1980s it did rise somewhat, but by August 1995, according to the *New York Times*/CBS Poll, it had fallen still further to only 20 percent.[5] The Harris Poll's aptly named "Alienation Index" likewise rose from 29 percent at the end of 1966 to 67 percent at the end of 1995.[6]

The statistics relating to the proportions of Americans who bother to turn out on polling day are equally telling. It is well known that, for many generations past, American citizens have turned out to vote in smaller numbers than the citizens of any other major democracy. What is less well known is that, even in the United States, turnout has been falling quite steadily since the early 1960s. In the Kennedy-Nixon presidential election of 1960, 65.4 percent of the eligible electorate turned out. In 1964 and 1968 the figures were still relatively high: 63.3 and 62.3 percent. But since then the proportion of eligible voters turning out in presidential elections has never exceeded 60 percent, and it has actually fallen at more elections than not.[7] In off-year congressional elections turnout is even lower. Since the Second World War it has on no occasion exceeded 50 percent. Since the mid 1970s it has only once exceeded 40 percent. The typical figure in recent midterm elections has been in the mid 30s. The image of a great, and growing, disconnectedness between governors and governed—of a growing alienation between the two—is reinforced.

Not only are ordinary American citizens at the end of the twentieth century dissatisfied with the functioning of American democracy; so, it would seem, is practically the whole of America's politically aware intelligentsia. America's intellectuals have always been among America's severest critics, but there has probably never been a time since the Progressive era nearly a century ago when so many writers, of so many differing political persuasions, have written so many books despairing of American democracy in its present form and advancing more or less concrete (and more or less realistic) proposals for change.

The books' titles in themselves capture the pervasive mood of democratic discontent: Jonathan Rauch, *Demosclerosis: The Silent Killer of American Government;* William Greider, *Who Will Tell the People: The Betrayal of American Democracy;* E. J. Dionne, Jr., *Why Americans Hate Politics;* George F. Will, *Restoration;* William E. Hudson, *American Democracy in Peril;* David Mathews, *Politics for People: Finding a Responsible Public Voice;* Kevin Phillips, *Arrogant Capital;* Jean Bethke Elshtain, *Democracy on Trial;* Kathleen Jamieson Hall, *Dirty Politics: Deception, Distraction, and Democracy;* Robert C. Grady, *Restoring Real Representation.*[8] All these and dozens more like them (though mostly not so good) were published in the first half of the 1990s. The publishers' catalogs suggested that many more were to come.

It goes without saying that the different authors offer different diagnoses of America's governmental disease and different prescriptions for curing it, and it would be quite wrong to lump all of them together as though all their ideas pointed in the same direction. They do not. E. J. Dionne maintains that "most of the problems of our political life can be traced to the failure of the dominant ideologies of American politics, liberalism and conservatism [which frame] political issues as a series of false choices."[9] Kevin Phillips emphasizes the power of Wall Street, William Greider that of corporate capital. Jonathan Rauch argues that the

proliferation of interest groups in the United States ("hyperplu-
ralism") is extremely costly in itself and skews the whole American system away from the production of wealth and toward its
distribution. Many writers deplore the decline, as they see it, of
deliberation, of "reasoning together" in American politics. And
their suggestions for reform are equally diverse.

That said, there is undeniably a widespread disposition in the
United States—at all levels of society, from the grass roots to the
editorial conference and the company boardroom—to want to
make American democracy "work better." But this presents
problems. Making democracy work better tends in America to
mean making politicians *more* responsive to the public; and making politicians more responsive to the public tends in practice to
mean trying to find ever more elaborate devices for bending
politicians to the people's will. In other words, the logic of agency
democracy, as distinct from division-of-labor democracy, is, in
the United States, an ever-attractive and deeply compelling logic.
In one of the largest countries in the world, with a population of
more than 250 million people, the myth of the town meeting
still holds sway.

It certainly does so at the level of rhetoric. David Mathews, a
former cabinet officer under President Ford, argues for "putting
the public back into politics" and for a resurgence of what he
terms "citizen politics."[10] William Greider maintains that "citizens are cut out of the politics surrounding the most important
governing questions" and calls for "democratic renewal," partly
for the sake of better government but partly also so that individuals' energies and creative ideas can be released in the interests of
the broader society. "If," he says, "there is a mystical chord in
democracy, it probably revolves around that notion—that unexpected music can resonate from politics when people are pursuing questions larger than self."[11] From a different point on the
political spectrum, Kevin Phillips insists that representative
democracy is now outdated and that various forms of direct
democracy—not merely what we have called agency democracy,
but actual direct democracy—constitute the only way forward.[12]

But much more than rhetoric is involved. In the mid and late 1990s, at the height of the current era of democratic discontent, concrete proposals abound in the United States for altering the relationship between governors and governed; and what strikes the foreign observer about all of them is that, without exception, they have as their primary purpose a weakening of the authority and autonomy of the governors and a strengthening of the power of the governed—in some cases, to the point where the distinction between governors and governed virtually ceases to exist. The current proposals, in other words, are precisely what one would expect given the historically dominant conception of democracy in America.

The 1990s proposals can be grouped loosely under four headings. First come those that, if implemented, would amount to the creation of an "electronic town meeting," taking advantage of technological developments such as closed-circuit television, interactive cable systems, electronic mail and information stored on CD-ROM. The more modest advocates of this kind of approach envisage little more than the creation of regional, national and transnational discussion groups. The more ambitious look forward to the day when, for example, interactive television or the Internet could be used for the purpose of holding America-wide referendums on major national issues. The *Wall Street Journal* referred in this general connection to "arranging a marriage of de Tocqueville and technology."[13]

Second, and related, are a variety of proposals for promoting democratic deliberation and citizen participation. The Kettering and Public Agenda Foundations already organize National Issues Forums which embrace some three thousand educational and civic groups across America. The Kettering Foundation's president links these modern forums directly to America's ancient "town meeting tradition."[14] Benjamin R. Barber would go further and create a nationwide network of neighborhood assemblies which could take actual decisions on strictly local matters and also debate and lobby on broader national questions.[15] There already exist similar bodies in Baltimore, San Antonio,

Portland, Oregon, and other American cities. James S. Fishkin likewise seeks to o'erleap the modern barriers to face-to-face democracy by means of what he calls "deliberative opinion polls" (which have already been tried out, with considerable success, in England).[16]

The third group of proposed reforms is equally radical but more old-fashioned. This group seeks to complete the work of the Progressive era reformers by extending to the federal level the characteristic state-level reforms that were introduced in that period: the initiative, recall and referendum. Kevin Phillips, for example, suggests that "the United States should propose and ratify an amendment to the Constitution setting up a mechanism for holding nationwide referendums to permit the citizenry to supplant Congress and the president in making certain categories of national decisions."[17] He would also like congressmen and senators to be subject to popular recall once they have been in office for a year.[18] Certainly proposed reforms of this type have broad public support. Depending on the precise question wording, more than 50 percent of Americans support the idea of national referendums and more than 80 percent support both the initiative and the recall.[19]

Finally, many commentators—and the majority of the American public—strongly back the newest and most fashionable item on the "making democracy work better" agenda: the imposition of term limits on both state and federal elected officials, notably members of Congress. The arguments advanced in favor of term limits vary. Some, like the columnist George F. Will, maintain that term limits would tend to create a Congress less parochial and less beholden to special interest groups than the present Congress and, therefore, more capable of genuinely deliberating in the public interest.[20] Will's line of argument deserves to be taken seriously, and we shall return to it in the final chapter.

But the great majority of those who favor term limits, true to the mainstream of the American democratic tradition, are less concerned with good government and the public interest as such than with the present generation of politicians' alleged lack of re-sponsiveness to the mass of ordinary people. At the center of this line of argument is the idea that the United States is now gov-erned by an unresponsive, self-perpetuating and increasingly re-mote class of professional politicians, a class that ought to be re-placed as soon as possible by "citizen legislators," men and women who will serve the people simply because they *are* the people. As one advocate of term limits puts it, ordinary people—the proposed citizen legislators of the future—"know things about life in America that people who have lived as very self-im-portant figures in Washington for thirty years have no way of knowing or have forgotten."[21] In other words, given that no na-tional town meeting does (or could) exist in modern America, Congress should be manned and womanned by the kinds of peo-ple who would turn up at such a national town meeting if one did exist. (The idea of direct democracy dies hard.)

Some of the items on this four-part shopping list of reforms designed to make American democracy more responsive are in-trinsically attractive; or at least a good case can be made out for them. There cannot be anything wrong—and there must be everything right—with institutions such as the National Issues Forums which seek to create a more informed citizenry and to encourage large numbers of citizens to participate more actively in political life at all levels. After all, civic engagement is one of the things democracy is, or is supposed to be, about. Similarly, there is a strong case for the holding of national referendums in the United States on a limited range of issues. On the face of it, it seems anomalous that proposed constitutional amendments, for example, are not submitted to the people for ratification.

All that is true. Nevertheless, taken as a whole, the mainstream reformist agenda, with its traditional American emphasis on agency democracy and politicians as mere servants of the people's will, rests on extremely tenuous conceptual foundations and, more important, is almost certainly inappropriate as a response to the practical needs of turn-of-the-century America. America's problem of governance is not one of insufficient responsiveness on the part of its elected leaders. On the contrary, as we have seen throughout this book, America's problem is one of their hyperresponsiveness. America's politicians do not need to be tied down still further, to be subjected to even more external pressures than they are already. Rather, they need to be given just a little *more* political leeway, just a little *more* room for policy maneuver. Any reforms should point in the direction of strengthening division-of-labor democracy and not in the direction of creating a still purer form of American-style agency democracy.

Several of the problems inherent in the various forms of participationist, agency and direct democracy are already familiar to students of democratic theory. One is simply the problem of time. As that affable cynic Oscar Wilde is said to have remarked about socialism, "It sounds like a good idea, but it would take up far too many evenings." Some reformers grossly underestimate the number of hours that their schemes for increased political participation would be bound to consume—and, alas, also grossly overestimate the willingness of large numbers of people to engage in such activity more than very occasionally. Even successful schemes, like the ones in some U.S. cities, actually involve only minuscule proportions of the total population.[22]

Another problem is the problem of bias. In any voluntary activity—and politics is always a voluntary activity—not everyone will volunteer, and those who do volunteer are most unlikely to constitute a true cross-section of the community. In the case of political activity, especially of a time-consuming character, the resulting biases are likely to favor the rich against the poor, the retired against those still in work, those with a lot of leisure time against those without, the educated against the uneducated, the assertive against the unassertive, the articulate against the inarticulate, those without small children against those with them, two-parent families against lone-parent families, those who stay at home against those who travel, the healthy against those who are ill in bed—and so on. Whatever its limitations as a democratic instrument, the ballot at least has the advantages of equality and universality. Even the citizen legislators envisaged by term limits are most unlikely to be "typical."

Those who advocate a more participatory style of politics also sometimes make the mistake of assuming that, if men and women of good will are brought together to exchange ideas and come up with solutions, they will sooner or later reach some broad consensual agreement. Embedded deep in the approach of many who favor more direct forms of democracy is the notion that, beneath all the squabbling of politicians, there exists, if only it could be discerned and lifted to the surface, a general will, a commonly shared conception of the public good—frequently dubbed a "common sense solution." This notion undoubtedly underlies much of the continuing pressure for term limits as well as new-style town meetings. Sadly, the notion, while attractive, is false to reality. It may—it probably does—apply to the internal life of most poker clubs and some university political science departments; but it seldom applies to the politics of nations. The differences of material interest and ideology among large and diverse populations are almost always far too great. More direct forms of democracy and greater participation would not eliminate them: they would, as with the effect of new roads on traffic jams in large cities, merely relocate them.

But the objection to most of the proposed reforms that is most pertinent to this book is simply that, if they were adopted, they would probably tend to increase, rather than diminish, the electoral vulnerability of America's politicians—and that vulnerability is already too great. Term limits would probably not have this effect; but, to take an extreme case, the recall certainly would.

So if the reformist prescriptions are bad ones there may be something wrong with the reformist diagnoses in the first place. What *are* the principal sources of so many Americans' dissatisfaction with the current state of American democracy? Is it conceivable that this widespread dissatisfaction in fact owes more to the hyperresponsiveness of American politicians than to their alleged unresponsiveness and more to the consequences of their spending so much of their time running scared than to their alleged remoteness and complacency? The experience of the past thirty years or so offers some clues.

Many commentators have gotten into the habit of blaming Americans' dissatisfaction, in an almost knee-jerk fashion, on "the Vietnam war and Watergate"; and it is certainly the case that the evidence of widespread dissatisfaction adduced earlier in this chapter began to appear during and shortly after the Vietnam and Watergate episodes, after having shown few or no signs of appearing before them. *Post hoc, ergo propter hoc?* Maybe. But, in the first place, Vietnam and Watergate led to a flowering of idealism as well as cynicism (and to the election, in 1974, of the "Watergate babies," one of the most idealistic and public-spirited cohorts ever to be elected to Congress); and, in the second place, it seems strange to attribute the dissatisfactions of the mid to late 1990s to events that took place in the 1960s and early 1970s.[23] The distance in time between Vietnam and Watergate and now is considerably greater than the distance in time between the two world wars; most of today's American college students were not yet born when President Nixon resigned. To be sure, subsequent scandals have undoubtedly (and deservedly) damaged the reputations of the White House and Congress; but some, at least, of the "sleaze" of the 1980s and 1990s is a consequence of elective politicians' increased reliance on the substantial funds needed to finance their reelection campaigns.

Two other hypotheses can be dismissed out of hand, or at least seriously downgraded. One is that America's politicians today are a poor lot compared with the intellectual and moral giants of the past. Admittedly it probably is the case, as we remarked earlier, that having to run scared all the time is tending to drive some able people out of politics and to discourage others from coming in; but the phenomenon is a relatively recent one, and for the time being there is no reason to think that today's average representative or senator is in any way inferior to his or her predecessors of years gone by. On the contrary, almost every close student of contemporary "inside the Beltway" politics comments favorably on the expertise, personal commitment and integrity of most of the people on Capitol Hill and in and around the White House. The quality of America's political class is, at most, a small part of the problem.

The same is almost certainly true of divided government, the phenomenon of one party's controlling one or both houses of Congress while the other controls the presidency. Divided party control has certainly characterized American government for most of the past thirty years, and it has certainly been associated with some of the more spectacular governmental and policy failures of that period: the Iran-Contra scandal of the 1980s (which arose out of a Republican administration's desire to circumvent a Democratic Congress) and successive shutdowns of parts of the U.S. government as presidents and Congress have failed to agree on timely taxing and spending measures. Other things being equal, divided government is probably to be regretted.

All the same, it is hard to credit the idea that Americans' disillusionment with their politics would today be significantly less if party control had been mainly undivided over the past thirty years. On the one hand, recent periods when the government has not been divided—the Carter years 1977–80 and the first two Clinton years 1993–94—have not been notably successful (Carter never surmounted the energy crisis and Clinton failed to reform America's health care system despite having been elected to do just that). On the other, as David R. Mayhew has shown, periods of divided government have often been extremely productive in legislative terms.[24] On balance, divided government appears to be more of a nuisance and a distraction than a root cause of either the U.S. government's difficulties or the public's disillusionment with them (quite apart from the fact that the public could, if it wanted to, bring divided government to an end).[25]

The idea that the American system suffers from the excessive

power of interest groups, however, needs to be taken more seriously. Jonathan Rauch in his recent book *Demosclerosis* argues
persuasively that America's interest groups have become larger,
more numerous and more powerful over the past three decades
and that during that time they have acquired the capacity to prevent the U.S. government from doing almost anything that
would disadvantage or offend any of the clients whom they represent—taking in, as it happens, virtually the whole American
population. Rauch writes:

> By definition, government's power to solve problems comes from
> its ability to reassign resources, whether by taxing, spending, regu-
> lating, or simply passing laws. But that very ability energizes
> countless investors and entrepreneurs and ordinary Americans to
> go digging for gold by lobbying government. In time, a whole in-
> dustry [the lobbying industry]—large, sophisticated, professional-
> ized, and to a considerable extent self-serving—emerges and then
> assumes a life of its own. This industry is a drain on the productive
> economy, and there appears to be no natural limit to its growth. As
> it grows, the steady accumulation of subsidies and benefits, each
> defended in perpetuity by a professional interest group, calcifies
> government. Government loses its capacity to experiment and so
> becomes more and more prone to failure.

"That," Rauch concludes, "is demosclerosis: postwar government's progressive loss of the ability to adapt."[26] And that, according to Rauch, is one of the major sources—if not the sole
source—of America's current democratic discontents.

Rauch is probably right; but of course, precisely because he is
probably right, one needs to go on to ask, as he does himself, what
the power of these pullulating and all-encompassing lobby groups
is based on. And the answer is straightforward. The group's power
depends ultimately on their money, on their capacity to make
trouble for elected officials, on the votes of their members (the
American Association of Retired Persons has more than thirty
million members, all of voting age) and on elective politicians'

fear of not being reelected. The groups' power, in other words, depends on politicians' electoral vulnerability; and America's interest groups are peculiarly powerful in large measure because America's elective politicians are, by international standards, peculiarly vulnerable. It is not quite as simple as that—but almost.

It is also important to take note of the precise timing of the developments described by Jonathan Rauch and by almost everyone else who has written on this subject. Readers will have noticed the frequent recurrence in these pages of the phrases "over the past thirty years" and "over the past three decades." Almost all of the developments described in this book are, almost uncannily, developments of the past thirty years: the rise in the number of interest groups, the growth in their membership and power, the sharply increased incidence of governmental failure, the decline in turnout at presidential and congressional elections, the decline in the public's trust in government officials, and the increased sense among voters that who they are and what they think do not matter to "them," the people in Washington. In other words, the origins of the present era of democratic discontent can be dated remarkably precisely to the end of the 1960s and the beginning of the 1970s. It was then that people began to think there was something wrong, not with this or that aspect of the system, but with the system itself.

What happened at that time, roughly thirty years ago? It is hard to escape the conclusion that the crucial developments, largely provoked by the Vietnam war and Watergate, were the moves from 1968 onward to open up the American system, to make it more transparent, to make it more accessible, to make it more, in a word, "democratic." These moves led to a sharp increase in the number of primary elections, they led to a further weakening of America's already weak political parties, they led to American electoral politics becoming even more expensive than they would have become anyway because of the need to buy time on television and they also led to American elective officials finding themselves increasingly isolated, in an increasingly hostile environment.[27] In short, the post-Vietnam, post-Watergate reforms led, as they were meant to lead, to individual American officeholders becoming even more vulnerable to their electorates than they had been in the past. If this analysis is correct, it is the long-term consequences of these reforms that we have, at least in part, been exploring in this book.

The paradox that has resulted is an obvious one. It is easily stated. Recent history suggests that when large numbers of Americans become dissatisfied with the workings of their government they call for more democracy. The more they call for more democracy, the more of it they get. And the more of it they get the more dissatisfied they become with the workings of their government. And the more they become dissatisfied with the workings of their government, the more they call for more democracy. And the more they call for more democracy, the more of it they get. And the more of it they get, the more dissatisfied they become. . . . And so it goes, the cycle endlessly repeating itself.[28]

The proximate result is very large numbers of politicians running scared—and engaging in the endless evasions and runnings-for-cover that frightened people do engage in. Senator Alan Simpson of Wyoming captured the spirit well when he addressed those few of his Senate colleagues who were listening in 1985:

> One of the things . . . that [lobby groups] do here so beautifully . . . is the use of fear, raw fear. You can do a lot with raw fear. You can do a lot with raw fear with people who do like nuclear power or do not like it. You can do a lot with raw fear with farmers. You can do a lot with raw fear with uranium workers. You can do a lot with raw fear with oil and gas workers. You can do a lot with raw fear with veterans. You can do a lot with raw fear with Social Security recipients.
>
> And that is what we do beautifully here in this place, because I guess we really are all impelled by a raw fear—and that raw fear is, I would guess, a fear of what the electorate will do to us, and, of course, maybe that is the primal fear in this place. It may well be.[29]

It certainly is. It is not often that politicians speak like that, but, on the rare occasions when they do, they speak from the heart and deserve to be listened to.

In the next chapter, we shall address the question of how America's cycle of greater democratization leading to greater dissatisfaction with democracy might be broken into. We shall also ask whether there are any institutional and procedural reforms that might usefully be put in place, not with a view to abolishing democracy in the United States (no one wants that), but precisely with a view to rendering American democracy more effective. Running scared may sometimes be the right thing to do; but it is always tiring—and never dignified.

9

WHAT, IF ANYTHING,
MIGHT BE DONE?

Before we consider how America's politicians might be made somewhat less vulnerable to the short-term vicissitudes of electoral politics, we need to notice an additional fact about many elective politicians in the United States. If it is true that genuine courage can be displayed only by those who are genuinely frightened, then American politicians frequently act with exemplary courage—which they are far too seldom given credit for. Anyone conscious of the extreme degree of U.S. politicians' electoral vulnerability is bound to be struck by the large number of occasions on which they do what they believe to be right, even though they know they may subsequently pay a price. As ever, adversity is the mother of courage.

Several instances have already been cited in these pages. Many more could have been. Many congressmen and senators over the years have taken electoral risks in refusing to vote in favor of capital punishment. Pete Domenici and the majority of Senate Republicans launched what many of them undoubtedly feared would prove "a kamikaze mission" against the budget deficit in

1985. Marjorie Margolies-Mezvinsky took her political life in her hands when she cast the deciding vote in favor of President Clinton's deficit-reduction package in 1993.[1] A House colleague praised another freshman Democrat, Gary Condit of California, for voting in the same year to axe $58 million in agricultural research projects despite the fact that he represented one of the richest agricultural districts in the country.[2] Precisely because American politicians are so electorally exposed, they probably have to display—and do display—more political courage more often than the politicians of any other democratic country. Not surprisingly, the number of political saints and martyrs in the United States is unusually large.[3]

There is, however, no special virtue in a political system that requires large numbers of politicians to run the risk of sainthood and martyrdom in order to ensure that tough decisions can be taken in a timely manner in the national interest. The number of such decisions requiring to be taken is always likely to be too large; human nature being what it is, the supply of would-be saints and martyrs is always likely to be too small. On balance, it would seem better, not totally to eliminate the electoral risks (that can never be done in a democracy), but to reduce somewhat their scale and intensity. There seems no reason why the risks run by American politicians should be so much greater than the risks run by elective politicians in other democratic countries.

If this is true, how might the risks be reduced? What, in practical terms, might be done? The suggestions to be made here undoubtedly go against the American grain, especially during an era when populist solutions are once again in fashion; but they are worth considering all the same.

To begin with, it would be no bad thing if Americans reexamined their long-standing, instinctive preference for agency or direct democracy and at least considered whether some version of division-of-labor democracy might not serve their national purpose better. After all, most other democratic countries—Great Britain, Canada, Australia, New Zealand, Denmark, Norway, Sweden, Finland, Belgium, the Netherlands, France, Germany,

Spain, Italy, Greece, Japan and so on—all work with some form of division-of-labor democracy, and it does not seem to do them any particular harm. Several of these countries have their problems, of course. Canada and Belgium are deeply divided on linguistic lines; Italy and Japan have both suffered from systemic corruption. But no one seriously suggests that the absence of agency or direct democracy caused these countries' problems or that more of it would in any way solve them. If solutions to their problems are to be found at all, they will be found elsewhere.

If Americans do wish to look again at the case for division-of-labor democracy, they have no need to look beyond their own shores; for, although agency democracy has been the dominant conception of democracy in America over the past hundred years, it has at no time been the only one. There has always existed an alternative American tradition, which might be called the tradition of leadership. According to this tradition, men and women elected to public office have a duty to govern in accordance with what they believe to be in the nation's best interests, which may, or may not, coincide with what the majority of the American people currently want. What the people currently want must be, and undoubtedly should be, one factor bearing on their decisions; but it should never be the only one. The people's task, according to this tradition, is not to dictate to their leaders in detail what they should do but is rather to pass, in the fullness of time, a broad judgment on the quality of the leaders' overall performance.

This alternative conception of the appropriate relationship between governors and governed has deep roots in American soil, even if sometimes it has had to struggle to survive. James Madison was always conscious of the difficulty, but also the desirability, of combining within one polity "the requisite stability and energy in government with the inviolable attention due to liberty and to the republican form."[4] His worry, which he shared with most of the other Federalists, was that "liberty and republican form" would triumph over "stability and energy." Hence his preference, referred to in Chapter 3, for three-year terms for members of the House of Representatives. Hence also his enthusiasm for the indirect election of members of the Senate and, even more, for their terms of six years.

In *Federalist* 63, praising the six-year terms that the constitutional convention proposed for senators, Madison drew attention to the unfortunate disjunction that could exist between the short-term outlooks of legislators elected for very short periods and the long-term needs of the nation:

> Responsibility, in order to be reasonable, must be limited to objects within the power of the responsible party, and in order to be effectual, must relate to operations of that power, of which a ready and proper judgment can be formed by the constituents. The objects of government may be divided into two general classes: the one depending on measures which have singly an immediate and sensible operation; the other depending on a succession of well-chosen and well-connected measures, which have a gradual and perhaps unobserved operation. The importance of the latter description to the collective and permanent welfare of every country needs no explanation. And yet it is evident that an assembly elected for so short a term as to be unable to provide more than one or two links in a chain of measures, on which the general welfare may essentially depend, ought not to be answerable for the final result any more than a steward or tenant, engaged for one year, could be justly made to answer for places or improvements which could not be accomplished in less than half a dozen years.[5]

Madison would probably have liked terms even longer than six years.

Some of the most celebrated American politicians of the nineteenth century likewise went on to advocate a division-of-labor conception of democracy and representation. John C. Calhoun of South Carolina was characteristically blunt:

> I never know what South Carolina thinks of a measure. I never consult her. I act to the best of my judgment and according to my

conscience. If she approves, well and good. If she does not and wishes anyone to take my place, I am ready to vacate. We are even.[6]

On another occasion, when the House of Representatives was about to bow to popular pressure and repeal an act it had passed only a few months before (in an almost audible pre-echo of the repeal of the Medicare Catastrophic Coverage Act), Calhoun was adamant. "This House," he insisted, "is at liberty to decide on this question according to the dictates of its best judgment." He asked rhetorically: "Are we bound in all cases to do what is popular? Have the people of this country snatched the power of deliberation from this body?"[7] His answer to both questions was a defiant "No."

Daniel Webster differed from Calhoun on most political questions, but on this point he agreed with his old adversary:

> Inconsistencies of opinion arising from changes of opinion are often justifiable. But there is one sort of inconsistency that is culpable: it is the inconsistency between a man's conviction and his vote, between his conscience and his conduct. No man shall ever charge me with an inconsistency of that kind.[8]

Later, preparing to speak in favor of the Clay Compromise in March 1850, Webster told his friends that, faced with the almost unanimous hostility of the people of his home state of Massachusetts, he intended nevertheless "to push my skiff from the shore alone."[9]

In the twentieth century, perhaps the most eloquent American advocate of division-of-labor democracy was John F. Kennedy, from whose 1956 book *Profiles in Courage* the above quotations from Calhoun and Webster are drawn. *Profiles in Courage* is sometimes dismissed as little more than a collection of morally uplifting folk tales (or, alternatively, as part of a crude effort to secure for the author the Democrats' 1956 vice-presidential nomination); but in fact, whatever its author's motives, the book constitutes a remarkably robust, and often explicit, statement of the division-of-labor view.

In a crucial passage toward the beginning of the book, Kennedy maintains that an elected representative like himself (he was then a U.S. senator) needs "to face squarely the problem of [his] responsibility to the will of his constituents."[10] It can be argued, he concedes, that the problem is not really a problem at all, that the democratically elected representative is obliged to vote as his constituents would vote if they were in his place. If he is not prepared to do this, "he is no longer representative in the true sense, he has violated his public trust, he has betrayed the confidence demonstrated by those who voted for him to carry out their views."

Kennedy acknowledges the simplicity and attractiveness of this agency-democracy view; but he rejects it utterly:

> It is difficult to accept such a narrow view of the role of United States senator—a view that assumes the people of Massachusetts sent me to Washington to serve merely as a seismograph to record shifts in popular opinion. . . . The voters selected us because they had confidence in our judgment and our ability to exercise that judgment from a position where we could determine what were their own best interests, as a part of the nation's interests. This may mean that we must on occasion lead, inform, correct and sometimes even ignore constituent opinion, if we are to exercise fully that judgment for which we were elected.

Still, he concludes, people who hold his view continue to be democrats: "they expect—and not without considerable trepidation—their constituents to be the final judges of the wisdom of their course. . . ."[11] But constituents, in Kennedy's view, are to be, indeed, "final judges," no more than that.

This tradition, the indigenous American leadership tradition, has much to commend it, especially in an era when, at so many levels, hyperresponsiveness and nonstop electioneering are among the factors causing the American system to malfunction, not least in the eyes of the very people it is meant to serve. The cause of democracy is inevitably damaged when circumstances make it almost impossible for democratically elected legislators and executives to function effectively.

If this plea for the introduction of some element of division-of-labor democracy into the U.S. system is accepted, then a number of reforms to the existing system suggest themselves. None of them may be politically feasible—Americans hold tight to the idea of agency democracy—but there should be no bar in principle to any of them.

One of the simplest would also be the most radical. That would be to lengthen the terms of members of the House of Representatives from two years to four. The proposal is by no means a new one. Far from it: at least 123 resolutions bearing on the subject were introduced in Congress in the eighty years between 1885 and 1965, and President Lyndon B. Johnson advocated the change in his State of the Union address in January 1966. Several resolutions in favor of lengthened terms have actually passed the House.[12] There seems general agreement that, if the Constitution were to be amended along these lines, quadrennial elections to the House should coincide with presidential elections (off-year elections would thus cease) and that sitting House members should not be allowed to challenge sitting members of the Senate without resigning their House seats (if nothing else, as a means of assuring senators that they would not themselves be running electoral risks in backing the change).

Such an amendment was introduced in both the House and the Senate early in 1966 following President Johnson's address. The relevant sections read:

> SECTION 1. The terms of Representatives shall be four years and shall commence at noon on the 3rd day of January of the year in which the regular term of the President is to begin.
>
> SEC. 2 No member of a House of Congress shall be eligible for election as a Member of the other House for a term which is to begin before the expiration of the term of the office held by him unless, at least thirty days prior to such election, he shall have submitted a resignation from such office which shall become effective no later than the beginning of such term.[13]

One of the congressmen participating in a Brookings Institution round table held at about the same time supported the change, using the kind of language that has been used throughout this book: "I think that the four years would help you to be a braver congressman, and I think what you need is bravery. I think you need courage."[14] Another congressman on the same occasion cited the example of a bill that he reckoned had the support of a majority in the House:

> That bill is not going to come up this year. You know why it is not coming up? . . . Because 435 of us have to face election. . . . If we had a four-year term, I am as confident as I can be the bill would have come to the floor and passed.[15]

A similar case could be made for extending the term of senators to eight years, with half the Senate retiring or running for reelection every four years. If the terms of members of both houses were thus extended, and were also made to coincide, the effect in reducing America's never-ending election campaign would be dramatic.

There is much to be said, too, on all the grounds mentioned so far, for scaling down the number of primary elections in the United States.[16] They absorb extravagant amounts of time, energy and money; they serve little democratic purpose; few people bother to vote in them; and they place additional, and unnecessary, pressure on incumbent officeholders. Since the main disadvantage of primaries is the adverse effects they have on incumbents, any reforms probably ought to be concerned with protecting their interests.

At the moment the primary laws of most states make no distinction between situations in which a seat in the House or Senate is already occupied and situations in which the incumbent is (for whatever reason) standing down. The current laws provide for the automatic holding of a primary in either case. Any incumbent is therefore treated as though the seat in question were open and as though he or she were merely one of the potential candidates for it. A relatively simple reform would be to distinguish between the two situations. If a seat were open, primaries would be held in both parties as now; but, if there were an incumbent who indicated that he or she intended to run for reelection, then a primary in his or her party would be held only if there were hard evidence that large numbers of supporters of the incumbent's party were determined to have one—i.e., were determined that the incumbent should be ousted. The obvious way to ascertain whether such determination existed would be by means of a petition supervised by the relevant state government and requiring a considerable number of signatures. The way to the holding of a primary would thus be left open; but those who wanted one would have to show that they were both numerous and serious. A primary would not be held simply because an ambitious, possibly discontented, possibly wealthy individual decided to throw his or her hat in the ring.

There are two possible variations on this theme. One possibility would allow for the holding of such a "petition primary" only if an actual challenger to the incumbent had come forward, in which case the petitioners would be saying, in effect, that they wanted a primary contest to be fought between the incumbent and some named individual. The other possibility would allow the petitioners to say merely that they wanted a primary to take place, without their having to name (or even agree on) a potential challenger. It is hard to say which kind of petition primary would be easier to organize; but both would have the effect of reducing somewhat the extreme electoral uncertainty that incumbents now face.

Any moves that had the effect of strengthening the Democratic and Republican parties as institutions would also be desirable on the same grounds. Lack of party cover in the United States means that American elective officeholders find it hard to take tough decisions partly because they lack safety in numbers. They can seldom, if ever, tell an aggrieved constituent or a political action committee out for revenge, "I had to vote that way because my party told me to" or even "I had to vote that way because we in my party all agreed that we would." Lack of party cohesion in the U.S. Congress compared with other democracies, together with American voters' disposition to "vote for the man" (or woman) rather than the party, means that individual congressmen and senators are always in danger of being picked off one by one. They need to be able more often to heed Benjamin Franklin's dictum: "We must all hang together or, most assuredly, we shall all hang separately." Fortunately, there are signs of party revival in the United States, especially on the Republican side. The parties nationally and in many states are better organized than they were a generation ago; they campaign more as parties; party cohesion in Congress has increased; and there are even signs that voters are somewhat readier than in the recent past to respond to party cues.[17]

Still, America's parties remain both invertebrate and anemic compared with those in other countries. What might be done to give them both more blood and a backbone? As the University of Virginia political scientist Larry J. Sabato has pointed out, the parties are in fact in a position to do much to strengthen themselves (and have already begun to do just that), but there are also a number of possible changes in federal and state laws that would do much to carry the process forward.[18]

In order to encourage voters to support one or other of the political parties rather than individual candidates (though without preventing them from voting for individual candidates if that is really what they want to do), the physical form of many American states' ballot papers could easily be amended, to give them a more sharply party-oriented focus. It could be made easier for voters in all states to vote a straight party ticket if that is what they were inclined to do (rather than their having to rummage through the whole of what may be a very long ballot in order to identify the names of their party's candidates). For the same reason, each party's candidates could, and should, be listed vertically on the ballot rather than being scattered all over the ballot, office by office, as they frequently are now. Quite apart from anything else, such party-focused ballots would encourage voters to take part in the election of minor officeholders rather than succumbing to what is sometimes known as "ballot fatigue." More important, it would also encourage the parties to mount joint, concerted, multioffice election campaigns, thereby promoting, among other things, their own long-term cohesion and strength.

Voters would also be more likely to respond to partisan cues, rather than individual personality cues, if more American elections took place simultaneously, so that the parties as a whole could campaign on, and be judged on, their platforms and records. The proposals outlined above for extending the terms of office of congressmen and senators would help achieve that effect. So would any moves to abolish not only off-year elections but also off-off-year elections—that is, the elections that are held in some states to fill state offices in odd-numbered years. Not only do such elections induce voter fatigue (as distinct from ballot fatigue); they make it impossible for the parties to mount unified campaigns covering the whole range of elective offices (federal, state and local). In addition, off-off-year elections sometimes serve further to undermine party cohesion by giving state and local candidates an opportunity to mount campaigns critical of their own party's officeholders in Washington. Consolidating national, state and local elections along these lines, so that the great majority of elections in the United States took place in presidential election years, would almost certainly lead to a substantial strengthening of the major parties' organizations at all levels; and it would probably also cause voters to take the two major political parties, as parties, more seriously than they do at present.

In addition, as Sabato points out in *The Party's Just Begun*, simultaneous elections would almost certainly enhance America's currently very weak "coattail effect," whereby strong candidates at the top of a party's ticket can attract votes to those at the bottom. An enhanced coattail effect would, in turn, provide more of what we have been calling party cover. In Sabato's words:

> The coattail effect . . . draws all of the party standard-bearers together since their fates are intertwined. It gives party officeholders a strong incentive to push for the strongest possible party nominees for president and governor, since these top-of-the-ballot can-

didates can sink or save their electoral chances. Similarly, all the party's legislators have a stake in seeing the executives succeed, once in office, so that at reelection time the party can boast a successful record.[19]

The parties, both as organizations and as cues to which voters can meaningfully respond, would be still further strengthened if the number of primary elections—not just primaries involving incumbents, but all primaries—were substantially reduced and if those that remained were also invariably "closed"—that is, restricted to those who publicly declared their allegiance to the party of their choice. One alternative to the holding of primaries as a means of choosing party candidates would be the holding of postal ballots confined to each of the two parties' card-carrying paid-up members.[20] Another would be the selection of candidates by state and local conventions and caucuses. Even in states that retained primaries, the parties' organizations would almost certainly be strengthened if party conventions and caucuses were invited as a matter of course, or even required, to make pre-primary endorsements of individual candidates (and if the party's endorsements were indicated on the ballot). Where they occur, primary contests are inevitably divisive. By contrast, a candidate-selection system based less on primaries and more on the parties as organizations would tend to promote processes of intraparty deliberation and compromise, thereby also promoting party cohesion.

Needless to say, the parties themselves would be strengthened—and the need for elective officeholders to raise large amounts of money to finance their own campaigns would be reduced—if each party organization itself became a major source of campaign funding. In the unlikely event (against the background of chronic budget deficits) that Congress ever gets round to authorizing the federal funding of congressional election campaigns, there would be a strong case for channeling as much of the money as possible through the political parties, with some of it being set aside to cover the parties' administrative and other ongoing costs. Such schemes work well in a considerable number of states, where they tend to promote party cohesion and a degree of bonding between parties and their candidates.[21] Pending full-scale funding of congressional campaigns, any surpluses in the existing Federal Election Campaign Fund (used for presidential contests) could be used to subvent the two parties at the national level.

Both the party organizations and the nexus between parties and their candidates would also be strengthened if it were made easier for ordinary citizens to give money to the parties and if it were made easier for the parties to give money to their candidates. Until their abolition in 1986, tax credits were available for income tax payers who contributed small sums to the political parties. These credits could be restored.[22] Sabato has similarly suggested that citizens entitled to an income tax refund could be enabled to divert a small part of their refund to the party of their choice.[23] Such party-strengthening measures would not, however, reduce individual candidates' dependence on donations from wealthy individuals and PACs unless they were accompanied by measures to enable the parties to contribute more generously to their candidates' campaigns on the ground. At the moment, there are quite strict legal limits on the amounts of money that the party organizations—both national and state—can contribute to the campaigns of individual candidates. These limits should be raised (and indexed to inflation). There is even a case for abolishing them altogether.[24]

All that said, there would be an even more straightforward way of reducing incumbents' dependence on campaign contributors. At present, incumbents have to spend so much time and energy raising campaign funds because the campaigns themselves are so expensive. There is a lot to be said for making them cheaper. One way to achieve this would be to make elections in the United States less numerous and less frequent than they are now (an outcome that we have already been advocating on other grounds). Another would be to provide candidates and parties (ideally both) with free air time on television and radio. The United States is one of the very few democracies that does not already require its broadcasters to provide politicians and parties with free time. A generous allocation of free (or lowest-rate) time would cut the cost of election campaigns. If some of the time were allocated to the political parties, one effect would probably also be "to introduce more collective responsibility into the political system."[25]

The aim of all the changes proposed so far—lengthening congressional terms, reducing the number and role of primaries, strengthening the political parties and making politicians less dependent on campaign contributions and contributors—is to enable elective officeholders in the United States to spend more time and energy on actually governing, to promote deliberation in Congress and to give the politicians in Washington greater leeway in the making of policy, including in the adoption of unpopular policies. In this context, it is clear that the case for term limits needs to be taken seriously. After all, if American politicians are thought to be excessively vulnerable at the moment, one way of rendering them invulnerable would be to prevent them from being reelected. No impending election contest, no need to worry overmuch about the voters.

As is evident, much of the actual campaigning in favor of term limits takes the form of ranting—ranting against big government, ranting against Washington, ranting against "them," ranting against taxes, ranting against the deficit. Much of the term-limiters' rhetoric is sulphurous, and the principal motive of many of them seems to be revenge. They claim that members of Congress are insufficiently responsive to their constituents when the evidence suggests that, on the contrary, they are far too responsive. In large part, the term-limits movement is of a piece with previous outbursts of frustrated American populism such as the Know-Nothing movement of the 1850s—an essay, as one historian has put it, in "the politics of impatience."[26]

Nevertheless, as we noted in the last chapter, there is an alternative case for term limits, one based not on American politicians' alleged lack of responsiveness to the voters but on their alleged willingness to do almost anything in the interests of both the voters and interest groups in order to secure their own reelection.[27]

The most persuasive and subtle advocate of this alternative line of argument is George F. Will—and certainly much that Will says is consistent with the themes being developed in this book. His principal goal, he says part way through *Restoration,* "is deliberative democracy through representatives who function at a constitutional distance from the people"; and he reiterates the point about distance in his final paragraphs: "Americans must be less demanding of government. They must give to government more constitutional space in which to think, more social distance to facilitate deliberation about the future."[28] Almost inevitably he quotes Edmund Burke's famous dictum about elected representatives owing those who elected them their judgment and not only their industry. According to both Will and Burke, the elected representative's will, based on his judgment, ought always to count for more than the wills of his constituents.[29]

The case for giving American politicians more "space" and more "distance" is undoubtedly a strong one; but, assuming these twin objectives to be desirable, it is still not entirely clear whether term limits are a suitable means for achieving them. Three questions arise. Would term limits as a matter of fact achieve the desired objectives? Would they do so at an acceptable cost in terms of other American goals and values? Might the desired objectives not be better achieved by other means? The first question is strictly empirical. The other two mix the empirical and the moral.

One way in which term limits might promote deliberation by giving legislators more distance and space is by causing some existing legislators—namely those serving out their final term under term limits—to think, speak and vote differently from the way they would have thought, spoken and voted if they had been eligible for, and also running for, reelection. In addition, for term limits to affect the behavior not just of identifiable individuals but of Congress as a whole, it would be necessary for any given Congress to contain a significant number of these final-term and therefore "voter-proofed" members. In other words, congressional lame ducks would have to quack differently from other ducks; and there would have to be a fair number of them on the pond.

It is impossible to be sure, but it seems unlikely that term limits would have significant effects along these lines. In the first place, existing research—and most human experience—suggests that a final-term congressman or senator, after eleven or twelve years on Capitol Hill, would be unlikely to alter his pattern of behavior in any radical way; he might send out fewer pieces of franked mail and make fewer trips back home, but he would be unlikely to execute more than a few U-turns in the way he spoke and voted.[30] In the second place, although the proportion of senators who would be in their final term under term limits would always be large (nearly half the Senate if senators were restricted to two terms), the proportion of lame-duck congressmen would normally be much smaller (an average of about 60–70 congressmen out of 435 if House members were limited to six terms).[31] The cumulative impact of term limits that would result from the presence and behavior of lame ducks in Congress would thus be much greater in the Senate than it would in the House, and in both houses it would probably be felt mainly at the margins (though the margins can, of course, be very important on occasion, as they were in the case of the final 1990 budget deal).

But those who advocate term limits in fact rest very little of their case on the expected future behavior of lame ducks. Rather, their emphasis is on the creation of a wholly new class of elected representatives. George Will, in particular, maintains that America's current difficulties stem in large part from the dominance of Washington politics by career politicians, men and women whose political horizons are dominated almost totally by the need to raise money and win votes in order to secure reelection. "A career legislator," Will writes, "is not only risk-averse, he or she lives by a perverse ethic that eliminates—indeed proscribes— any moral misgivings about the policy of avoiding politically risky decisions."[32] Holding on to one's job is all—even if it means, as Will says, "buying votes with the voters' money."[33]

Will holds out the prospect that mandatory term limits would

have the effect of replacing today's political careerists with nonca-
reerists—in other words, of replacing today's ducks with crea-
tures more closely resembling swans.[34] The new legislators, because they were not careerists, would not be driven by the need
to secure reelection, and for that reason they would be more
likely to concern themselves with the national interest. Also because they were not political careerists, they would be more likely
to have some personal, hands-on understanding of America and
its real concerns. Will writes:

> The absence of term limits is a temptation to legislative careerism.
> Enactment of limits will perform a winnowing function, discour-
> aging certain kinds of people from seeking legislative offices. Lim-
> its also will discourage occupants of those offices from entertaining
> the kind of aspirations that result in behavior that subordinates the
> public interest to the tactics useful for prolonging legislative ca-
> reers.[35]

Later he adds:

> Many Americans wish that a lot of legislators had a better sense of
> American life, and particularly of what it is like to be on the re-
> ceiving end of the high-minded laws and regulations that gush like
> a cataract from Washington. Term limits, guaranteeing a steady ro-
> tation of offices, would help. They would make it impossible for
> anyone to come to Congress counting on a long career there.
> [They would therefore] increase the likelihood that people would
> come to Congress from established careers, with significant experi-
> ence in the private sector. Furthermore, term limits would increase
> the likelihood that people who come to Congress would anticipate
> returning to careers in the private sector and therefore would, as
> they legislate, think about what it is like to live under the laws they
> make.[36]

The prospect is undoubtedly attractive. But is it also realistic?
Would term limits in fact diminish the number of careerists and
produce a larger number of legislators who were more national-
minded and disinterested? It is again impossible to be sure; but it

again seems unlikely. It seems more probable that Congress would continue to be dominated by career politicians, but ones who had merely followed different career paths. George Will himself half concedes this point when he notes that "a typical career sequence early in the nineteenth century would be local office, state office, U.S. House, and back to the state House"— not, note, from some nonpolitical position into politics and then back again, but simply from one kind of political position to another.[37]

The principal difficulties with Will's hypothesis are twofold. One is that modern politics at all levels, local and state as well as national, is an immensely time-consuming, energy-consuming activity, one that demands enormous commitment from those who are attracted to it. Legislative sessions are long, constituents' demands are exigent, the policy problems themselves are increasingly complicated. As a result, politics all over the world, not just in the United States, is becoming professionalized. Men and women in all countries increasingly choose a political career at an early age and then stick to it.[38] It seems likely that the great majority of congressmen and senators, even under term limits, would be drawn from this professional political class. It would be they who had not only the commitment to politics but the requisite patience, skills and contacts. To be sure, people's political careers would take a different shape; but they would still be political careers.[39]

The other difficulty with Will's hypothesis is the obverse of the first. Just as politics is becoming more professionalized, so is almost every other occupation. As many women, in particular, know to their cost, career breaks are becoming harder and harder to take, and those who jump off the career ladder in any profession find it increasingly hard to jump back on (even at the level they were on when they left, let alone the level they would have attained had they stayed). For this reason, it is hard to imagine many upwardly mobile corporation executives or successful professionals, or men and women busy running small businesses, taking time off to serve, on a citizen-legislator basis, in Congress.

The citizens who sought to serve on this basis would probably be largely the rich and the old.

Rep. Henry J. Hyde of Illinois underscored both difficulties when he intervened in the House of Representatives debate on term limits in March 1995:

> Term limits limit the field of potential candidates. What successful person in mid life will leave a career at 50 and try and pick up the pieces at 56 or 62? This job will become a sabbatical for the well-to-do elite and bored retirees. And [he added] if you listen carefully, if this ever becomes law, that shuffling sound you [will] hear is the musical chairs being played in every legislature in the country.[40]

Thus, although the vision of creating a broad spectrum of citizen-legislators is in many ways an attractive one, it is probably unrealizable in modern circumstances.

Even if it were realizable, however, Americans would still need to consider whether it could be realized at an acceptable cost in terms of other considerations. As the old saying goes, every silver lining has a cloud. One cloud hanging over term limits is the obvious one that they would represent a substantial infringement on people's right to choose whomever they wanted to represent them (the Twenty-second Amendment limiting presidents to two terms can be called in question on the same grounds). Another is that the ways of Washington take time to learn and that members of Congress would be forced to retire just as they were learning them.[41] Yet another, arguably the most serious, is that, had term limits existed in previous periods, they would have arbitrarily foreshortened the careers of some of the most distinguished politicians and statesmen in U.S. history, including Daniel Webster, Henry Clay, John C. Calhoun, Joe Cannon, Arthur H. Vandenberg, J. William Fulbright, Robert A. Taft, Sam Rayburn, Barry Goldwater, Everett McKinley Dirksen, Howard Baker, Sam Ervin, Henry M. "Scoop" Jackson and Thomas P. "Tip" O'Neill.[42] During the House debate on term limits in 1995, much was made of the fact that, had term limits been in force in Britain in 1940, Winston Churchill could not have become prime minister. It is perhaps worth adding that term limits of the kind proposed in the United States would also have prevented two of Britain's greatest nineteenth-century premiers, Gladstone and Disraeli, from ever reaching Downing Street.

Whatever the merits and demerits of term limits, we also need to ask whether the ends of those who seriously advocate them—those who seek greater "space" and "distance" for America's political leaders—could not be better achieved by other means. On the face of it, the reforms proposed earlier in this chapter—notably longer terms, fewer primaries and stronger parties—seem more likely to achieve the desired ends. The political obstacles to their being adopted may be greater than in the case of term limits; but, if adopted, they would tackle the problem of American politicians' excessive vulnerability much more directly.

Despite their differences, term limits and the proposals offered here have in common the fact that they point to major changes in America's political institutions, in some cases involving amendments to the Constitution. But of course it is possible for America's politicians to alter the way they behave in the context of the country's existing political and governmental institutions. They can try to find alternative ways of insulating at least some aspects of policymaking from the intense campaigning and electioneering pressures they are now under. There are precedents after all. The Supreme Court and to a lesser extent the Federal Reserve Board—to take two admittedly extreme examples—are already thus insulated.

Short of taking difficult issues out of electoral politics altogether, on the model of the Supreme Court and the Federal Reserve Board, there are nevertheless other tactics that could be employed. Most of them are out of keeping with the contemporary American preferences for direct democracy, high levels of political participation and the maximum exposure of all political processes to the public gaze; but that is precisely their strength. Bismarck is reputed to have said that there are two things one should never watch being made: sausages and laws. Laws, like sausages, should be judged more in terms of their quality and their capacity to do good than in terms of the precise circumstances of their manufacture.

One available tactic might be called "the collusion of elites." There may be occasions on which the great majority of America's politicians, in both the executive and the legislative branches, are able to agree, first, that an issue is of such overriding importance to the nation as a whole that it must be dealt with at almost any cost; second, that therefore the politicians involved must be prepared to sink all their ideological and other differences in the interests of finding a workable solution (almost any solution); and, third, that having found a solution they must then stick together in presenting it to what may well be a disgruntled or even hostile electorate. In order to be successful, the collusion-of-elites tactic requires not only a substantial degree of bipartisanship (or, better still, nonpartisanship) but also, in practice, unusually small teams of negotiators, complete secrecy (not a single ray of "sunshine" must penetrate the proceedings) and, at the end, the presentation to Congress and the public of a comprehensive, all-or-nothing, take-it-or-leave-it package of proposals.

The number of occasions on which politicians will be prepared to sink their ideological differences, and also pool their political risks, in this fashion will inevitably—and sadly—be rare. There were no signs of such a spirit prevailing as President Clinton and the Republican majorities in Congress wrangled over how to cut the budget deficit in the winter of 1995–96. But there have been instances of the successful collusion of elites, even in relatively recent times.

One of them occurred in 1983 when representatives of President Reagan and the two party leaderships on Capitol Hill colluded to save the entire Social Security system, which at that time was in imminent danger of bankruptcy. Paul Light's classic account of the 1983 Social Security reform, *Artful Work,* is in effect a case study of how to conduct collusion-of-elites politics and of the circumstances in which it may succeed.[43] The so-called Gang of Seventeen that was originally put together to hammer out a deal (and was later reduced to a Gang of Nine) excluded all the more extreme ideologues and met in circumstances of great secrecy, including the use, according to one participant, of "unmarked limos."[44]

Of the Gang of Seventeen's activities, Light writes:

> The meetings seemed to inaugurate a new form of presidential-congressional government. The meetings were secret. There were no minutes or transcripts. All conversations were strictly off the record. The gang was free to discuss all of the options without fear of political retaliation. It . . . [existed] completely outside of the constitutional system. This was not just separate institutions sharing power; this was a new kind of government body involving a single chamber of national leadership.[45]

Ultimately, as Light relates, the "secret gang built a compromise, wrapped it in a bipartisan flag, and rammed it through Congress. There was no other way to move. It was government by fait accompli."[46] It was also successful government—and none of the participants suffered electoral damage.

Another instance of the collusion of elites occurred only three years later in 1986, when Senator Bob Packwood of Oregon and Representative Dan Rostenkowski of Illinois, with President Reagan in the background, were the principal authors of a sweeping and largely unexpected reform of the U.S. tax system. The reform involved ignoring the demands of large numbers of once-powerful lobby groups; and, again, the politicians' willingness to provide one another with political cover, a substantial element of secrecy and a final set of proposals that had to be accepted or turned down on an all-or-nothing basis were crucial to the enterprise. On this occasion, it was left to one of the final package's most vehement critics, Senator John Danforth of Missouri, to put his finger on both what was happening and why:

> In the backroom of the Senate Finance Committee earlier today . . . I said that this should be ventilated, and there is no reason not

to put it out before the public and give us and our staffs a chance to look at it before we sign the [Senate-House] conference report. The position that was taken by our chairman, by Secretary [of the Treasury] Baker, and several other senators who were present was: "Well, we can't do that. We can't put it public, we've got to sign the conference report now." Why? Well the reason given was that if we don't do it now, people are going to find out what we're doing before we do it. And if they find out, they're going to bring pressure on us. . . . Lobbyists, interest groups, people who have concerns about the bill are going to bring pressure on the Congress, and we can't have that.[47]

Danforth did not like the tax reform, but he was right about its authors' tactics. Such tactics, including insulating the Congress from pressure, are sometimes essential if radical change is to be achieved.

Another possible tactic, with many similarities to the collusion of elites, might be called "putting it into commission." If taking tough decisions is too politically risky, then get someone else to take them. If someone else cannot be got to take them, then make someone else *appear* to take them. The "someone else" in question need not be, but usually will be, a bipartisan or nonpartisan commission of some kind.

Such a commission, the National Commission on Social Security Reform, played a role in the passage of the 1983 act; but an even better, indeed an almost perfect, example was the procedure adopted by Congress in the early 1990s for closing redundant U.S. military bases. The previous practice had been almost a caricature of Congress's traditional decision-making process. The president or defense secretary proposed a program of base closures. Senators and representatives immediately leapt to the defense of the targeted bases in their own home state or district. They of course had the backing of their colleagues, who were threatened with, or feared, base closures in *their* home state or district. Almost no bases were closed.

Realizing that the process was absurd and that huge sums of

taxpayers' money were being wasted in keeping redundant bases open, Congress decided to protect itself from itself. It established the Defense Base Closure and Realignment Commission, which operated on the basis of an extraordinarily simple formula. The defense secretary every two years published a list of the bases he proposed to close together with a statement of the criteria he had used in compiling his list. The commission then examined the list in the light of the criteria, held public hearings and recommended its own list (with additions as well as deletions) to the president. The president was then obliged to accept the commission's list as a whole or reject it as a whole. If, as invariably happened, he accepted it, Congress could only intervene if, within forty-five legislative days, it passed a bill overriding the president's decision and rejecting the commission's whole list. This it never did.

The formula was a near-miracle of voter-proofing. Members of Congress were left entirely free to protest against the closure of bases in their home district or state; Steny Hoyer did so effectively in the case of the Patuxent Naval Air Test Center. But the ultimate decision was taken by the president, and all Congress had to do for the president's decision to take effect was to do nothing. In the event, hundreds of bases were closed and millions of dollars saved, but no member of Congress ever had to vote— and be seen by his constituents to be voting—in *favor* of a base closure close to home.

Former senator Alan J. Dixon of Illinois was nominated by President Clinton in 1994 to be chairman of this base-closing commission. As a senator, Dixon had waged fierce battles in defense of bases that were under threat in his home state. Nevertheless, he wholly approved of the commission procedure. "You've got to understand," he told a reporter. "This process was designed to *stop* a guy like me."[48] Unsurprisingly, the process had yet another voter-proofing feature. The law provided that lists of base closures were to be published only in odd-numbered years, well in advance of the next round of congressional elections. Senators and representatives thus not only insured themselves against having to take the blame for closing bases; they reinsured themselves. The results were, beyond any question, in America's national interest.

For obvious reasons, putting major but electorally tricky problems like base closures into commission is not a device that can be employed more than occasionally. Ideological divisions cannot often be overcome in such a simple fashion, and many government programs, unlike individual base closures, have a real impact on the lives of millions of people living all over the country. Even so, the possibility of proceeding by commission ought at least to be in the mental repertoire of any policymaker contemplating, for example, how to eliminate redundant federal programs and facilities—such as peanut subsidies and superfluous veterans hospitals—in addition to military bases. It is not wholly fantastic to suppose that the president in odd-numbered years might, on the basis of advice received from a bipartisan commission, announce a list of "program eliminations," which, like the existing program of base closures, Congress could countermand only by legislating to reject the list as a whole. Presidents would probably prefer to put forward such lists during the first years of their first term in office—or at any time during their second term when they, at least, were not up for reelection.

A final tactic, which could also be adopted without major institutional change, might be described as "thinking big." Proposals that are put forward on a piecemeal basis can also be opposed, and in all probability defeated, on a piecemeal basis. By contrast, large-scale, broad-based proposals may have a better chance of success simply by virtue of their comprehensiveness. They can provide something for everyone—conservatives as well as liberals, deficit cutters as well as program defenders, sunbelters as well as rustbelters. Gains as well as losses can be broadcast widely. The 1983 Social Security reform and the 1986 tax reform were certainly "big thoughts" of this character. So, in its way, was the 1990s base-closure program.

Jonathan Rauch advances the same proposition in *Demosclerosis.* Advocating a reduction in the power of special interest groups by killing off the low-priority programs and ancient subsidies on which so many of them depend, Rauch insists that:

> The strategy can work, but only on a relatively big scale. No group wants to be singled out (that's "unfair"), and isolated hits don't save any visible amount of money anyway. Why take on a powerful lobby for a lousy half-billion dollars? Even if you succeed, the voters won't notice the difference. The key, instead, is to round up as many programs as possible—hundreds, preferably—and shove them all over the cliff together. Then you save money and create real maneuvering room.[49]

Thinking big is ideologically neutral. It might mean more activist government; it might mean less.[50] For his part, Rauch wants to cut many existing programs not merely because they are wasteful and as a means of reducing the budget deficit, but also to leave room for more innovative and possibly more effective programs.

Tactics like these—the collusion of elites, putting issues into commission and thinking big—all have their virtues; but they also suffer from being tactics in the pejorative as well as the descriptive sense. At bottom, they are somewhat cynical devices for getting round the real difficulty, which is the hyperresponsiveness of American politicians that is induced by their having to run scared so much of the time. Although more difficult, it would be better in the long run to confront this core difficulty directly and to try to bring about at least some of the more fundamental institutional changes proposed earlier in this chapter. Above all, what is needed if American democracy is to function more effectively in the future than in the recent past is a profound attitudinal change: away from the airy myths of agency or direct democracy and toward a more realistic and down-to-earth form of division-of-labor democracy. The American people cannot govern themselves. They need therefore to find appropriate means of choosing representatives who can do a reasonably decent job of governing on their behalf. And that means giving those whom they choose some distance, some space, some time—in a word, some freedom—to take decisions, knowing they will have to live with the consequences.

We end where we began. America's problems are not unique. Italy has much larger per capita budget deficits than the United States; crime is rising fast in other industrial countries like Great Britain, Germany and France; discontent with government is a fact throughout the western world—and is likely to intensify as low economic growth and aging populations combine almost everywhere to place greater and greater strains on the public services.

Nor is it being claimed here that the electoral vulnerability of America's politicians is the sole cause of America's current woes. Of course it is not. Some problems, such as crime, are emanations of the broader society that governments and politicians, with the best will in the world, can do relatively little about. Some purely political problems arise from causes that have little to do with vulnerability. The traditional conservative/liberal dichotomy has long outlived its usefulness in the United States (as it has in many other countries). The procedures for nominating and electing American presidents seem almost guaranteed to drive out the experienced, the able and the emotionally well-balanced and to suck in, at best, the inexperienced and superficially genial and, at worst, the super-wealthy and slightly demented. To repeat: no simple, monocausal explanation is being offered here.

All that is being claimed here, but it is a good deal, is that high-exposure, high-risk politics of the American kind is exceedingly time-consuming and exceedingly expensive, that it is degrading to those who actively participate in it and depressing to those who merely watch it and that, in policy terms, it results far more often than is necessary in fear, paralysis and fraud, ceaseless activity becoming a substitute for calm deliberation and effective action. The best decisions are seldom taken or implemented on a fast-moving rollercoaster.

American readers may protest that other countries indeed have similar or even greater political and other problems than the United States and that it is unfair to pick on America, which is, after all, rich, powerful and one of the world's oldest democracies (arguably *the* oldest). That is true, but it is also beside the point. America's problems are America's and will often have causes that are unique to America. There is no point in Americans consoling themselves, as the British often do, by drawing attention to the faults and failings of others. The present writer happens to think that the political system of the country in which he lives, Great Britain, is also in pretty bad shape—but for different reasons. The vulnerability of America's politicians is peculiar to America. It has adverse effects on the American system. It is up to Americans to decide what, if anything, they want to do about it.

NOTES

Chapter 2. Why American Politicians Are Vunerable

1. It should be stressed that the point being made here is largely unrelated to other aspects of the political systems existing in the United States and other countries. For example, it has very little to do with whether they have proportional or winner-take-all electoral systems. All countries *could* have primaries. The important point here is that only the United States actually does have them.
2. David S. Broder, "Democrats Worrying," *Washington Post,* June 9, 1993, p. A1.
3. *Ibid.*
4. Elizabeth Drew, *On the Edge: The Clinton Presidency* (New York: Simon & Schuster, 1994), p. 69. See also Bob Woodward, *The Agenda: Inside the Clinton White House* (New York: Simon & Schuster, 1994). For a broader analysis of the influence of opinion polls on presidents, see Paul Brace and Barbara Hinckley, *Follow the Leader: Opinion Polls and the Modern Presidents* (New York: Basic Books, 1992).
5. Since the ratification of the Twenty-second Amendment in 1951, only two presidents, Dwight D. Eisenhower and Ronald Reagan, have served two full terms. Another, Richard Nixon, was elected for a second term but served only part of it. Perhaps because there have been so few second-term presidencies since 1951, oddly little atten-

tion has been paid to how the political position of second-term presidents differs from that of those in their first term and to how, if at all, second-term presidents comport themselves differently.

6. The best brief introduction to the subject remains Austin Ranney, "Candidate Selection," in David Butler, Howard R. Penniman and Austin Ranney, eds., *Democracy at the Polls: A Comparative Study of Competitive National Elections* (Washington, D.C.: American Enterprise Institute, 1981), pp. 75–106.

7. By 1960 congressional primaries were so prevalent that in 1960 itself all but three states held at least one such contested primary, and two of those three held at least one contested congressional primary two years later, in 1962. Currently, Virginia allows its state parties to select congressional candidates by primaries or at a party convention, and Connecticut and Utah allow parties to dispense with primaries if their conventions favor one candidate overwhelmingly. Richard M. Scammon and Alice V. McGillivary, eds., *America Votes 21: A Handbook of Contemporary American Election Statistics 1994* (Washington, D.C.: Congressional Quarterly, 1995), pp. 464, 134, 446.

8. Norman J. Ornstein, Thomas E. Mann and Michael J. Malbin, *Vital Statistics on Congress 1993–1994* (Washington, D.C.: CQ Press, 1994), Table 2–7, p. 58.

9. Calculated using data from *Congressional Quarterly Weekly Report.*

10. At one level, "swing" is simply an arithmetical calculation: the average of the winning party's gain since the previous election and the losing party's loss. But the point about swing between the parties in Britain is that it tends to be relatively uniform across all districts and regions. To the losers, therefore, swing has the aspect of a deadly scythe, lopping off the heads of those who get in its way, irrespective of their personal merits and demerits.

11. On Japan, especially the *Koenkai,* see Hitoshe Abe, Muneyuki Shindo and Sadafumi Kuwato, *The Government and Politics of Japan,* trans. James W. White (Tokyo: University of Tokyo Press, 1994), chapter 5. On Italy, see Douglas Wertman, "The Italian Electoral Process: The Elections of June 1976," in Howard R. Penniman, ed., *Italy at the Polls: The Parliamentary Elections of 1976* (Washington, D.C.: American Enterprise Institute, 1977), pp. 48, 51, 76–79.

12. Gary C. Jacobson, *The Politics of Congressional Elections,* 3rd edn. (New York: HarperCollins, 1992), p. 7.

13. Ornstein et al., *Vital Statistics on Congress 1993–1994,* Table 2–17, pp. 67–68.

14. "Evolution of a Crime Bill," *Time,* September 5, 1994, p. 25.

15. The funding and regulation of election campaigns is, needless to say, a complicated topic. For a general introduction, see Khayyam Zev Paltiel, "Campaign Finance: Contrasting Practices and Reforms," in Butler et al., *Democracy at the Polls,* pp. 138–72.

16. Gerald L. Curtis, *The Japanese Way of Politics* (New York: Columbia University Press, 1988), p. 177.

17. See, among others, Frank J. Sorauf, *Money in American Elections* (Glenview, Ill.: Scott, Foresman, 1988), and Herbert E. Alexander, *Financing Politics: Money, Elections, and Political Reform,* 4th edn. (Washington, D.C.: CQ Press, 1992).

18. Jacobson, *The Politics of Congressional Elections,* p. 65.

19. Richard F. Fenno, Jr., *Home Style: House Members and Their Districts* (Boston: Little, Brown, 1978), p. 13.

20. *Ibid.*

21. *Ibid.,* p. 14.

22. *Ibid.,* p. 16.

23. *Ibid.*

24. *Ibid.,* p. 190.

25. *Ibid.,* pp. 217–18.

26. Richard F. Fenno, Jr., *Learning to Legislate: The Senate Education of Arlen Specter* (Washington, D.C.: CQ Press, 1991), p. 130.

27. Richard F. Fenno, Jr., *When Incumbency Fails: The Senate Career of Mark Andrews* (Washington, D.C.: CQ Press, 1992), p. 251.

28. David R. Mayhew, *Congress: The Electoral Connection* (New Haven, Conn.: Yale University Press, 1974), pp. 5–6.

29. See Jacobson, *The Politics of Congressional Elections, passim.*

30. Ornstein et al., *Vital Statistics on Congress 1993–1994,* Table 2–7, p. 58.

31. *Ibid.,* Table 2–8, p. 59.

32. Calculated using data from *Congressional Quarterly Weekly Report.*

33. Mayhew, *Congress: The Electoral Connection,* pp. 81–82.

34. Jacobson, *The Politics of Congressional Elections,* pp. 37–42.

35. Ornstein et al., *Vital Statistics on Congress 1993–1994,* Table 6–8, p. 163.

36. *Ibid.,* Table 2–8, p. 59.

37. See Thomas E. Mann, *Unsafe at Any Margin: Interpreting Congres-*

sional Elections (Washington, D.C.: American Enterprise Institute, 1978).

Chapter 3. How They Came to Be Vulnerable

1. Joseph A. Schumpeter, *Capitalism, Socialism, and Democracy,* 2nd edn. (New York: Harper, 1947), p. 269.
2. The distinction being made here between division-of-labor democracy and agency or direct democracy is first cousin to a set of distinctions long familiar to students of democratic theory and representation—for instance, the distinction between the representative as "trustee" and the representative as "delegate" as expounded in John C. Wahlke, Heinz Eulau, William Buchanan and Leroy C. Ferguson, *The Legislative System: Explorations in Legislative Behavior* (New York: John Wiley, 1962), chapter 12. These distinctions are, however, most commonly used to describe actual or desirable relationships between individual representatives and those they claim to represent rather than those that occur, within whole political systems, between the class of governors (or politicians) on the one hand and the class of the governed (or voters) on the other. To put it another way, the approach adopted here is a "macro" approach rather than a "micro" one.
3. Alexis de Tocqueville, *Democracy in America,* Phillips Bradley, ed. (New York: Alfred A. Knopf, 1946), Volume I, pp. 57–58.
4. Robert A. Dahl, *Democracy in the United States: Promise and Performance,* 4th edn. (Boston: Houghton Mifflin, 1981).
5. *The Book of the States,* 30, 1994–95 edn. (Lexington, Ky.: Council of State Governments, 1994), pp. 294, 305–6.
6. For a brief summary of the Founding Fathers' conception, see Richard Hofstadter, *The American Political Tradition and the Men Who Made It* (New York: Alfred A. Knopf, 1948), chapter 1.
7. It is strange that no full-scale history of the theory and practice of democracy in America has yet been attempted. Part of the gap is filled by Robert H. Wiebe, *Self-Rule: A Cultural History of American Democracy* (Chicago: University of Chicago Press, 1995).
8. De Tocqueville, *Democracy in America,* p. 40.
9. See Sam Bass Warner, Jr., *The Private City: Philadelphia in Three Periods of Growth* (Philadelphia: University of Pennsylvania Press, 1968), p. 225.

10. Jonathan Elliot, ed., *Debates on the Adoption of the Federal Constitution* (Washington, D.C.: Printed for the Editor, 1845), pp. 183–84.

11. *Ibid.,* pp. 225, 184.

12. *Ibid.,* pp. 183–84.

13. *Ibid.,* pp. 184, 225.

14. *Ibid.,* p. 226.

15. *Ibid.*

16. *Ibid.,* p. 241.

17. For a brief history of the direct primary, see Austin Ranney and Willmoore Kendall, *Democracy and the American Party System* (New York: Harcourt, Brace, 1956), pp. 276–77; for more details, see Charles E. Merriam and Louise Overacker, *Primary Elections* (Chicago: University of Chicago Press, 1928). Even before primary elections became commonplace, campaigning in the United States could be a virtually nonstop affair. See, for example, the detailed account of how the young Abraham Lincoln found his way to the House of Representatives in the 1840s provided by David Herbert Donald in *Lincoln* (New York: Simon & Schuster, 1995), pp. 111–15. Lincoln would have had no trouble adapting to 1990s-style electioneering.

18. Merriam and Overacker, *Primary Elections,* p. 5.

19. See Samuel P. Huntington, *American Politics: The Promise of Disharmony* (Cambridge, Mass.: Belknap Press, 1981), chapter 5.

20. Richard H. Hofstadter, *The Age of Reform: From Bryan to F.D.R.* (New York: Alfred A. Knopf, 1955), p. 257.

21. *Ibid.,* p. 262.

22. *Ibid.*

23. *Ibid.,* p. 263.

24. *Congressional Quarterly Almanac 1960* (Washington, D.C.: Congressional Quarterly, 1961), p. 774.

25. See Nelson Polsby, *Consequences of Party Reform* (New York: Oxford University Press, 1983), chapters 1–2, and Byron E. Shafer, *Quiet Revolution: The Struggle for the Democratic Party and the Shaping of Post-Reform Politics* (New York: Russell Sage Foundation, 1983).

26. "1980 Convention Delegate Breakdowns," *Congressional Quarterly Weekly Report,* vol. 38, no. 27, July 5, 1980, p. 1873.

27. See Martin P. Wattenberg, *The Rise of Candidate-Centered Politics: Presidential Elections of the 1980s* (Cambridge, Mass.: Harvard University Press, 1991), chapter 3.

28. See above, page 33.

29. See Wattenberg, *The Rise of Candidate-Centered Politics, passim.*

30. John Kenneth White and Jerome M. Mileur, eds., *Challenges to Party Government* (Carbondale: Southern Illinois University Press, 1992), p. 97, quoting Richard Hofstadter, *The Idea of a Party System: The Rise of Legitimate Opposition in the United States, 1780–1840* (Berkeley: University of California Press, 1969), p. 13.

31. Martin P. Wattenberg, *The Decline of American Political Parties, 1952–1988* (Cambridge, Mass.: Harvard University Press, 1990), p. 163.

32. Larry J. Sabato, *The Party's Just Begun* (Glenview, Ill: Scott, Foresman/Little, Brown, 1988), p. 133.

33. Wattenberg, *The Decline of American Political Parties*, pp. 92–100.

34. Paul S. Herrnson, *Congressional Elections: Campaigning at Home and in Washington* (Washington, D.C.: CQ Press, 1995), pp. 132–33, 140–41, 146, 151.

35. *Ibid.*, p. 133.

36. *Ibid.*, p. 149.

37. Polsby, *Consequences of Party Reform*, pp. 37–38. One consequence of *Buckley et al. v. Valeo*, taken together with other changes in America's campaign finance laws, has been to give a comparative electoral advantage to candidates who are personally very wealthy. Compared with most other democracies, the United States shows signs of becoming a genuine plutocracy.

38. Quoted in Wattenberg, *The Rise of Candidate-Centered Politics*, p. 165.

Chapter 4. Why Their Vulnerability Matters

1. Norman J. Ornstein, Thomas E. Mann and Michael J. Malbin, *Vital Statistics on Congress 1993–94* (Washington, D.C.: CQ Press, 1994), p. 128.

2. *Ibid.*, p. 121.

3. *Ibid.*, pp. 130–31.

4. *Ibid.*, p. 163.

5. Morris P. Fiorina, *Congress: Keystone of the Washington Establishment*, 2nd edn. (New Haven, Conn.: Yale University Press, 1989), p. 120; see also Michael J. Malbin, *Unelected Representatives: Con-*

gressional Staff and the Future of Representative Government (New York: Basic Books, 1980).

6. See above, p. 32.

7. Fiorina, *Congress,* pp. 91–92.

8. See Roger H. Davidson and Walter J. Oleszek, *Congress and Its Members,* 4th edn. (Washington, D.C.: CQ Press, 1994), p. 145; and John R. Hibbing, *Congressional Careers: Contours of Life in the U.S. House of Representatives* (Chapel Hill: University of North Carolina Press, 1991), pp. 134–39.

9. The most searching analysis of these phenomena is still David R. Mayhew, *Congress: The Electoral Connection* (New Haven, Conn.: Yale University Press, 1974).

10. Suzanne Garment, *Scandal: The Culture of Mistrust in American Politics* (New York: Anchor Books, 1992), p. 207. (A House committee was, of course, bound to be larger in any case.)

11. *Ibid.,* p. 153.

12. James L. Payne, "The Rise of Lone Wolf Questioning in House Committee Hearings," *Polity,* 14 (Summer 1982), p. 632.

13. Michael J. Robinson, "Three Faces of Congressional Media," in Thomas E. Mann and Norman J. Ornstein, eds., *The New Congress* (Washington, D.C.: American Enterprise Institute, 1981), p. 65; Stephen Hess, *Live from Capitol Hill!—Studies of Congress and the Media* (Washington, D.C.: Brookings Institution, 1991), pp. 62–76.

14. Davidson and Oleszek, *Congress and Its Members,* p. 154.

15. The phrase "I am on TV, therefore I am" is from Hess, *Live from Capitol Hill!,* p. 109.

16. Davidson and Oleszek, *Congress and Its Members,* p. 132.

17. See Linda L. Fowler and Robert D. McClure, *Political Ambition: Who Decides to Run for Congress* (New Haven, Conn.: Yale University Press, 1989); and L. Sandy Maisel, *From Obscurity to Oblivion: Running in the Congressional Primary* (Knoxville: University of Tennessee Press, 1982).

18. Alan Ehrenhalt, *The United States of Ambition: Politicians, Power, and the Pursuit of Office* (New York: Times Books, 1991), p. 230.

19. On voluntary retirements from Congress, see Stephen E. Frantzich, "Opting Out: Retirement from the House of Representatives, 1966–1974," *American Politics Quarterly,* 6 (July 1978), pp.

251–73; Michael K. Moore and John R. Hibbing, "Is Serving in Congress Fun Again?—Voluntary Retirements from the House since the 1970s," *American Journal of Political Science,* 36 (August 1992), pp. 824–28; John R. Hibbing, "The Career Path of Members of Congress," in Shirley Williams and Edward L. Lascher, Jr., eds., *Ambition and Beyond: Career Paths of American Politicians* (Berkeley, Calif.: Institute of Governmental Studies Press, 1993), pp. 109–33; Steven G. Livingston and Sally Friedman, "Reexamining Theories of Congressional Retirement: Evidence from the 1980s," *Legislative Studies Quarterly,* 18 (May 1993), pp. 231–53; Richard L. Hall and Robert P. Houweling, "Avarice and Ambition in Congress," *American Political Science Review,* 89 (March 1995), pp. 121–36.

20. This view appears to be contradicted by some of the scholarly literature cited in n.19; but most of those who have written on the subject of congressional retirements have relied mainly on readily available quantitative data and have not introduced any direct measures of job satisfaction (or the lack of it) into their analyses. A strong correlation between premature retirements and, say, improved pensions does not mean that lack of job satisfaction did not play a part in causing some members of Congress to leave and enjoy their pensions rather than stay and pursue their careers.

21. John R. Hibbing, *Choosing to Leave: Voluntary Retirement from the U.S. House of Representatives* (Washington, D.C.: University Press of America, 1982), p. 57.

22. Janet Hook, "Will the Flood of Retirements Arrive in 1992? Maybe Not," *Congressional Quarterly Weekly Report,* vol. 49, no. 2, January 12, 1991, pp. 72–79.

23. Michael Wines, "Many in Congress Deciding They Want Out," *New York Times,* April 28, 1994, p. A1.

24. Hibbing, *Choosing to Leave,* p. 59.

25. *Ibid.*

26. Adam Clymer, "Citing Rise in Frustration, Dozens of Lawmakers Quit," *New York Times,* April 5, 1992, p. 1.

27. Fiorina, *Congress,* p. 79.

28. The congressional parties are a good deal stronger than they used to be—both organizationally and in terms of party cohesion—though they remain weaker than the legislative parties in most other democracies. On recent developments, see David W. Rohde,

Parties and Leaders in the Postreform House (Chicago: University of
Chicago Press, 1991); Gary W. Cox and Mathew D. McCubbins,
Legislative Leviathan: Party Government in the House (Berkeley:
University of California Press, 1993); John Aldrich, *Why Parties?
The Origin and Transformation of Political Parties in America*
(Chicago: University of Chicago Press, 1995), chapter 7; and Dan
Carney, "As Hostilities Rage on the Hill, Partisan-Vote Rate
Soars," *Congressional Quarterly Weekly Report,* vol. 54, no. 4, Janu-
ary 27, 1996, pp. 199–201.

29. Gary C. Jacobson, *The Politics of Congressional Elections,* 3rd edn.
(New York: HarperCollins, 1992), p. 210.
30. Mayhew, *Congress: The Electoral Connection,* p. 128.
31. R. Douglas Arnold, "The Local Roots of Domestic Policy," in
Mann and Ornstein, *The New Congress,* p. 272.
32. Fiorina, *Congress,* p. 131.
33. Jacobson, *The Politics of Congressional Elections,* p. 214.
34. Mayhew, *Congress: The Electoral Connection,* pp. 132–40; see also
Murray Edelman, *The Symbolic Uses of Politics* (Urbana: University
of Illinois Press, 1967).
35. No one has ever attempted a comparative study of the incidence
of, and the uses of, political bullshit in different countries. A foreign observer can only offer his impression that there is substantially more of it in the United States than elsewhere. It may be no
accident that most of the examples of the genre given in *The Oxford English Dictionary* are of American provenance. See *The Oxford English Dictionary,* 2nd edn. (Oxford: Clarendon Press, 1989),
Volume II, p. 645.
36. Anyone who has ever spent time watching C-SPAN or sitting in
on congressional hearings can add their own examples. As in the
case of bullshit, no one has ever attempted to study symbolic politics comparatively, but anyone who did would almost certainly
conclude that there is more of it in the United States than in most,
possibly all, other democracies. (Symbolic politics should not, of
course, be confused with political symbols. Most countries have
lots of the latter.)
37. Mayhew, *Congress: The Electoral Connection,* p. 138.
38. *Bartlett's Familiar Quotations,* 16th edn. (Boston: Little, Brown
1992), p. 317.
39. Ehrenhalt, *The United States of Ambition,* p. 236.

40. *Ibid.*
41. Timothy J. Penny and Major Garrett, *Common Cents: A Retiring Six-Term Congressman Reveals How Congress Really Works—and What We Must Do to Fix It* (Boston: Little, Brown, 1995), p. 72.
42. Jacobson, *The Politics of Congressional Elections,* pp. 232–38; David E. Price, *The Congressional Experience: A View From the Hill* (Boulder, Colo.: Westview Press, 1992), pp. 166–67.
43. Ehrenhalt, *The United States of Ambition,* p. xiv.
44. *Ibid.,* p. 235. See also a more recent contribution to the discussion: Robert Wright, "Hyper Democracy," *Time,* January 23, 1995, pp. 51–56. Wright maintains (p. 52) that the United States is "a nation that, contrary to all Beltway-related stereotypes, is thoroughly plugged into Washington—too plugged in for its own good." He stresses that modern communications technology—notably e-mail and fax machines—further intensify constituent pressures on elective officeholders.

Chapter 5. A Case of Fright: The First Oil Shock

1. On the first oil shock and its political aftermath, see Franklin Tugwell, *The Energy Crisis and the American Political Economy: Politics and Markets in the Management of Natural Resources* (Stanford, Calif.: Stanford University Press, 1988); Harvey Feigenbaum, Richard Samuels and R. Kent Weaver, "Innovation, Coordination, and Implementation in Energy Policy," in R. Kent Weaver and Bert A. Rockman, eds., *Do Institutions Matter?—Government Capabilities in the United States and Abroad* (Washington, D.C.: Brookings Institution, 1993), pp. 42–107; and R. Douglas Arnold, *The Logic of Congressional Action* (New Haven, Conn.: Yale University Press, 1990).
2. See Paul Pierson, *Dismantling the Welfare State?—Reagan, Thatcher, and the Politics of Retrenchment* (New York: Cambridge University Press, 1994).
3. The rest of this chapter draws heavily on Arnold, *The Logic of Congressional Action,* chapter 9. Arnold's analysis is elegant and his conclusions correct, although his focus is different from the one adopted here.
4. *Ibid.,* p. 232.
5. These are, of course, two separate points. The price mechanism it-

self, in the circumstances of the 1970s, would have had the effect of reducing oil consumption. It certainly had that effect in most of the industrial world. The point of any petroleum tax would have been to reduce consumption still further if an additional reduction had been thought desirable on other grounds—for example, energy conservation.

6. But not in Canada: see Feigenbaum et al., "Innovation, Coordination, and Implementation in Energy Policy," pp. 65–74.
7. Gerald R. Ford, *A Time to Heal* (New York: Harper & Row, 1979), p. 242.
8. Arnold, *The Logic of Congressional Action*, p. 233.
9. *Ibid.*, p. 234.
10. Jimmy Carter, *Keeping Faith: Memoirs of a President* (New York: Bantam Books, 1982), p. 91. Carter has a whole chapter with that title.
11. Arnold, *The Logic of Congressional Action*, p. 236.
12. Carter, *Keeping Faith*, p. 111.
13. Arnold, *The Logic of Congressional Action*, p. 234–35.
14. John E. Chubb, "U.S. Energy Policy: A Problem of Delegation," in John E. Chubb and Paul E. Peterson, eds., *Can the Government Govern?* (Washington, D.C.: Brookings Institution, 1989), p. 92; see also Morris P. Fiorina, *Congress: Keystone of the Washington Establishment*, 2nd edn. (New Haven, Conn.: Yale University Press, 1989), pp. 60–61; Feigenbaum et al., "Innovation, Coordination, and Implementation in Energy Policy," p. 54.
15. Carter, *Keeping Faith*, p. 97.
16. Arnold, *The Logic of Congressional Action*, p. 237.
17. Carter, *Keeping Faith*, p. 97.
18. "Energy Situation," *The Gallup Poll: Public Opinion 1979* (Wilmington, Del.: Scholarly Resources, 1980), p. 200.
19. *Ibid.*, p. 202.
20. Arnold, *The Logic of Congressional Action*, pp. 47–51.
21. That said, the United States was not quite unique. France managed to have three elections—one presidential and two for the National Assembly—during the same period.
22. Arnold, *The Logic of Congressional Action*, p. 232.
23. *Ibid.*, p. 233.
24. *Ibid.*, p. 236.
25. Alan Ehrenhalt, *The United States of Ambition: Politicians, Power, and the Pursuit of Office* (New York: Times Books, 1991), p. 246.

26. *Ibid.*
27. Feigenbaum et al., "Innovation, Coordination, and Implementation in Energy Policy," p. 53.

Chapter 6. A Case of Paralysis: The Budget Deficit

1. U.S. Office of Management and Budget, *Budget of the United States Government Fiscal Year 1996: Historical Tables* (Washington, D.C.: U.S. Government Printing Office, 1995), Table 1–3, "Summary of Receipts, Outlays, and Surpluses or Deficits in Current Dollars, Constant (FY 1987) Dollars, and as Percentage of GDP: 1940–2000," pp. 17–18.
2. David Stockman, *The Triumph of Politics: How the Reagan Revolution Failed* (New York: Harper & Row, 1986), p. 271.
3. *Historical Tables, Budget of the United States Government Fiscal Year 1996:* Table 1-3, pp. 17–18.
4. David P. Calleo, *The Bankrupting of America: How the Federal Budget is Impoverishing the Nation* (New York: W.W. Morrow, 1992), p. 50. Any New Yorker or anyone visiting New York can always get an update on the current size of America's national debt by consulting the "national debt clock" now located at the corner of 43rd Street and the Avenue of the Americas. It was erected in 1989 by a real estate developer named Seymour B. Durst. In 1996 it had been stalled for some years at just below the $5 trillion mark. Copycat signs can be found elsewhere in the country.
5. *Statistical Abstract of the United States 1996* (Washington, D.C.: U.S. Government Printing Office, 1995) Table 504, p. 330.
6. See James D. Savage, *Balanced Budgets and American Politics* (Ithaca, N.Y.: Cornell University Press, 1988).
7. Steven E. Schier, *A Decade of Deficits: Congressional Thought and Fiscal Action* (Albany: State University of New York Press, 1992), pp. 31–32, 159. The supply-siders did not think it was a major problem area because they believed that low taxes would lead to higher economic growth, which would lead to higher federal revenues, which in turn would have the effect of reducing the deficit. In other words, if everyone was patient the deficit problem would simply go away.
8. Joseph White and Aaron Wildavsky, *The Deficit and the Public In-*

terest: The Search for Responsible Budgeting in the 1980s (Berkeley: University of California Press, 1989), pp. 427–28.

9. *Ibid.*, p. xv.

10. *Ibid.*, pp. 154–55.

11. David S. Cloud, "Big Risk for Margolies-Mezvinsky," *Congressional Quarterly Weekly Report*, vol. 51, no. 32, August 7, 1993, p. 2125.

12. Quoted in Savage, *Balanced Budgets*, p. 203.

13. John H. Makin and Norman J. Ornstein, *Debt and Taxes* (New York: Times Books, 1994), p. 284.

14. R. Douglas Arnold, *The Logic of Congressional Action* (New Haven, Conn.: Yale University Press, 1990), p. 188.

15. Quoted in Schier, *A Decade of Deficits*, p. 117.

16. Allen Schick, "Governments versus Budget Deficits," in R. Kent Weaver and Bert A. Rockman, eds., *Do Institutions Matter?—Government Capabilities in the United States and Abroad* (Washington, D.C.: Brookings Institution, 1993), p. 207.

17. *Budget of the United States Government Fiscal Year 1996: Historical Tables*, Table 1-3, pp. 17–18.

18. White and Wildavsky, *The Deficit and the Public Interest*, p. 427.

19. *Ibid.*

20. *Ibid.*, p. 513.

21. Tim Penny appears a prime example: see Timothy J. Penny and Major Garrett, *Common Cents: A Retiring Six-Term Congressman Reveals How Congress Really Works—and What We Must Do to Fix It* (Boston: Little, Brown, 1995), p. 4.

22. Makin and Ornstein, *Debt and Taxes*, p. 283.

23. During the 1980s and early 1990s many commentators ascribed the failure to deal with the deficit to divided government, and certainly the presidency and both houses of Congress were seldom in the hands of the same party from 1980 onwards. Against that, Ronald Reagan as president was not prepared to accept any deficit-reduction package that was acceptable to his own party, let alone the Democrats. Moreover, divided government clearly played different roles, if any, on the three occasions when frontal assaults were launched on the deficit, 1986, 1990 and 1993. In 1986 the government was divided (Republican president, Republican Senate, Democratic House), but a certain amount of progress was

made. In 1990 the government was still divided (Republican president, whole Congress Democratic), but rather more progress was made. In 1993 the government was no longer divided (the Democrats controlled the presidency as well as Congress); but, although still more progress was made, the bill of that year hardly constituted a quantum leap forward.

24. Stockman's prophecies were seriously apocalyptic. For example, he wrote in *The Triumph of Politics* in 1986 (p. 380): "The clock is thus ticking away inexorably toward another bout of inflationary excess. If we stay the course we are now on, the decade [the 1980s, not the 1990s] will end with a worse hyperinflation than the one with which it began. Indeed, the increased fragility and instability of the global economy . . . will make this inflationary cycle even more violent and destructive." It did not happen.

25. *Budget of the United States Government Fiscal Year 1996: Historical Tables,* Table 1-3, pp. 17–18.

26. On public opinion and the deficit, see White and Wildavsky, *The Deficit and the Public Interest, passim.*

27. "Federal Budget Deficit," *The Gallup Poll: Public Opinion 1985* (Wilmington, Del.: Scholarly Resources, 1986), pp. 93–95.

28. Roger H. Davidson and Walter Oleszek, *Congress and Its Members,* 4th edn. (Washington, D.C.: CQ Press, 1994), p. 405.

29. Quoted in the memoirs of a BBC journalist: John Cole, *As It Seemed to Me* (London: Weidenfeld & Nicolson, 1995), p. 75.

30. Arnold, *The Logic of Congressional Action,* p. 182.

31. *Ibid.,* pp. 181–82; Stockman, *The Triumph of Politics,* chapter 6.

32. White and Wildavsky, *The Deficit and the Public Interest,* p. 163.

33. Steven V. Roberts, "Democrat Leads Foes of Party's Budget," *New York Times,* April 9, 1981, p. B14; Irwin B. Arieff, "Conservative Southerners Are Enjoying Their Wooing As Key to Tax Bill Success," *Congressional Quarterly Weekly Report,* June 13, 1981, vol. 39, no. 24, p. 1024.

34. Steven V. Roberts, "44 Democrats Are Objects of White House Attentions," *New York Times,* May 1, 1981, p. A19.

35. White and Wildavsky, *The Deficit and the Public Interest,* p. 178.

36. Darrell M. West, *Congress and Economic Policy Making* (Pittsburgh: University of Pittsburgh Press, 1987), p. 55.

37. *Ibid.,* pp. 78–80.

38. *Ibid.,* p. 55.

39. Stockman, *The Triumph of Politics,* p. 271.
40. Richard F. Fenno, *The Emergence of a Senate Leader: Pete Domenici and the Reagan Budget* (Washington, D.C.: CQ Press, 1991), p. 58.
41. Stockman, *The Triumph of Politics,* p. 305.
42. *Ibid.,* p. 310.
43. *Ibid.,* p. 311.
44. *Ibid.,* pp. 312–13.
45. Arnold, *The Logic of Congressional Action,* p. 184.
46. Quoted in Steven V. Roberts, "99th Congress Opens Somberly in Deficit Shadow," *New York Times,* January 4, 1985, p. A17.
47. *Ibid.*
48. The best account of this episode is in Penny and Garrett, *Common Cents,* p. 101.
49. Quoted in White and Wildavsky, *The Deficit and the Public Interest,* p. 433.
50. Quoted in Fred R. Harris, *Deadlock or Decision: The U.S. Senate and the Rise of National Politics* (New York: Oxford University Press, 1993), p. 223. See also Warren B. Rudman, *Combat: Twelve Years in the U.S. Senate* (New York: Random House, 1996), esp. chap. 2, which deals with the politics of deficit reduction. Rudman offers a number of ruminations on the impact of impending elections on his and his colleagues' efforts to reduce the deficit. He comments on p. 76, for example: "Some senators felt relatively secure with their constituents [in 1985]. They felt strong enough to take political risks, because they could go home and give interviews and hold town meetings and win public support. But many of our colleagues lived in fear of an unpopular vote that might cost them their seats." Later (p. 105) he observes ruefully: "In the end, Gramm-Rudman was defeated by politics as usual. The way it was undermined stands today as a textbook example of how politicians trick the American people into thinking they're acting on a problem when in fact they're ducking it."
51. Quoted in White and Wildavsky, *The Deficit and the Public Interest,* p. 436.
52. Quoted in *ibid.,* p. 434.
53. *Ibid.*
54. Penny and Garrett, *Common Cents,* pp. 101–2.
55. Makin and Ornstein, *Debt and Taxes,* pp. 179–86.
56. *Public Papers of the Presidents: George Bush 1990,* Book II, p. 1327.

57. For a brief account of the 1990 budget deal, see Anthony King and Giles Alston, "Good Government and the Politics of High Exposure," in Colin Campbell and Bert Rockman, *The Bush Presidency: First Appraisals* (Chatham, N.J.: Chatham House, 1991), pp. 251–62.

58. Quoted in Penny and Garrett, *Common Cents,* p. 170.

59. David E. Price, *The Congressional Experience: A View From the Hill* (Boulder, Colo.: Westview Press, 1992), p. 105.

60. Penny and Garrett, *Common Cents,* p. 172.

61. For details, see Gary C. Jacobson, "Deficit-Cutting Politics and Congressional Elections," *Political Science Quarterly,* 108 (Fall 1993), pp. 375–402. Jacobson shows that a kind of division of labor operated in Congress in 1990. Safer senators and representatives carried the burden of casting politically risky, but necessary, votes in favor of the deficit-cutting measure, thus enabling their more vulnerable congressional colleagues to vote defensively. Jacobson throughout his article emphasizes the extent to which electoral considerations made it difficult to cut the deficit. Indeed, as he says (p. 377), "The first step in understanding how electoral politics shaped the battle to tame the deficit monster in 1990 is to recognize that the monster itself is a creature of electoral politics."

62. It goes without saying that other countries also suffered massive budget deficits during the 1980s and 1990s, and some were even less successful than the United States in curbing them. What differentiated the United States was the intensity and duration of national concern and national debate over the issue. Useful comparative studies are United States General Accounting Office, *Deficit Reduction: Experiences of Other Nations,* GAO/AIMD-95-30 (Washington, D.C.: General Accounting Office, 1994), and Salvatore Pitruzzello, "Political Control of Budget Deficits?," paper delivered at the 1994 Annual Meeting of the American Political Science Association, New York.

Chapter 7. A Case of Fraud: The Wars on Crime

1. David R. Mayhew, *Congress: The Electoral Connection* (New Haven, Conn.: Yale University Press, 1974), pp. 138–39.

2. Michael R. Rand, "Crime and the Nation's Households, 1992," *Bureau of Justice Statistics Bulletin,* August 1993, pp. 1–2.

3. James Q. Wilson and Joan Petersilia, eds., *Crime* (San Francisco: ICS Press, 1995), pp. 411–13; also 95–96. Wilson and Petersilia offer by far the most comprehensive study and assessment of public policy relating to crime in the United States. This chapter is heavily based on it.

4. Michael G. Hagen, "The Crime Issue and the 1994 Elections," paper delivered at the 1995 Annual Meeting of the American Political Science Association, Chicago, pp. 3–4.

5. Neil A. Lewis, "Crime Rates Decline: Outrage Hasn't," *New York Times,* December 8, 1993, p. B6.

6. See, for instance, Wilson and Petersilia, eds., *Crime,* pp. 333–34, 339–41, and 495–98.

7. Timothy J. Penny and Major Garrett, *Common Cents: A Retiring Six-Term Congressman Reveals How Congress Really Works—and What We Must Do to Fix It* (Boston: Little, Brown, 1995), p. 93.

8. Margaret Edwards, "Mandatory Sentencing," *CQ Researcher,* May 26, 1995, pp. 473–74.

9. Don J. DeBenedictis, "How Long Is Too Long?" *American Bar Association Journal,* 79 (October 1993), p. 78.

10. Quoted in *ibid.,* p. 75.

11. Quoted in *ibid.*

12. Quoted in Edwards, "Mandatory Sentencing," p. 482.

13. *Ibid.,* pp. 472–73.

14. Barbara S. Vincent and Paul S. Hofer, "The Consequences of Mandatory Minimum Prison Terms: A Summary of Recent Findings," paper published by the Federal Judicial Center, Washington, D.C., 1994, p. 21.

15. *Ibid.*

16. Edwards, "Mandatory Sentencing," pp. 468–69.

17. House Report No. 1441, 91st Congress, 2nd Session (1970), cited in U.S. Sentencing Commission, *Special Report to Congress: Mandatory Minimum Penalties in the Federal Criminal Justice System,* August 1993, pp. 6–7.

18. Quoted in Vincent and Hofer, "Consequences of Mandatory Minimum Prison Terms," p. 11.

19. DeBenedictis, "How Long Is Too Long?" p. 77.

20. Edwards, "Mandatory Sentencing," p. 471; Vincent and Hofer, "Consequences of Mandatory Minimum Prison Terms," p. 14.
21. Vincent and Hofer, "Consequences of Mandatory Minimum Prison Terms," pp. 11–12.
22. Edwards, "Mandatory Sentencing," p. 471.
23. Vincent and Hofer, "Consequences of Mandatory Minimum Prison Terms," p. 11.
24. Edwards, "Mandatory Sentencing," pp. 468–69. See David B. Kopel, "Prison Blues: How America's Foolish Sentencing Policies Endanger Public Safety," Cato Institute Policy Analysis No. 208, May 17, 1994, p. 6.
25. Wilson and Petersilia, eds., *Crime,* p. 319. Mandatory sentences also, of course, increased costs. Edwards writes in "Mandatory Sentencing" (pp. 474–75): "Getting tough on crime is not cheap. As the U.S. inmate population grows, the cost of the criminal justice system is skyrocketing. In just 14 years, federal outlays for criminal justice, including corrections, skyrocketed from $4.6 billion in 1980 to $16.5 billion in 1994. The corrections costs alone increased sevenfold—from $342 million to about $2.5 billion. Total criminal justice expenditures for state and local government were $65 billion, of which $23.5 billion were for housing inmates."
26. "'Three Strikes': Serious Flaws and a Huge Price Tag," *RAND Research Review,* 19 (Spring 1995), p. 1.
27. For details of the California experience, see Edwards, "Mandatory Sentencing," p. 480.
28. "'Three Strikes'," *RAND Research Review,* p. 1.
29. Timothy Egan, "A 3-Strike Law Shows It's Not As Simple As It Seems," *New York Times,* February 15, 1994, p. A1.
30. Wilson and Petersilia, eds., *Crime,* p. 494.
31. Quoted in Wendy Kaminer, *It's All the Rage: Crime and Culture* (Reading, Mass.: Addison-Wesley, 1995), p. 180.
32. Wilson and Petersilia, eds., *Crime,* p. 460.
33. Quoted in Kaminer, *It's All the Rage,* p. 128.
34. "For the Record: The Federal Death Penalty," *New York Times,* September 14, 1994, p. A16.
35. David Johnston with Steven A. Holmes, "Experts Doubt Effectiveness of Crime Bill," *New York Times,* September 14, 1994, p. A16.
36. Robert J. Spitzer, *The Politics of Gun Control* (Chatham, N.J.: Chatham House, 1995), p. 161.

37. Edwards, "Mandatory Sentencing," p. 467; DeBenedictis, "How Long Is Too Long?" p. 77.
38. See above, p. 140.
39. The evidence that the voters wanted tougher laws is both voluminous and overwhelming. For example, the *Los Angeles Times* asked a nationwide sample of voters in 1994: "Do you favor or oppose a 'three strikes and you're out' law, which requires any criminal convicted of three violent felonies to be imprisoned for life without the possibility of parole?" More than three-quarters, 79 percent, said they were in favor of such a law—and almost as many, 74 percent, said they would still be in favor even if it meant raising taxes or taking money from other programs to build more prisons. Edwards, "Mandatory Sentencing," p. 473. In 1994, one Gallup poll found 60 percent of respondents in favor of extending the death penalty to some serious crimes other than murder, while another found that 62 percent believed that the use of Singapore-style canings would be a deterrent to crime in the United States. *The Gallup Poll: Public Opinion 1994* (Wilmington, Del.: Scholarly Resources, 1995), pp. 134, 216.
40. David R. Mayhew, *Congress: The Electoral Connection* (New Haven, Conn.: Yale University Press, 1974).
41. *Congressional Quarterly Almanac 1986* (Washington, D.C.: Congressional Quarterly, 1986), p. 95.
42. *Congressional Quarterly Almanac 1988* (Washington, D.C.: Congressional Quarterly, 1989), p. 103.
43. David E. Price, *The Congressional Experience: A View From the Hill* (Boulder, Colo.: Westview Press, 1992), 167.
44. *Congressional Quarterly Almanac 1991* (Washington, D.C.: Congressional Quarterly, 1992), p. 269.
45. *Congressional Record—Senate,* November 9, 1993, p. S15384.
46. *Ibid.,* p. S15385.
47. Kaminer, *It's All the Rage,* p. 211.
48. Kaminer, *It's All the Rage,* p. 218–19.
49. Todd S. Purdum, "Anticrime Bill Will Not End U.S. Violence, Bradley says," *New York Times,* May 12, 1994, p. A22.

Chapter 8. More Democracy, More Dissatisfaction

1. "Extracts from Powell's News Conference on Political Plans," *New York Times,* November 9, 1995, p. B13.

2. Richard Himelfarb, *Catastrophic Politics: The Rise and Fall of the Medicare Catastrophic Coverage Act of 1988* (University Park: Pennsylvania State University Press, 1995), p. 96.

3. Warren E. Miller and Santa A. Traugott, *American National Election Studies Data Sourcebook, 1952–1990* (Cambridge: Harvard University Press, 1992), p. 264.

4. *Ibid.,* p. 265.

5. Ruy A. Teixeira, *The Disappearing American Voter* (Washington, D.C.: Brookings Institution, 1992), p. 32; *New York Times*/CBS News Poll, August 5–9, 1995, p. 7.

6. Humphrey Taylor, "Americans More Alienated Than At Any Time in Last 30 Years," Harris Poll 1996 #2, January 1996, p. 3.

7. Teixeira, *The Disappearing American Voter,* p. 9; Paul R. Abramson, John H. Aldrich and David W. Rohde, *Change and Continuity in the 1992 Elections* (Washington, D.C.: CQ Press, 1994), p. 104.

8. Jonathan Rauch, *Demosclerosis: The Silent Killer of American Government* (New York: Times Books, 1994); William Greider, *Who Will Tell the People: The Betrayal of American Democracy* (New York: Simon & Schuster, 1992); E. J. Dionne, Jr., *Why Americans Hate Politics* (New York: Simon & Schuster, 1991); George F. Will, *Restoration: Congress, Term Limits, and the Recovery of Deliberative Democracy* (New York: Free Press, 1992); William E. Hudson, *American Democracy in Peril: Seven Challenges to America's Future* (Chatham, N.J.: Chatham House, 1995); David Mathews, *Politics for People: Finding a Responsible Public Voice* (Urbana: University of Illinois Press, 1994); Kevin P. Phillips, *Arrogant Capital: Washington, Wall Street, and the Frustration of American Politics* (Boston: Little, Brown, 1994); Jean Bethke Elshtain, *Democracy on Trial* (New York: Basic Books, 1995); Kathleen Jamieson Hall, *Dirty Politics: Deception, Distraction, and Democracy* (New York: Oxford University Press, 1992); Robert C. Grady, *Restoring Real Representation* (Urbana: University of Illinois Press, 1993).

9. Dionne, *Why Americans Hate Politics,* p. 11.

10. Mathews, *Politics for People,* p. 12, chapter 7. To be fair to Mathews, his preferred model is not strictly a town meeting.

11. Greider, *Who Will Tell the People,* pp. 11–12, 408, 410.

12. Phillips, *Arrogant Capital,* chapter 8.

13. Frederick Rose, "In the Lab: Democracy Goes On-Line in Califor-

nia," *Wall Street Journal,* October 26, 1994, p. B1; see also Lawrence K. Grossman, *The Electronic Republic: Reshaping Democracy in the Information Age* (New York: Viking, 1995).

14. Mathews, *Politics for People,* pp. 105–9.

15. Benjamin R. Barber, *Strong Democracy: Participatory Politics for a New Age* (Berkeley: University of California Press, 1984).

16. James S. Fishkin, *The Voice of the People: Public Opinion and Democracy* (New Haven, Conn.: Yale University Press, 1995); see also Hudson, *American Democracy in Peril,* especially pp. 303–8.

17. Phillips, *Arrogant Capital,* p. 190.

18. *Ibid.,* p. 191.

19. Gordon S. Black and Benjamin D. Black, *The Politics of American Discontent: How a New Party Can Make Democracy Work Again* (New York: Wiley, 1994), pp. 201–4.

20. See Will, *Restoration.*

21. Cleta Deatherage Mitchell quoted in Keith A. Boeckelman, "Term Limitation, Responsiveness, and the Public Interest," *Polity,* 26 (Winter 1993), p. 192. On the term limits movement in general, see Gerald Benjamin and Michael J. Malbin, edns., *Limiting Legislative Terms* (Washington, D.C.: CQ Press, 1992).

22. As Robert Dahl has pointed out, "severe upper limits are set on effective participation in 'democratic' decisions by the sheer number of persons involved." (In the modern world, he notes, "six hundred seems to be about the limit for legislative bodies.") Participation requires time: "if an association were to make one decision a day, allow ten hours a day for discussion, and permitted each member just ten minutes . . . then the association could have no more than sixty members." Robert A. Dahl, *After the Revolution? Authority in a Good Society,* rev. edn. (New Haven, Conn.: Yale University Press, 1990), pp. 118, 54, 52.

23. On the Watergate babies, see Burdett A. Loomis: *The New American Politician: Ambition, Entrepreneurship, and the Changing Face of Political Life* (New York: Basic Books, 1988).

24. See David R. Mayhew, *Divided We Govern: Party Control, Lawmaking, and Investigations, 1946–1990* (New Haven, Conn.: Yale University Press, 1991).

25. All people have to do is stop splitting their tickets and stop voting for candidates of the party opposed to the president in off-year

elections. This would not absolutely guarantee divided government's end—the Anglo-American electoral system and America's
electoral college could have perverse effects—and the whole
process could take time, as presidents, with their four years, and
senators, with their six, worked their way out of the system. It
would nevertheless have a high probability of achieving the desired
objective in the end. Needless to say, people are most unlikely to
stop splitting their tickets and are, if anything, even more unlikely
to stop voting, on anti-divided government grounds, for candidates of the opposition party in off-year elections.

26. Rauch, *Demosclerosis,* pp. 17–18.
27. See, in particular, Nelson W. Polsby, *Consequences of Party Reform*
   (New York: Oxford University Press, 1983).
28. On this point, see Teixeira, *The Disappearing American Voter,* chap.
   2, and, more generally, John R. Hibbing and Elizabeth Theiss-
   Morse, *Congress as Public Enemy: Public Attitudes Toward American
   Political Institutions* (Cambridge: Cambridge University Press,
   1995).
29. Quoted in Rauch, *Demosclerosis,* p. 7.

Chapter 9. What, If Anything, Might Be Done?

1. See above, p. 115. She lost her seat.
2. Timothy J. Penny and Major Garrett, *Common Cents: A Retiring
   Six-Term Congressman Reveals How Congress Really Works—and
   What We Must Do to Fix It* (Boston: Little, Brown, 1995), p. 192.
   Condit in fact retained his seat (by a comfortable majority.)
3. The phrase is not meant to be taken literally, but it is meant to be
   taken seriously. When committed career politicians step out of
   line—act in defiance of those upon whom their careers depend—
   they are putting their careers on the line. It is easy, and cheap, for
   any nonpolitician to say that people in government should always
   "do the right thing" irrespective of the consequences; but any nonpolitician who says that has probably never contemplated putting
   at risk his or her entire career as a doctor, lawyer, political science
   professor or whatever. Politicians, like everyone else, can seldom be
   better than circumstances allow them to be. Hence, it is important
   to get the circumstances right.

4. Federalist 37, *The Federalist Papers* (New York: New American Library, 1961), p. 226.

5. Federalist 63, *ibid.,* pp. 383–84.

6. Quoted in John F. Kennedy, *Profiles in Courage* (New York: Harper, 1956), p. 239.

7. Quoted in *ibid.,* pp. 231–32.

8. Quoted in *ibid.,* p. 69.

9. Quoted in *ibid.*

10. *Ibid.,* p. 15.

11. *Ibid.,* pp. 16–17. James A. Morone comes to similar conclusions in *The Democratic Wish: Popular Participation and the Limits of American Government* (New York: Basic Books, 1990). He disputes (pp. 322–23) John Dewey's claim that "the cure for the ailments of democracy is more democracy" and calls (p. 332) for "a new political environment [which] would require public officials with a far richer set of skills and a far greater discretion—bluntly, more power—than Americans have ever been willing to concede to their public officials."

12. Charles O. Jones, *Every Second Year: Congressional Behavior and the Two-Year Term* (Washington, D.C.: Brookings Institution, 1967), pp. 14, 1.

13. *Ibid.,* pp. 24–25.

14. Quoted in *ibid.,* p. 28.

15. Quoted in *ibid.,* pp. 28–29.

16. There is an almost equally strong case for eliminating primaries altogether. They consume prodigious amounts of time, money and energy. They engage only small (and biased) subsamples of the electorate. They weaken the party organizations. They place a premium on the possession of campaigning skills rather than governing skills—and disproportionately attract into politics people with those skills. They should really never have been invented. Party conventions and caucuses would produce a wider variety of candidates more cheaply. Still, primaries were invented and it is probably too late to shove that particular genie back into the bottle.

17. See L. Sandy Maisel, ed., *The Parties Respond: Changes in the American Party System* (Boulder, Colo.: Westview Press, 1990).

18. Larry Sabato, *The Party's Just Begun: Shaping Political Parties for America's Future* (Glenview, Ill.: Scott, Foresman/Little, Brown,

1988), chapter 6. Sabato's is much the most comprehensive discussion of possible party-strengthening reforms. See also Gerald M. Pomper, *Passions and Interests: Political Party Concepts of American Democracy* (Lawrence: University Press of Kansas, 1992), chapter 8.

19. Sabato, *The Party's Just Begun*, p. 227.

20. In January 1996, Oregon's special election to replace departing Senator Bob Packwood was conducted entirely by mail; the primaries were also conducted by mail and achieved an unusually high turnout of 57 percent. See Juliana Gruenwald, "Wyden, Smith Vie for Center in Race for Packwood Seat," *Congressional Quarterly Weekly Report*, vol. 53, no. 48, December 9, 1995, pp. 3755–56.

21. By the mid 1980s some ten states had established schemes for the public funding of politics, with the political parties being among the direct beneficiaries or being used as the means of funneling public money to party candidates. The schemes in North Carolina and Iowa were the most comprehensive. See Sabato, *The Party's Just Begun*, p. 217.

22. For details of possible schemes, see Sabato, *The Party's Just Begun*, pp. 212–13; and Paul S. Herrnson, *Congressional Elections: Campaigning at Home and in Washington* (Washington, D.C.: CQ Press, 1995), pp. 254–55.

23. Sabato, *The Party's Just Begun*, pp. 213–15.

24. For specific proposals on this subject, see *ibid.*, pp. 221–23; Herrnson, *Congressional Elections*, p. 253.

25. Herrnson, *Congressional Elections*, pp. 250–51; detailed proposals can be found in Herrnson, and also in Sabato, *The Party's Just Begun*, pp. 218–21. A few tentative steps in the direction of providing candidates (though not parties) with free air time were taken during the 1996 presidential campaign when the four main television networks and CNN all agreed to provide the main presidential candidates with a limited amount of free time which they could use as they saw fit. See Lawrie Mifflin, "ABC Joins Others in Offering TV Time," *New York Times*, May 9, 1996, p. A1.

26. John A. Garraty, *The American Nation: A History of the United States*, 5th edn. (New York: Harper & Row, 1983), p. 344.

27. These two lines of argument are not only alternatives; they are actually incompatible. As Congressman Henry H. Hyde said during

the March 1995 House debate on term limits, "There are two con-
tradictory arguments which support this term-limits issue. One is
that we are too focused on reelection, not close enough to the people. Then you have the George Will theory that we are too close to
the people, too responsive, and we need a constitutional distance
from them. I suggest any cause that is supported by two contradic-
tory theories like this is standing on two stools which, as they separate, will give you an awful hernia." *Congressional Record—House,*
vol. 141, no. 58, March 29, 1995, p. H3906.

28. George F. Will, *Restoration: Congress, Term Limits, and the Recovery
of Deliberative Democracy* (New York: Free Press, 1992), pp. 110,
231.

29. *Ibid.,* pp. 99–101.

30. Little has been written on this subject (just as little has been writ-
ten on post–Twenty-second Amendment second-term presidents);
but see Rebekah Herrick, Michael K. Moore and John R. Hibbing,
"Unfastening the Electoral Connection: The Behavior of U.S.
Representatives when Reelection is No Longer a Factor," *Journal of
Politics,* 56 (February 1994), pp. 214–27.

31. The calculation for the Senate assumes that almost all first-term
senators run for reelection and are reelected. Absent either of these
considerations, the proportion of lame-duck senators would, of
course, be lower. The calculation for the House similarly assumes
that almost all congressmen in their first, second, third, fourth and
fifth terms run for reelection and are reelected. Again, absent either
of these conditions, the proportion of lame-duck congressmen
would be lower. In the case of the House, given that each lame-
duck congressman would have to be reelected on five separate occasions (as distinct from senators' one), the attrition rate would almost certainly be quite high. In other words, the estimate of 60–70
given in the text probably errs, possibly by a wide margin, on the
high side. If it does, this impact of term limits on the House might
be even smaller than is suggested here.

32. Will, *Restoration,* p. 177.

33. *Ibid.,* p. 32.

34. Actually that formulation is a little unfair to Will, who, consistent
conservative that he is, does not imagine that the introduction of
term limits will, in some automatic and inevitable way, transform

American politics for the better. As he himself says (*Restoration,* p. 145) term limitation is not a "silver bullet."

35. *Ibid.,* p. 145.

36. *Ibid.,* pp. 200–201.

37. *Ibid.,* p. 84. Will is here quoting Samuel Kernell, "Toward Understanding 19th Century Congressional Careers: Ambition, Competition, and Rotation," *American Journal of Political Science,* 21 (November 1977), but Will himself points out (p. 225) that as more states adopt term limits "term limits for Congress will be attractive to those state legislators who are themselves forced by term limits to make an 'up or out' choice—moving up to other offices or out of politics."

38. See Alan Ehrenhalt, *The United States of Ambition: Politicians, Power, and the Pursuit of Office* (New York: Times Books, 1991); Anthony King, "The Rise of the Career Politician in Britain—And Its Consequences," *British Journal of Political Science,* 11 (July 1981), pp. 249–85, and Peter Riddell, *Honest Opportunism: The Rise of the Career Politician* (London: Hamish Hamilton, 1993).

39. One possibility is that friendly politicians of the same party would try to keep political positions warm for each other, with a member of the House trading places on a prearranged basis with, say, a state senator from the same state. In Washington itself, lame-duck senators and congressmen would be on the lookout, even more than they are now, for post-congressional job opportunities. Because of term limits, the supply of such persons would be larger, but the demand for them seems to be insatiable. The revolving door would simply revolve faster. Paradoxically, term limits would also be likely to have the effect of making serious challenges to congressional incumbents less frequent, since would-be challengers would frequently prefer to wait for the next seat that they had their eye on to become vacant, i.e., "open," as a result of an impending enforced retirement. For a trenchant critique of the term-limits idea, see Nelson W. Polsby, "Constitutional Mischief: What's Wrong with Term Limitations" in Walter Dean Burnham, ed., *The American Prospect Reader in American Politics* (Chatham, N.J.: Chatham House, 1995), pp. 309–14.

40. *Congressional Record—House,* vol. 141, no. 58, March 29, 1995, p. H3906.

41. Much was made of the loss-of-experience argument in the March 1995 House debate on term limits. Henry J. Hyde in the speech quoted earlier was eloquent on the point (p. H3905): "Have you ever been in a storm at sea? I have, and I knew real terror until I looked up on the bridge and the old Norwegian skipper, who had been to sea for 45 years, was up there sucking on his pipe. And I can tell you that was reassuring." The argument about experience clearly has some validity, but, as George Will points out (*Restoration*, pp. 56–59), it can be overstated. For example, most executive branch posts, including the presidency, are held for much shorter periods than the twelve years envisaged by most term-limiters.

42. At one time or another all of these politicians would have fallen foul of modern term-limit advocates for spending more than twelve consecutive years in either the House or Senate; see individual entries in the *American Dictionary of Biography* (Scribner's).

43. Paul C. Light, *Artful Work: The Politics of Social Security Reform* (New York: Random House, 1985).

44. *Ibid.*, p. 143.

45. *Ibid.;* italics in original removed.

46. *Ibid.*, p. 232.

47. Quoted in Jeffrey H. Birnbaum and Alan S. Murray, *Showdown at Gucci Gulch: Lawmakers, Lobbyists, and the Unlikely Triumph of Tax Reform* (New York: Random House, 1987), p. 281. The Birnbaum-Murray volume is easily one of the best case studies of American politics produced in recent years.

48. *Congressional Quarterly Almanac 1994*, p. 436. Accounts of the base-closing procedure can be found in the *CQ Almanacs* for 1990 (pp. 693–95), 1991 (pp. 427–31), 1993 (pp. 465–73) and 1994 (pp. 435–37).

49. Jonathan Rauch, *Demosclerosis: The Silent Killer of American Government* (New York: Times Books, 1994), p. 174.

50. All the reforms suggested in this book are ideologically neutral, in the sense that it is virtually impossible to predict their policy consequences in simple right-left or conservative-liberal terms. Given more room for policy maneuver, Republican politicians might use them to cut both spending and taxes; Democratic politicians might use them both to slash redundant federal programs and to spend more on health care. George Will makes the same point in

connection with term limits in *Restoration* (p. 180): "No one can know that term limits will serve 'the conservative agenda,' whatever that might be. Neither can anyone say with certainty that term limits would help or hinder the liberal agenda, whatever that is in the 1990s." Will adds, rightly: "In any case, such partisan political calculations have no legitimate place in debates about constitutional change."

INDEX